GODS MEN AND HEROES

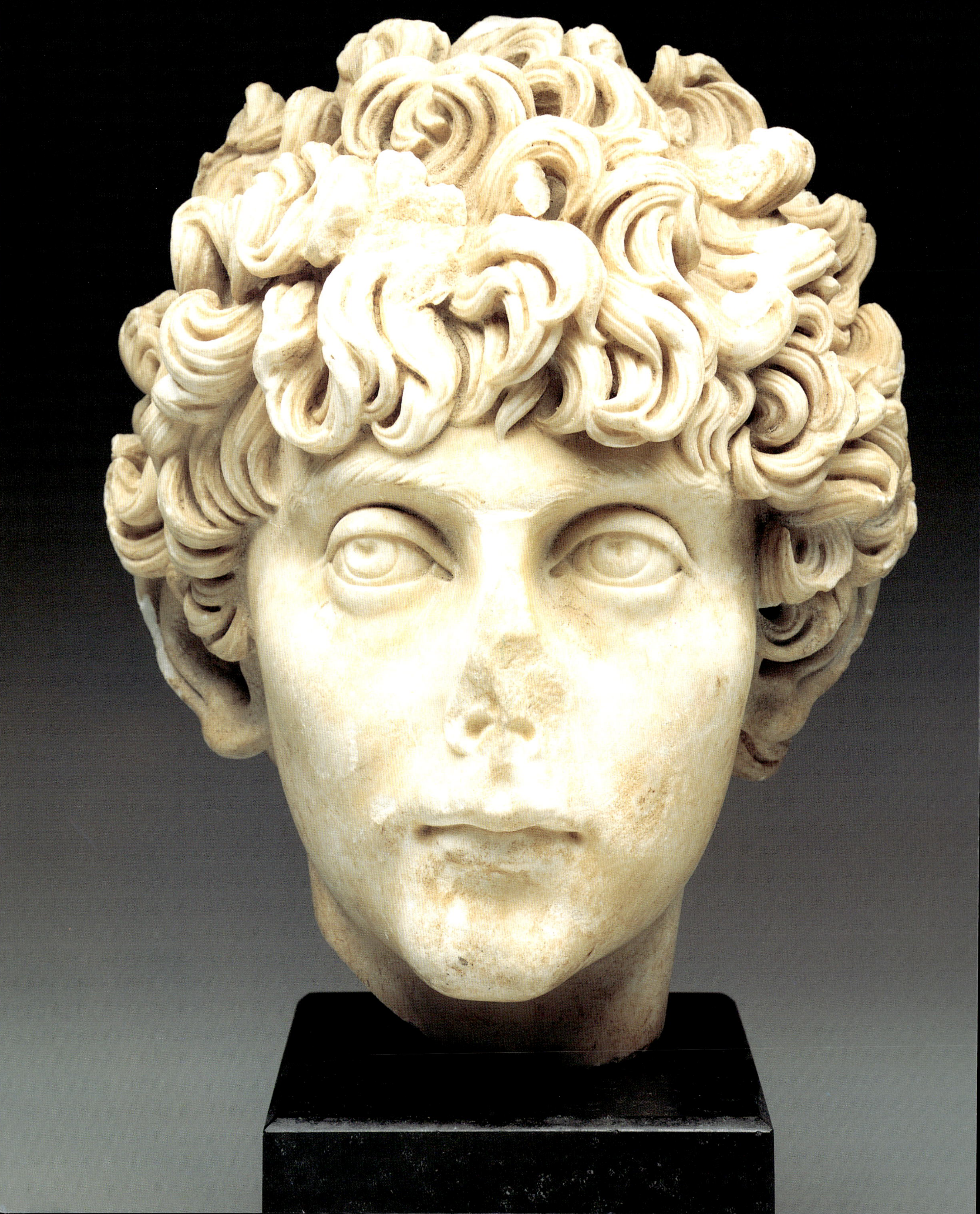

GODS MEN AND HEROES

Ancient Art at the Dallas Museum of Art

Anne R. Bromberg and Karl Kilinski II
Tom Jenkins, Photographer

Dallas Museum of Art
In association with
University of Washington Press

To Cecil H. Green and the late Ida M. Green,
for their farseeing support of ancient art

This catalogue was funded by the Wendover Fund of Dallas.

Funds for research on these collections and the photography of the objects came from the Andrew W. Mellon Foundation. Additional funding came from the Texas Committee for the Humanities.

Published 1996 by the Dallas Museum of Art

Distributed by the University of Washington Press,
P.O. Box 50096, Seattle, WA 98145

Library of Congress Cataloging-in-Publication Data
Bromberg, Anne R.
Gods, men, and heroes : ancient art at the Dallas Museum of Art / Anne Bromberg and Karl Kilinski II ; Tom Jenkins, photographer.
p. cm.
Includes bibliographical references and index.
ISBN 0-936227-18-4
1. Art, Ancient—Catalogs. 2. Art—Texas—Dallas—Catalogs. 3. Dallas Museum of Art—Catalogs. I. Kilinski, Karl. II. Title.
N5335.D35D353 1996
709´.01´0747642812—dc20 96-22975

Queta Moore Watson, editor, with assistance from Patricia Draher and Pamela Zytnicki
Debra Wittrup, managing editor
Shirley Reece-Hughes, research assistant
Ed Marquand, John Hubbard, and Susan E. Kelly, designers

Produced by Marquand Books, Inc., Seattle
Type composed in Munkton and Octavian
Printed and bound by C & C Offset Printing Co., Ltd., Hong Kong

Cover: Detail of coffin, Egyptian (cat. no. 4)
Frontispiece: Head of a youth, Roman (cat. no. 38)

Contents

Foreword

The antiquities collection of the Dallas Museum of Art is an unusually choice group of artifacts. Major objects in the collection were first acquired in the 1960s and 1970s, when DMA Director Merrill Rueppel identified ancient Mediterranean art as a particularly worthy area for the Museum to pursue. Rueppel's similar interest in pre-Columbian, Asian, and contemporary art led to the acquisition of artworks that are still today among the DMA's major strengths. Through these efforts, the DMA began to acquire important Greek ceramics; Near Eastern metalwork; classical marble sculptures, including one of the finest fourth-century-B.C. Greek funerary figures in America; and Etruscan works in bronze, clay, and gold. Important examples of Roman portrait sculptures and glass were to come later.

In 1990, under Director Richard Brettell, the DMA once again began to collect in this field, the most important recent acquisition being a selection of Greek, Etruscan, and Roman gold ornaments from the collection of Dr. Athos Moretti that added one hundred fifty major examples of ancient Mediterranean jewelry to the Museum's holdings. More recently, the DMA has purchased an important Twenty-fifth Dynasty Egyptian coffin, a remarkable Syro-Roman portrait of a priest, further examples of Greek and Roman jewelry, a Greco-Roman-period mummy mask of a woman, and a rare South Italian red-figure *patera* with an Atlas handle.

Special thanks are due to Cecil Green, who with his late wife, Ida, donated both of the Greek and Roman funerary statues, among other important works. Funds from the estate of Mrs. Green continue to underwrite the acquisition of antiquities at the Museum. The Greens' enlightened patronage has made it possible to enjoy the splendor of the classical tradition at the DMA and to better understand the impact of the ancient world on later European art.

It is a source of great personal pleasure to preside over this fertile period of increased acquisitions, when collections that date to the early years of the institution's growth are now expanding with rare and beautiful additions, and to anticipate a future bearing treasures yet to come.

Jay Gates
The Eugene McDermott Director
Dallas Museum of Art

Preface

The prospect of publishing the Dallas Museum of Art's ancient art collection led both authors of this book to consider not only the art historical meaning of the works, but also their wider meaning. For many years, one of the Museum's chief concerns has been its role as an educational force in the Dallas community. In considering how best to interpret these fine antiquities, it seemed desirable to concentrate on the great themes of ancient culture and history, which the DMA artworks embody. The authors have tried to make clear how these pieces reveal the religion, social values, political events, and commerce of the Mediterranean world. These artifacts, most of them made by anonymous craftsmen, are a record of peoples' beliefs and desires in the form of marble sculpture, bronze work, gold, and ceramics.

Ancient art is presently installed in the Ida and Cecil Green Classical Galleries on the Museum's floor devoted to European art. The many artworks from the sixteenth to the twentieth century that have been inspired by the art of the ancient world can now be studied in close proximity to the antiquities themselves. The story of European humanism may be seen in visual form. Although the DMA has few works that reflect the great systems of Christian and classical symbolism in Renaissance art, it does have a fine painting by Giulio Procaccini entitled *The Mocking of Christ*, painted in 1600, in which the naked body of Christ clearly owes a great deal to antique sculpture. From the seventeenth century on, some of the major works in the collections reflect the inspiration of the classical world. Pietro Paolini's *Bacchic Concert*, Jean Arp's *Sculpture Classique*, and René Magritte's *The Light of Coincidences* turn ancient sculpture into powerful visions of classic form. The Greek and Roman statues at the DMA have a lengthy heritage.

The text of this book was therefore conceived as a continuous story of the arts of antiquity, as seen at the Museum. The sequence of chapters is historical, with the oldest Mediterranean civilizations in Egypt and the Near East coming first. The arts of Greece are divided into two chapters, partly because the DMA has more Greek works and partly because some of the earlier Cycladic and Orientalizing/Archaic works fit naturally into a discussion of the relationship of man and nature in antiquity, a theme of the first two chapters. The second Greek chapter, a study of the human image, addresses the more centrally humanist types of Greek art. This leads easily into the Etruscan and Roman arts, which had a profound and complex relationship with Greek art that is too often dismissed as a matter of "copies." This survey includes a chapter on the gold collection at the Museum, since studying the techniques and forms of ancient gold jewelry is one of the best ways to explore the network of trade and artistic imagery that bound together Mediterranean societies. The chapters on ancient art consist of unifying essays on ancient culture followed by catalogue entries. The last chapter illustrates some of the Museum's finest examples of the classical heritage in later European and American art.

Both authors of this volume have worked on the interpretive essays, the catalogue entries, and the bibliographic citations. Karl Kilinski for many years has done research on the DMA pieces, especially the Greek vases, which are one of his specialties. Anne Bromberg has written two of the previous guidebooks to the Museum collections. The authors hope this publication, illustrating the blood, passion, piety, and nobility so remarkably portrayed in ancient art, will inspire people to look at antiquities with a keener eye and with a mind attuned to the real and intractable meanings of human history. Ancient art is fairly called classical because its ideal forms crystallize the painful yet ennobling struggle of mankind to achieve civilization.

The transliteration of Greek and Roman words in this publication and the standard for technical terms follow the *Oxford Classical Dictionary*.

Anne R. Bromberg
Curator of Ancient and South Asian Art
Dallas Museum of Art

Karl Kilinski II
Professor of Ancient Art History
Southern Methodist University

Acknowledgments

Many people have been very helpful in the preparation of this book. We gratefully acknowledge the suggestions and expertise of Charles Venable, Associate Director for Collections and Exhibitions and Chief Curator, Eleanor Jones Harvey, Associate Curator of American Art, and Douglas Hawes, Assistant Curator of Decorative Arts. Outside the Museum, the staff of the Department of Egyptian, Nubian, and Near Eastern Art at the Museum of Fine Arts, Boston, under Rita Freed, were very helpful with information on the background of our Egyptian works. Sue D'Auria, who has worked closely with the DMA staff on the large long-term loan of Egyptian art from the Museum of Fine Arts, Boston, provided tremendous assistance. Cornelius C. Vermeule III, former Head of the Department of Greek and Roman Art at the Museum of Fine Arts, Boston, once again provided insights into our marble sculptures; he did the original research on many of these pieces when they were acquired by the DMA. Barbara Deppert-Lippitz of Frankfurt did the basic research on the gold collection, and her later work on the pieces has been extremely helpful. Her volume *Ancient Gold Jewelry at the Dallas Museum of Art* is the catalogue of the DMA collection. Gerry D. Scott III of the San Antonio Museum of Art made important contributions to the chapter on Egyptian art.

Other members of the DMA staff have contributed to this book. Tom Jenkins created the superb color photography of all the pieces. Debra Wittrup, Head of Exhibitions and Managing Editor; Queta Moore Watson, Editor; Shirley Reece-Hughes, McDermott Curatorial Assistant; Cathy Zisk, Library Cataloger; Darin Marshall, Research Librarian; John Dennis, Conservator; Kevin Comerford, former Manager of Visual Resources; Rita Paschal-Bibb, Manager of Visual Resources; and Allen Townsend, former Librarian, offered invaluable help in the research and editing of the manuscript. Gary Wooley and Carol Griffin helped to process the publication. Karen Zelanka, Associate Registrar, investigated old files. Without the hard work and timely assistance of these people, the book would have been far more difficult to accomplish.

This publication was underwritten by the Wendover Fund of Dallas. We are deeply grateful for this support, which has made it possible to share with the public and the scholarly community an important part of the DMA's permanent collection. This support is primarily due to the enlightened interest of Juanita K. Bromberg and her late husband, Alfred L. Bromberg, founders of the Wendover Fund, and lifelong supporters of the Dallas Museum of Art. The Wendover Fund has also generously underwritten the publication of the DMA's collection of ancient Mediterranean gold ornaments.

Funds for research on these collections and the photography of the objects came from the Andrew W. Mellon Foundation. Additional support for research came from the Texas Committee for the Humanities.

Anne R. Bromberg and Karl Kilinski II

Introduction

The Aphrodite, to see which many have sailed to Knidos, is the finest statue not only by Praxiteles, but in the whole world. He had made and was offering for sale two figures of Aphrodite, one whose form was draped, and which was therefore preferred by the people of Kos, to whom the choice of either figure was offered at the same price, as the more chaste and severe, while the other which they rejected was bought by the Knidians and became immeasurably more celebrated. King Nikomedes wished to buy it from the Knidians, and offered to discharge the whole debt of the city, which was enormous: but they preferred to undergo the worst, and justly so, for by that statue Praxiteles made Knidos famous.

—Pliny, *Natural History*

That Greek art was essentially humanist is a truism; that ancient art is a foundation of European civilization is a truism too often left unexamined. What meaning *does* Greek art convey? What do these works, some battered or headless or repaired, say to us today? What, for that matter, does "humanism" actually mean? In what way was the Knidians' shrewd commercial acquisition of a famous statue by Praxiteles a humanist enterprise?

Artists, archaeologists, linguists, art historians, religious scholars, and classical philologists have been trying to answer these questions since the Renaissance—with stimulating results if no definitive conclusions. Each generation tries anew to understand the monuments of pharaonic Egypt, the glorious sculptures of Classical Greece, and the majestic world order of the Roman Empire. In the last years of the twentieth century, ancient art does not present a timeless, impersonal, "classical" face, but rather reveals the efforts of living, breathing people to find meaning in human experience and history.

In ancient art, images of gods in human form or superhuman heroes are created in counterpoint to deities of nature, who have animal heads or animal familiars. Man and nature have a debatable relationship, which can become outright conflict, as with the battle of Lapiths and Centaurs depicted on the Parthenon metopes. This complex effort to imagine human activity as separate from the natural realm of fruits, crops, and animals, and yet intertwined with it, produced fascinating visual forms in the Mediterranean world. Such visualizations underlie the abstract concepts of early philosophy. The earth goddess Demeter—"lovely haired," "fair wreathed"—"sent up fruit on the rich-soiled fields, and the whole broad earth teemed with leaves and flowers." The Homeric *Hymn to Demeter* imagines the earth goddess not as merely a life force, but as an actual human woman. She grieves for her daughter, who has been raped and taken from her, and displays the all too human emotions of rage, sorrow, revenge, love, and gloom.

On the other side of the coin, mortals struggled with a universe in which the gods were kind or cruel as their passions moved them. "The gods follow no laws but their own. What mortals hope for never happens, and what they least expect occurs" (Euripides, *The Bacchae* [trans. Vellacott] 1389–91). Except for Egypt, a civilization so rich as to have few metaphysical conflicts, and whose divine king was a beneficent force, most ancient Mediterranean civilizations visualized mankind as living a life of struggle, with the gods on the other side. Mesopotamian kings were worshipers before all-powerful deities, like the Israelite King David dancing before the Ark of the Covenant. The Mesopotamian hero Gilgamesh fought monsters and Death itself. In Greek culture, a descendant of these early civilizations, man and the deathless gods were opposed, although a unique hero like Heracles might join the Olympian deities after death. The Hellenistic Greeks and the Romans of the empire saw their kings as semidivine, taking upon themselves a protective role, as the Egyptian pharaohs had done.

How should we understand these visions from early civilizations, which depended on crops and herds, and engaged in farming, war, and commerce? We must think of the Nile River valley, where the early Egyptians were blessed with a dependable water supply every year, or the Near East, where the Tigris-Euphrates river plains were equally fruitful, while in the surrounding mountains nomadic grazers traveled with their herds. In Greek-speaking lands, the terrain was often harsh and difficult to farm, as it is today, while much wealth could be gained from trading and the sea. In the interchange of visual ideas, trade by sea played a vital role for millennia.

The Mediterranean Basin was a melting pot of peoples and cultures. Colonists, settlers, wine and oil shippers, traders in luxury goods from Egypt and the Levant, entrepreneurs looking for metal sources, warring bands looking for new territory, and artisans looking for new markets laid the groundwork for an artistic world in which Egyptian faience could be found in Cyprus, Cretan vessels in Egypt, Mycenaean Greek wares in Italy, Minoan artworks all over the Aegean, Phoenician ornaments and Greek ceramics in Etruria, and a Greek bronze krater in Celtic southern France. Many *koines*, worldwide styles, throughout Mediterranean history were shipped along the sea-lanes and caravan routes.

The purpose of this book is to discuss this vital trade network, whose coinage was ideas and artworks as much as wealth. From pre-Christian Egypt and the Near East to Greece and the Roman Empire, a huge body of visual imagery remains to illuminate the nexus of religious and social ideas in the ancient world. Offerings. Food. Animals. Fertility deities. Kingship. War. Heroes and gods. The afterworld. Men and women. Imaginary monsters. The intense and brilliant landscape of the human imagination, whose sun still shines after thousands of years.

Chronology

Egypt

ARCHAIC PERIOD
First–Second Dynasties
3100–2700 B.C.

OLD KINGDOM
Third–Sixth Dynasties
2700–2250 B.C.

FIRST INTERMEDIATE PERIOD
Seventh–Tenth Dynasties
2250–2040 B.C.

MIDDLE KINGDOM
Eleventh–Twelfth Dynasties
2040–1785 B.C.

SECOND INTERMEDIATE PERIOD
Thirteenth–Seventeenth Dynasties
1785–1550 B.C.

NEW KINGDOM
Eighteenth–Twentieth Dynasties
1550–1070 B.C.

THIRD INTERMEDIATE PERIOD
Twenty-first–Twenty-fifth Dynasties
1070–664 B.C.

LATE PERIOD
Twenty-sixth–Thirtieth Dynasties
664–332 B.C.

Near East

NEOLITHIC AGE
8000–3000 B.C.

EARLY BRONZE AGE
3000–2000 B.C.
Sumerian
Akkadian

MIDDLE BRONZE AGE
2000–1500 B.C.
Old Babylonian
Canaanite
Old Elamite
Old Hittite

LATE BRONZE AGE
1500–1200 B.C.
Mitannian
Middle Assyrian
Hittite Empire
Middle Elamite

IRON AGE
1200–331 B.C.
Assyrian Empire
Phoenician
Judaean
Urartian
Phyrigian
Carian
Lydian
Chaldaean
Persian

Aegean and Greece

BRONZE AGE
Cycladic 3000–1450 B.C.
Minoan (Crete) 3000–1450 B.C.
Early Helladic (Greece) 3000–2100 B.C.
Middle and Late Helladic (Greece) 2100–1150 B.C.
Trojan 3000–1150 B.C.

IRON AGE
Dark Age 1150–750 B.C.
Orientalizing Period 750–625 B.C.
Archaic Period 625–480 B.C.
Classical Period 480–323 B.C.
Hellenistic Period 323–31 B.C.

Italic and Roman

VILLANOVAN 1000–750 B.C.

ETRUSCAN 750–50 B.C.

ROMAN REPUBLIC 509–27 B.C.

ROMAN EMPIRE 27 B.C.–A.D. 476
Augustan 27 B.C.–A.D. 14
Julio-Claudian A.D. 14–69
Flavian A.D. 70–98
Trajanic A.D. 98–117
Hadrianic A.D. 117–138
Antonine A.D. 138–192
Severan A.D. 192–235

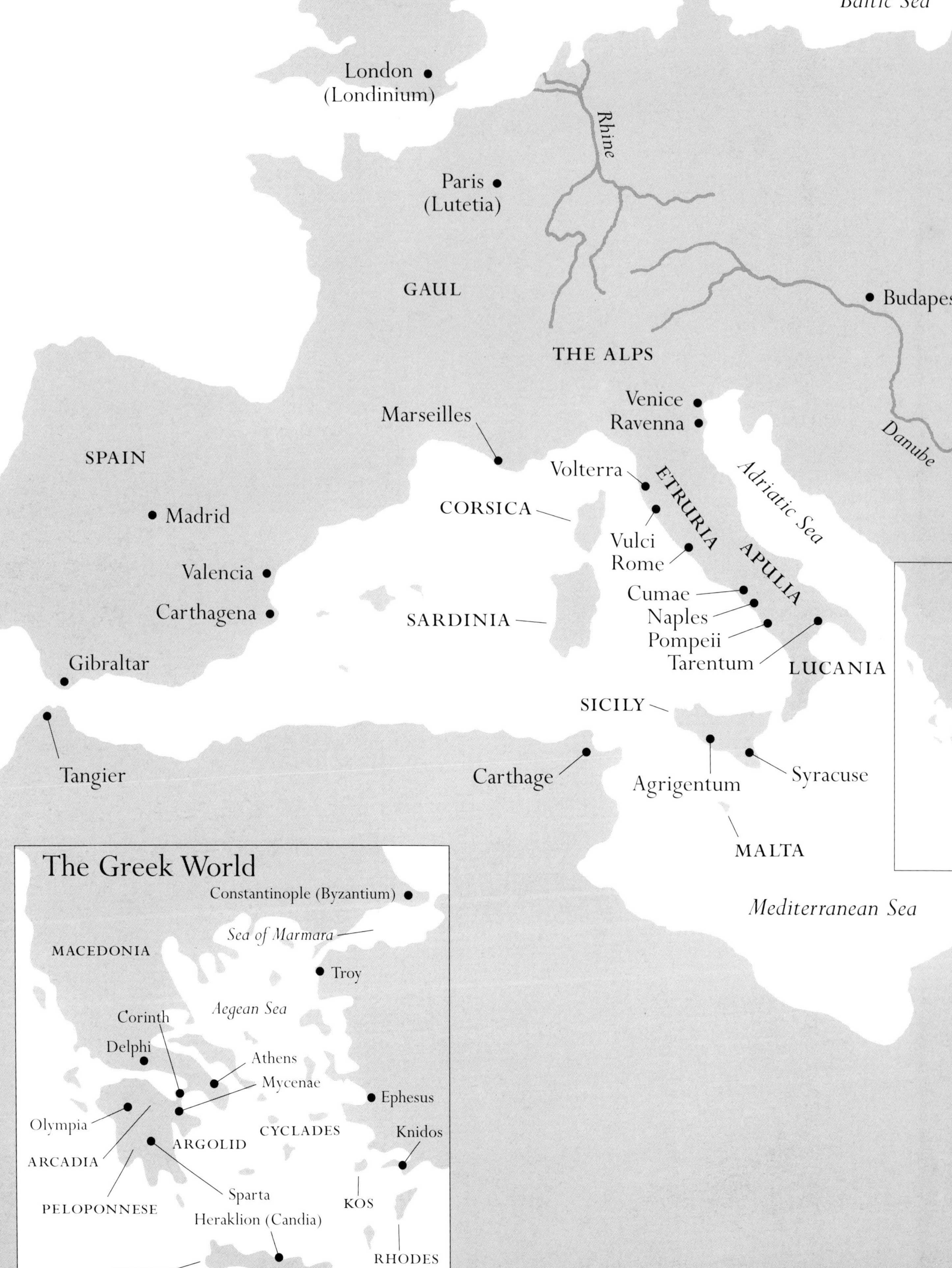

Baltic Sea
London
(Londinium)
Rhine
Paris
(Lutetia)
GAUL
Budapest
THE ALPS
Venice
Ravenna
Marseilles
Danube
SPAIN
Volterra
ETRURIA
Adriatic Sea
CORSICA
Madrid
Vulci
Rome
APULIA
Valencia
Cumae
Naples
Carthagena
SARDINIA
Pompeii
Tarentum
Gibraltar
LUCANIA
SICILY
Tangier
Carthage
Agrigentum
Syracuse
MALTA
Mediterranean Sea
The Greek World
Constantinople (Byzantium)
Sea of Marmara
MACEDONIA
Troy
Aegean Sea
Corinth
Delphi
Athens
Mycenae
Ephesus
Olympia
CYCLADES
Knidos
ARGOLID
ARCADIA
Sparta
KOS
PELOPONNESE
Heraklion (Candia)
RHODES
CRETE

The Ancient World

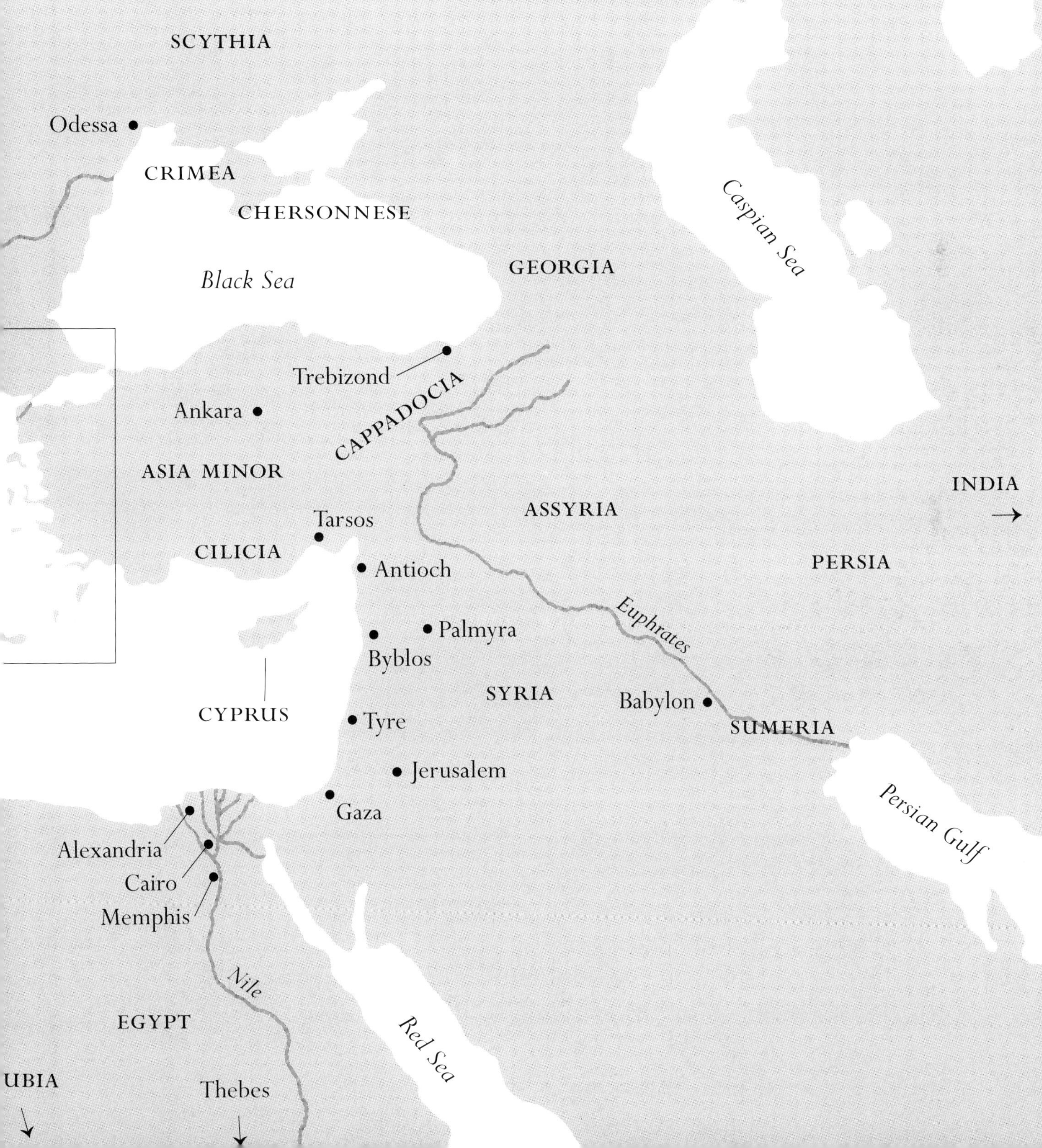

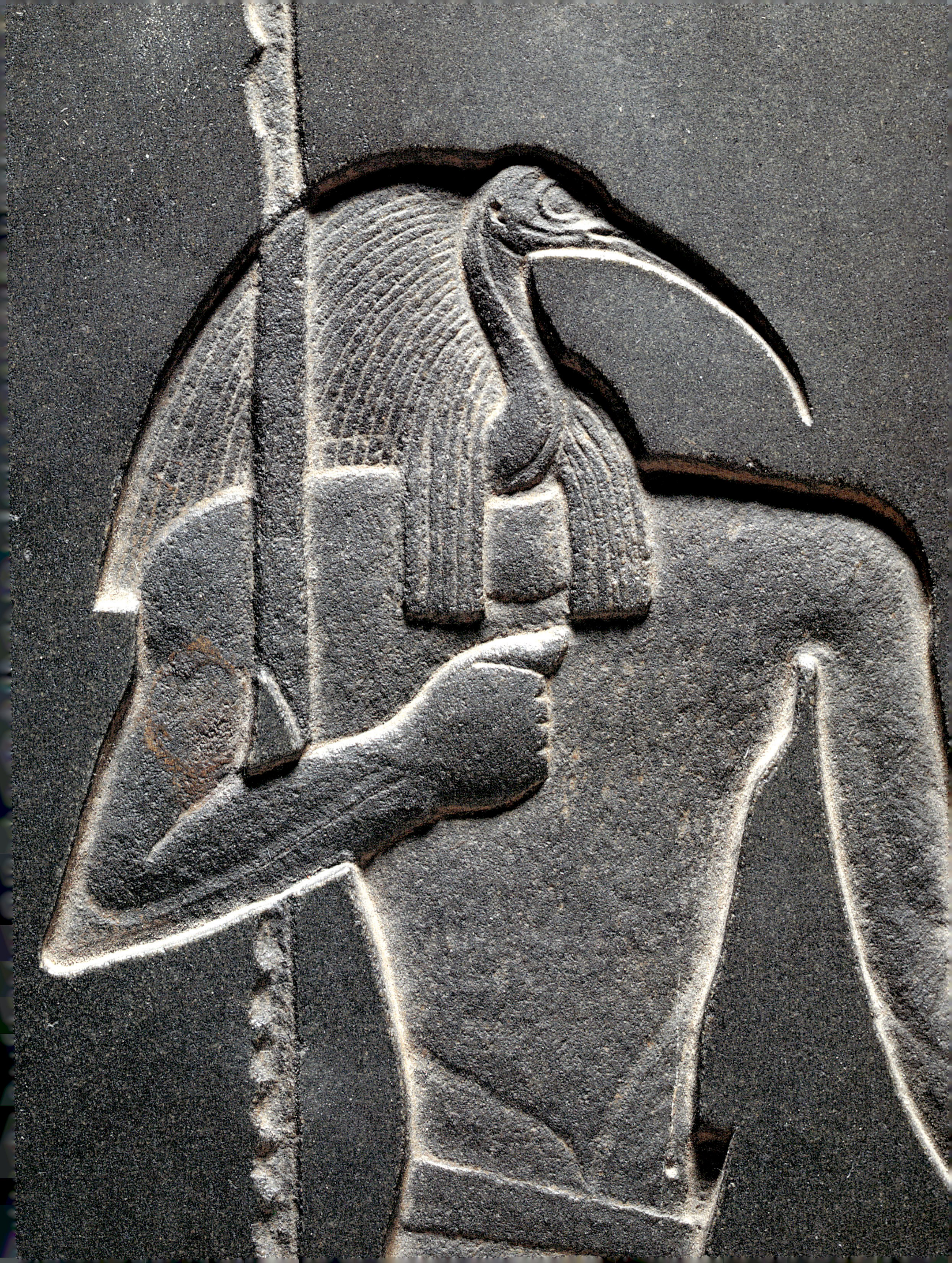

Chapter 1

Egypt: Royalty and the Afterlife

The living Horus: Strong Bull, Arisen in truth; Two Ladies; Giver of Laws; Pacifier of the Two Lands; Gold-Horus: Great of strength, Smiter of Asiatics; the King of Upper and Lower Egypt: *Nebmare*; the Son of Re; *Amenhotep, Lord of Thebes*, Beloved of Amun-Re, Lord of Thrones-of-the-Two-Lands, who presides over Ipet-Sut, given life; who rejoices as he rules the Two Lands like Re forever. The good god, lord of joy, very vigilant for his maker Amun, King of the Gods; who enlarged his house and contented his beauty by doing his *ka*'s desire.

It pleased his majesty's heart to make very great monuments, the likes of which had not existed since the beginnings of the Two Lands."

—Stela of Amenhotep III, the pharaoh's mortuary temple, Thebes

Possessing one of the most naturally fertile areas around the Mediterranean Sea, Egypt had a settled and agriculturally prosperous society along the Nile River valley from the fifth millennium B.C. onward. Whether the union of Upper and Lower Egypt really occurred under the king called Menes, or Narmer, as described in Egyptian texts, the crystallization of the Egyptian monarchy around 3100 B.C. created social forms and artistic imagery that would endure through the Greco-Roman period. The dominance of a divine king at an early stage of Egyptian society was clearly related to the defining elements of life in Egypt, which revolved around the annual Nile flood. The king was believed to have a magical and religious relationship with the gods of nature, who brought the fertilizing silt to Egyptian fields along the narrow river valley of Upper Egypt and the broad Delta of Lower Egypt each summer. This relationship was symbolized by the king's identity with the celestial god Horus, often depicted as a falcon or hawk.

As in early China, the divine king played a critical role in the development of society. The Egyptian king, imagined to be Horakhte (Horus of the Horizons), was the embodiment of the land's power and renewal, the guarantor of life and mediator between the gods and mankind. "How great is the lord of his city: he is a canal that restrains the river's flood water. How great is the lord of his city: he is a cool room that lets a man sleep till dawn" (A Cycle of Hymns to King Sesostris III [trans. Lichtheim], p. 199). The actual social hierarchy from king to royal family, nobles and priests, tax collectors and stewards, soldiers, artisans, and farmers was paralleled by the symbolic hierarchy of Egyptian belief, in which the king was a son of the gods whose power spread outward from a magic center. Lesser and local deities played the same role in myth that the lower classes of Egyptian society played in the mundane world.

Just as the earliest stages of this royal symbolism appear on the First Dynasty Narmer palette in the Cairo Museum, where the king defeats enemies in battle and embodies natural powers, so the earliest example of Egyptian monumental architecture, the Third Dynasty Step Pyramid complex of King Djoser, symbolizes the idea of the king's eternal life. Djoser's Heb-Sed courtyard was designed for a ritual emphasizing the regenerative powers of the king as a force of nature and as a divine ruler, ever young and victorious. After his death, the king's funerary complex became a visible paradigm of immortality as the Egyptians imagined it.

The great pyramids at Giza represent this immutable power of Egyptian kings, who could command an enormous workforce to build an image of eternity. Surrounding these tremendous monuments to the divine nature of royal power were many lesser tombs of the royal family, nobles, priests, and officials, forming a kind of suburb of the dead. Recent excavations at Giza have unearthed the cemetery of the artisans and workers who built the Great Pyramid, undeniable proof that the belief in immortality had spread to the far reaches of Egyptian society. Relatives and associates of the king, as well as more humble people, could also hope to achieve eternal life through tomb magic and the divine immortality of their monarchs. Their portraits, mummified bodies, inscribed names, artifacts, and the verbal or visual charms buried with them would ensure a fortunate life in the afterworld, much like earthly life but on a richer scale. Artistic representations in tombs showed the dead person supplied by servants with all the necessary food, drink, flowers, and emblems of immortality that one might wish for in eternity. Such a scene appears on the DMA's late Fifth–Sixth Dynasty relief showing a procession of offering bearers (cat. no. 1).

The basic formulations of Egyptian style established by the Old Kingdom were to survive, though with many breaks and innovations, for three thousand years. The concept of permanence, indelibly imprinted on the Egyptian psyche through the natural forces of their environment (e.g., the daily passage of the sun, the annual flooding of the Nile, and the arid climate, which promoted preservation), contributed immensely to their regimented notions of visual imagery. The lasting strength of Egyptian art was its hieroglyphic purity of design, fusing written symbols and pictorial form. Originating in carved stone, Egyptian art had an adamantine clarity. Whether in painted line, relief, or three-dimensional sculpture, Egyptian figural form reads as a verbal, as well as visual, charm. Inherent in this blend of verbal and visual image was the magical ability to evoke eternity. This marvelous capacity to model human features as tense with energy as nature itself still speaks to us from artworks that in their own time were primarily intended to achieve magical ends. The combination of pure line and sensuous warmth of modeling occurs in all media, from small wooden statuettes to colossal royal sculptures. Person and ideogram become one.

The human form played a vital role in Egyptian art, and the most prominent person was the pharaoh. The royal image was not only instilled with the elements of power and permanence, but also communicated to its audience the essence of divine being. The DMA bust of the great Nineteenth Dynasty king Seti I (cat. no. 2) has this sculptural embodiment of ultimate power. The king in his royal *nemes* headdress and false beard, the back of his head supported by his cartouche, seems to pulse with supernal energy. His perennially vibrant features convey a sense of serene majesty, one clearly capable of ordering the recurrent life of plants in nature, a cycle celebrated in the royal Heb-Sed ceremony. The pharaoh was a living symbol of the renewal of life and the return of crops every year, and so his human strength was emphasized and linked with divinity in the idealization of art. The black granite chosen for this statue symbolically represents the dark alluvial soil brought by the Nile flood to replenish the land and restore its vital force.

Seti I lived to an advanced age (his mummy still survives in the Cairo Museum), but the essence of this artistic representation has little to do with the course of human life or Seti's very successful career as a militant ruler who campaigned in the Near East and established his family dynasty. His image is that of a god-king, firmly and benignly presiding over Egypt, ensuring its prosperity. Although New Kingdom pharaohs had abandoned the practice of pyramid building so notable in the Old Kingdom, Seti's rock-cut tomb is one of the largest and most richly decorated in the Valley of the Kings, testifying to his power and preeminence as well as to the refined sense of artistic taste of his age, traits that are duly reflected in his royal portrait.

A late representation of the fertility of the Nile River, which supported Egyptian life, occurs on the DMA's two slate reliefs from the Twenty-sixth Dynasty (cat. no. 3), both probably from a shrine or the base of a throne supporting a seated figure. The elegant sunk reliefs demonstrate how nature served as a central component in Egyptian art and design. The image of the Nile god Hapi is represented as a pair of corpulent, androgynous figures with heavy breasts who tie together the lotus and papyrus, respective symbols of Upper and Lower Egypt. It is the Nile, represented by Hapi, that unifies the broad Delta of Lower Egypt with the long narrow valley cut through the mountains of Upper Egypt. The curving stemlike line of the valley blossoms into the flaring bulblike form of the Delta to create the unifying floral design. Like the sacred lotus flower of Buddhism farther east in Asia, the symbolic plants of Egypt spring, pure and powerful, from the Nile mud. The annual flood sent by Hapi inundates and submerges the land, but also carries the life-giving forces of water and fertile soil, which invigorate the land and the people who work it. This duality explains the androgynous image of Hapi, personifying the masculine aspects of the turbulent water and the feminine characteristics of the nourishing soil.

The other relief, showing Thoth, god of wisdom, learning, science, and medicine, who also recorded the judgment on the dead in the afterworld, is an even more concise symbolic blend of the human and the natural. As a patron of art and scribes, and archivist for the gods, Thoth represented both the beauty of visual imagery and the divine word. The god is human from the neck down, with the graphically drawn head of a sacred ibis. Thoth's role as scribe in the judgment of the dead made him a common figure in funerary art, but no matter how conventional the image, the sense of a powerful and beautiful water bird occurs in the god's piercing head with its curving beak. Much of the power of Egyptian art lies in its physicality. Flowers, flesh, birds, food, clothing, farms and gardens, and elegant equipment: the Egyptians liked the good things of life and immortalized them.

1.

Relief: procession of offering bearers, from the tomb of Ny-Ankh-Nesut

Egyptian, late Fifth–Sixth Dynasty, c. 2300 B.C.
Painted limestone
H. 44.5 cm, W. 169.5 cm, D. 8.9 cm
Munger Fund, 1965.28M

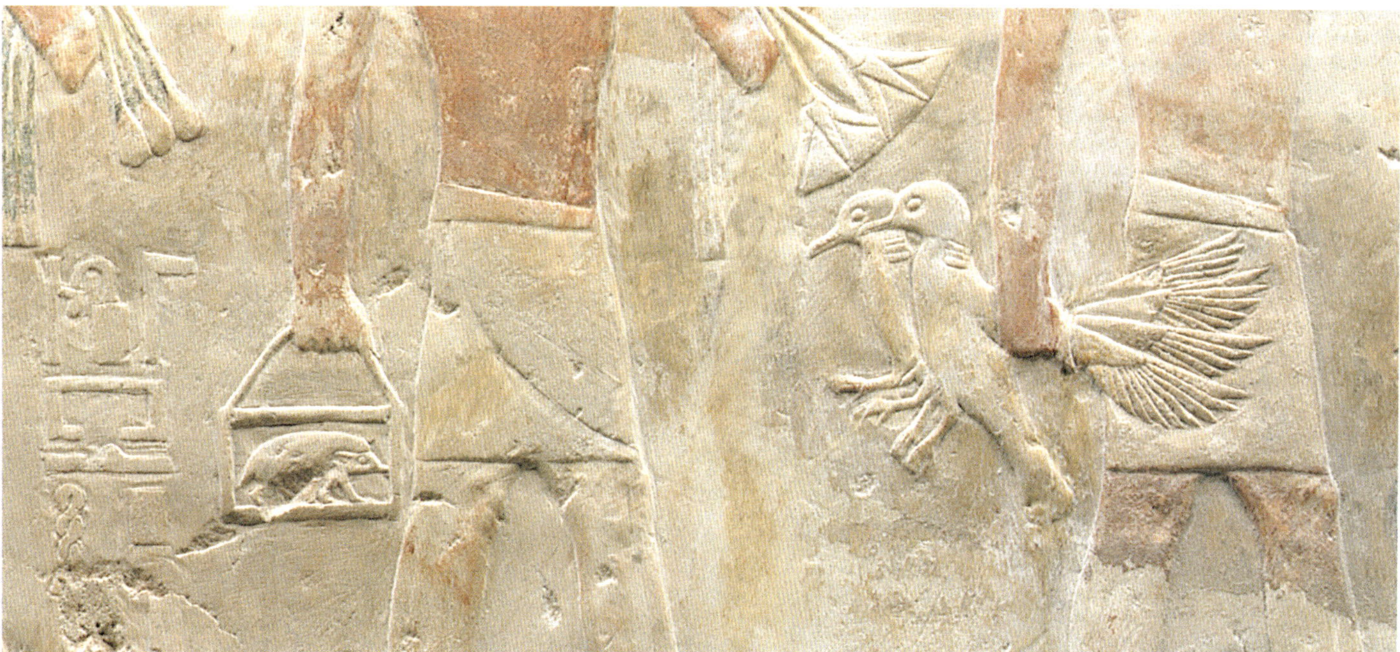

THIS RELIEF IS ONE OF almost sixty surviving examples that come from the tomb of Ny-Ankh-Nesut at Saqqara. These reliefs may be found in a number of museums and collections. The Cleveland Museum of Art currently has several on display, including portraits of Ny-Ankh-Nesut. The low carving on the DMA work suggests a date in the late Fifth or early Sixth Dynasty. Edward Brovarski, of the Museum of Fine Arts, Boston, associates the names inscribed beside several of the subsidiary figures on the reliefs with the use of names compounded from king names of the Sixth Dynasty. He speculates that Ny-Ankh-Nesut, who was clearly an important court official, may have been a High Priest of Re at Heliopolis. The style of the tomb sculptures seems related to important contemporary tombs, such as those of Mereruka and Kagemeni.

The DMA relief consists of a group of servant figures who move in procession from left to right, bearing offerings. There are eight male figures, evenly spaced across the plane. The servants' feet rest on a common register line, the stone frame of the relief, on which they appear to be walking. Each person wears a short kilt and has a similar short, rounded wig. They are depicted in the customary Egyptian convention for walking figures, with a combination of profile and frontal views of the body.

The figures bring the following offerings (pages 18–19, right to left). The hindquarters of an animal, perhaps a sheep, precede the first man, who carries in his left hand a tray

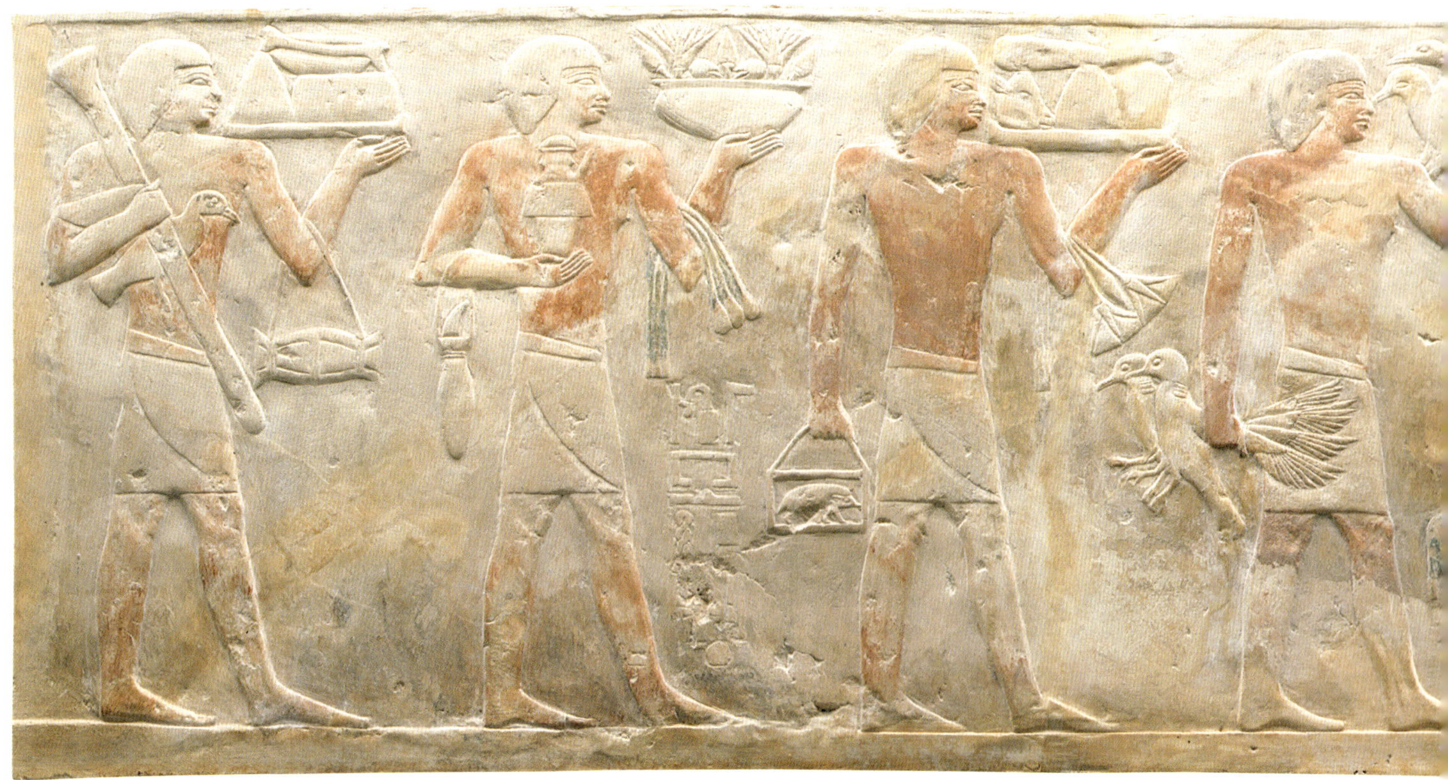

with loaves, and in his right, a cloth roll. The next man carries a live goose in both hands, his left hand holding the beak closed. The third man carries a tray of food in his left hand and a vessel in his right hand. Lotus flowers hang over his left arm, and there are traces of an object, perhaps a bag or basket, below his right arm. The fourth man carries a tray with loaves in his left hand and an ox leg in his right. A bag hangs over the right arm. The fifth man has pairs of ducks in each hand. The sixth man holds a tray with a calf head and other foods in his left hand and a small cage with a hedgehog in the right. The seventh man has a carinated bowl with flowers and buds in his left hand and a bag-shaped vessel slung over his right arm, as well as flower stems over his left arm. The last man carries a tray with loaves in the left hand, a basket or creel over the left arm, and a roll of cloth, as well as a bird, in the right hand.

Offering scenes like this one derive from the Egyptian concept of life after death. Since the dead person was presumed to live after death much as a priest or noble would in life, Egyptian funerary art, as an essential aspect of the funerary cult, served a magical function to ensure that the dead person was fully equipped for life in the afterworld. First in importance was the person's physical body, which was preserved in several different ways. The actual mummified corpse was placed in the tomb, but there were also images, statues, and relief depictions, accompanied by hieroglyphic inscriptions with the person's name, in case the mummy should come to grief. Next in importance was food for the person in the afterlife. Relatives of the deceased might leave actual food offerings for some time after the burial, but representations in the tomb were believed to magically assure a luxurious food supply. This relief ensures that bread, beer, ducks

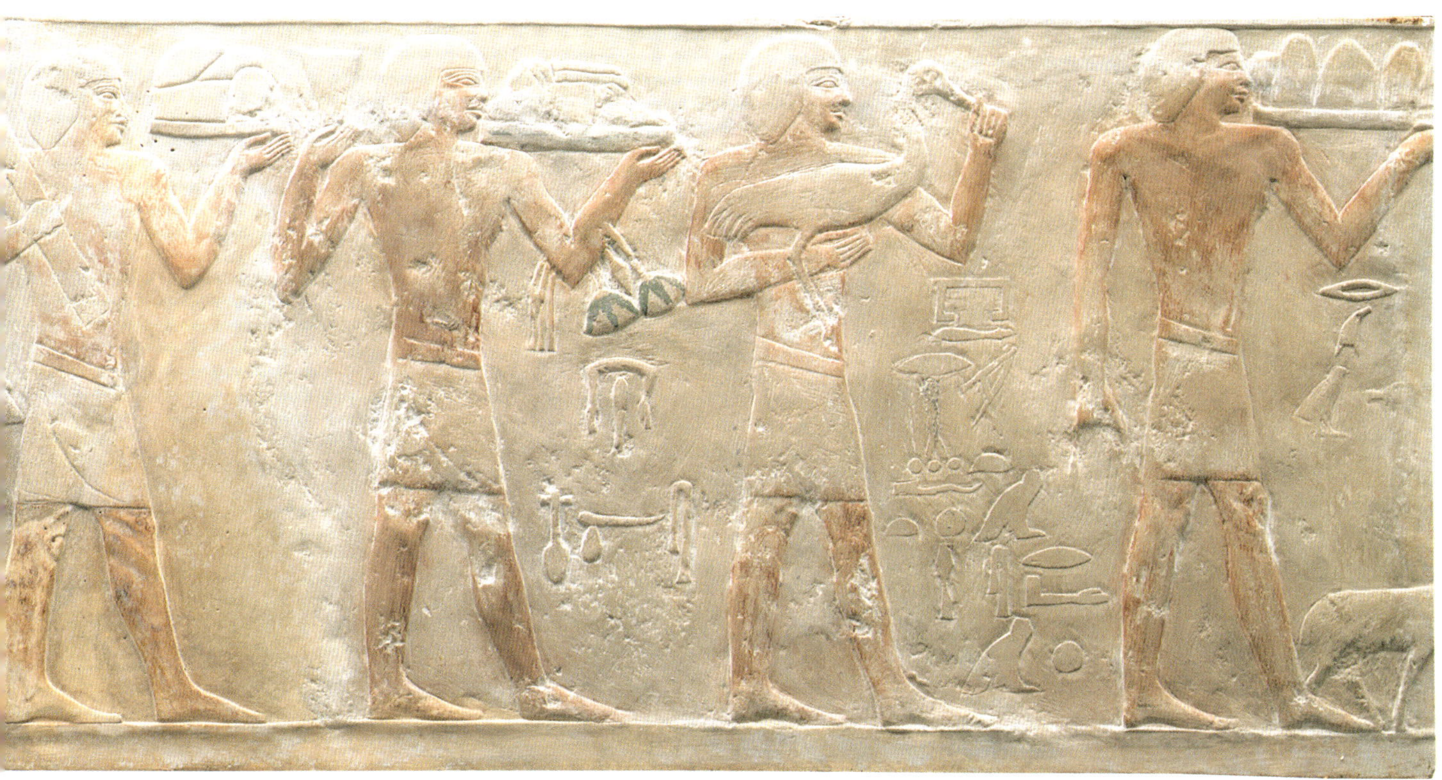

and geese, beef, flowers, cloth, and live animals are supplied for Ny-Ankh-Nesut's use at a kind of immortal banquet or picnic. In life, the dead person was an official who lived in luxury; after death, he wished to enjoy the same lifestyle.

The false door of Sat-In-Teti, which is on long-term loan to the DMA from the Museum of Fine Arts, Boston, lists such a food supply for the afterlife, with a servant described as "carrying the choice parts of the bull for the spirit of the honored one, Sat-In-Teti."

PUBLICATIONS: DMFA 1966. For a summary of work Brovarski has done with J. Malek on this tomb see Brovarski 1989.

REFERENCES: Hayes 1990a 96, fig. 54; Saleh and Sourouzian 1987, no. 62; Smith 1978, pl. 34c and fig. 74 (Mereruka); Basta 1982. For a discussion of some of the Cleveland Museum of Art's reliefs from the Ny-Ankh-Nesut tomb see Finkenstaedt 1988, 76–77.

2.

Head and upper torso of Seti I

Egyptian, Nineteenth Dynasty, c. 1303–1290 B.C.
Black granite
H. 38.1 cm, W. 29.9 cm, D. 18.7 cm
Purchased in Honor of Betty B. Marcus with the Art Museum League Funds, the Melba Davis Whatley Fund, and the General Acquisitions Fund, 1984.50

THIS SUPERB SCULPTURE is a very rare portrait of one of the great kings of Egyptian history, Seti I, a dominant figure of the early Nineteenth Dynasty. The Eighteenth Dynasty had fallen on difficult times when the heretic king Akhenaten attempted to revolutionize Egyptian religion by introducing the cult of a sun god, the Aten, and moved the Egyptian capital from Thebes to a new location at the modern site of El Amarna. More traditionally powerful figures of Egyptian society, especially the priesthood at Thebes, reasserted the values of older Egyptian theology after Akhenaten's death. His successors, Tutankhamun (whose tomb is the richest known royal burial to survive), the Priest Ay, and General Horemheb, attempted to restore the political, religious, and military order of Egypt. Egyptian power both at home and abroad was not fully restored until Seti's father, Ramses I, a general of Horemheb with no connection to the old imperial family, took control of the kingdom and inaugurated a new dynasty.

Ramses I was an old man at his accession and ruled briefly; it was Seti I who regenerated the Egypt of his time. A tough and effective military man, Seti fought in Palestine against armies of the Hittite kingdom, the Phoenician city-states, and the coastal cities of Syria, thus reestablishing sea trade between Egypt and the Levant. In Egypt itself, he decisively defeated the Libyans of the western Delta. Like the militant kings of the Eighteenth Dynasty, Seti made Egypt an international power. This course was also followed by his son Ramses II, who had one of the longest reigns in Egyptian history.

The works Seti I commissioned within Egypt also followed the Eighteenth Dynasty pattern. Seti supported the traditional gods and was therefore supported by the priesthood of Amun. He engaged in a large-scale building program, extending existing monuments and designing his splendid tomb at Thebes and funerary temple at Abydos. He was responsible for the first stages of the giant Hypostyle Hall in the Great Temple of Amun at Karnak. The north walls of this great pillared area are covered with reliefs depicting Seti's campaigns, some in raised relief and some in sunk relief. The painted reliefs of Seti's funerary temple at Abydos, which were completed by Ramses II, are among the finest examples of Egyptian monumental art, as Seti's marble sarcophagus, now in the Sir John Soane Museum in London, is one of the loveliest of decorated coffins. Seti's artists raised the elegant court art of Amenhotep III to a colossal scale. The arts created under Ramses II retained this monumentality but usually lacked the refinement of design found under Seti I.

Seti I could be considered one of ancient Egypt's greatest kings. He displayed the energy of Thuthmosis III and Amenhotep III as well as their creative visions of Egyptian culture and religion. Like the great pharaohs of the Old Kingdom, Seti was a god-king, the living embodiment of the Two Lands.

The DMA bust, actually a head and torso remaining from a statue that was perhaps in a kneeling position, is a fitting representation of the great king. It is one of the finest of the very rare three-dimensional portraits of Seti to survive. Along with the relief portraits of Seti in the funerary temple at Abydos, in the Great Temple at Karnak, and in his tomb in the Valley of the Kings, there remain only a handful of portraits, including sculptures at the Metropolitan Museum of Art, New York, and in Hildesheim, Germany. The DMA figure is a noble and powerful sculptural conception, the ruler calm and aloof, yet imbued with vital power. Seti wears the traditional royal *nemes* headcloth and false beard. Supporting the back of the figure is the royal cartouche. Despite damage to the face and the headdress, the sculpture still gives a very vivid image of the king's physical presence. The boldly plastic modeling of Seti's self-confident head emphasizes the pharaoh's divine majesty and his role as ruler of Egypt and its people.

PUBLICATIONS: Nash 1984, 1; *Gazette des beaux-arts* 1985, 26, pl. 147.

REFERENCES: Michalowski 1969, 223–24. For an illustration of the Metropolitan Museum of Art's kneeling statue of Seti I see Hayes 1990b, 326–31. For an illustration of the Hildesheim head see Woldering 1967, 162, pl. 84. To compare Seti's mummy with the portrait at Abydos see Spanel 1988, 2–3. For a discussion on Seti I in relation to his son see Freed 1987, 25–29. For representations of Seti I in relief see Gardiner 1933–1958 and Hornung 1991.

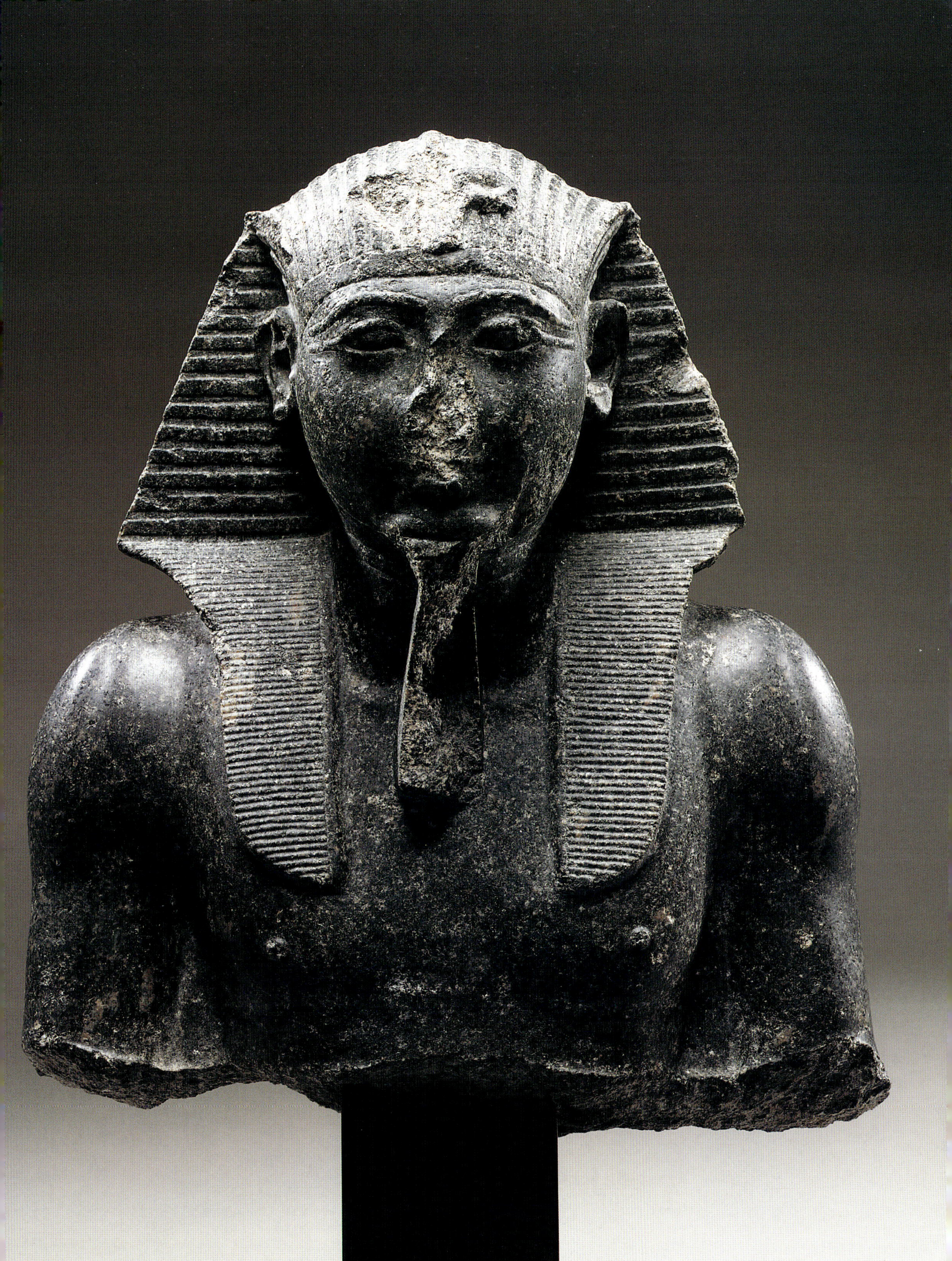

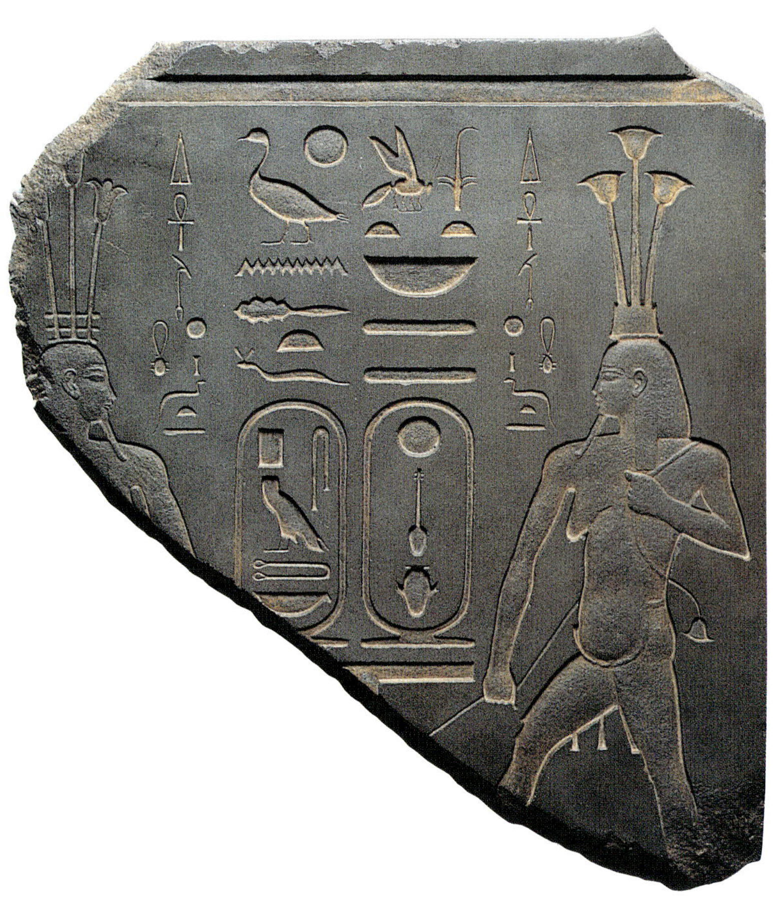

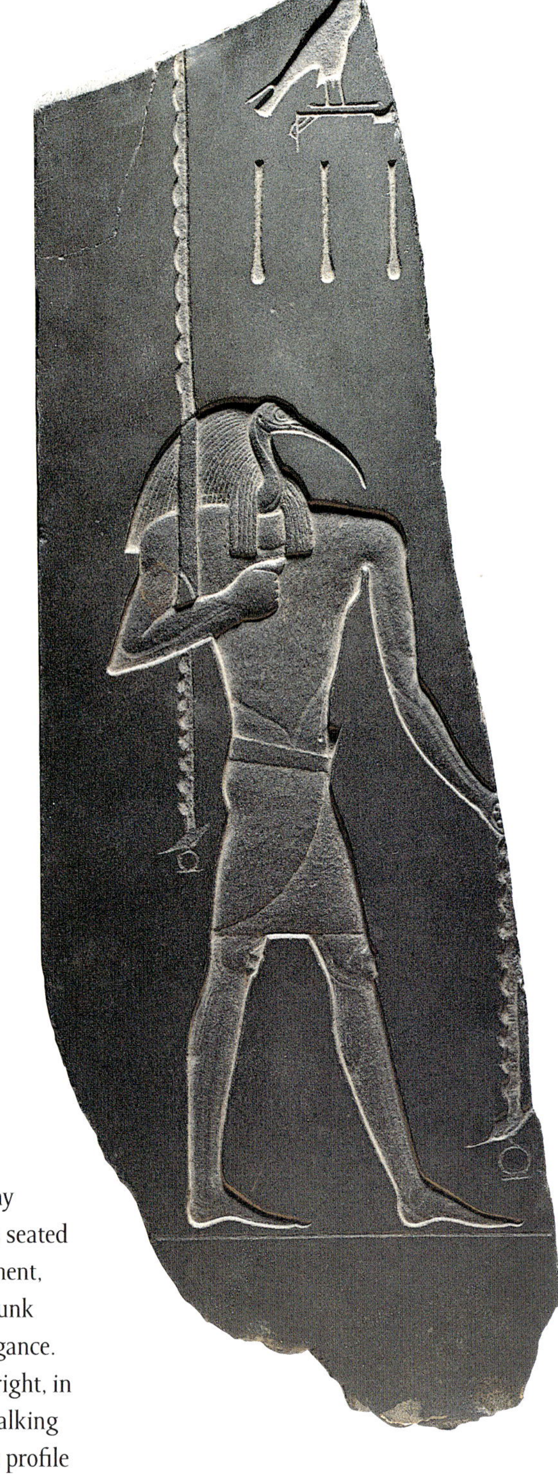

3.

Two reliefs from a throne or architectural monument

LEFT: The Nile god Hapi ritually tying together Upper and Lower Egypt
Egyptian, Twenty-sixth Dynasty, 664–525 B.C.
Schist slate
H. 29.5 cm, W. 26.7 cm, D. 1.1 cm
Gift of Melba Davis Whatley, 1991.114

RIGHT: Thoth, god of learning and patron of scribes
Egyptian, Twenty-sixth Dynasty, 664–525 B.C.
Schist slate
H. 36.5 cm, W. 12 cm, D. 1.1 cm
Gift of Elsa von Seggern, 1979.1

THESE TWO SCHIST SLATE reliefs may have come from a throne supporting a seated figure or from an architectural monument, such as a shrine. Both figures are in sunk relief of an exceptional purity and elegance.

The figure of Thoth strides to the right, in the usual Egyptian convention of a walking man, with the lower body and head in profile and the torso in a frontal posture. The god's left hand is extended and holds a twisted staff, while the right arm is crooked and holds another twisted staff at the elbow. The ibis head is framed in a formal wig. The figure wears a short kilt belted at the waist. Each staff bears symbols of the years of the king's life and hopes for a long reign. At the bottom of each staff is the circular hieroglyph meaning "a million" or "eternity." The fragmentary hieroglyphic inscription at the top of the relief signifies "divine speech," presumably the words Thoth will utter.

The intense vitality of the relief is remarkable. Each part of the body, including the naturalistic head of the sacred ibis, is outlined with iconographic clarity. Thoth, the god of wisdom, writing, scribal learning, and lunar activity as well as scribe to the judges of the dead in the afterworld, blesses the king's reign in a formal convention dating back to the Old Kingdom.

The large object from which these reliefs come was intended for the pharaoh Psamtik II. This is clear on the relief with the double-figured Nile god Hapi. Above the deity tying together Upper and Lower Egypt is the following inscription: "The King of Upper and Lower Egypt. The Lord of the Two Lands. Nefer-ib-re. The son of Re, of his body, Psamtik [II]." Flanking the central inscription and appearing before each part of the Nile god are two hieroglyphic texts, both of which read: " [I] give [you] all life and dominion, like Re, forever."

As in the earliest stages of Egyptian history, the kings of the Late Period are described as immortal saviors of the land, embodying in themselves the fertility of the Nile River and the blessings of the gods. The Nile floods, which brought rich silt from Ethiopia, the highlands of Africa, and the Sudan to feed Egyptian fields, appear graphically as the god Hapi. An androgynous figure with a drooping belly and pendulous breasts, he wears the divine false beard and ties together the lotus and the papyrus, the sacred water plants of Upper and Lower Egypt. Although Hapi is a more grotesque combination of man and nature than Thoth, he, too, is depicted here in an elegant way, looking grand, upright, and full of vital energy.

These reliefs belong to the very end of traditional Egyptian art made for native rulers. The kings of the Twenty-sixth Dynasty, who came from Sais in the western Egyptian Delta, had returned Egypt to native rule after the Nubian dominance of the Twenty-fifth Dynasty. Following these Saite kings, Persian, Greek, and Roman rulers largely controlled Egypt. In a span of less than a hundred and fifty years, the Twenty-sixth Dynasty kings briefly recalled the grandeur of earlier Egypt. Throughout the Late Period, including the Twenty-sixth Dynasty, the scribes and priests of Egypt, followers of Thoth, kept the art, writing, and symbolic traditions of ancient Egypt alive in troubled times. In one way, this scribal tradition even has links with the twentieth century, since the ritual language of the modern Egyptian Christian Church is Coptic, the last remnant of the old Egyptian tongue, which has continued to be used from the first centuries of the Christian (or Common) Era.

The period of Psamtik II is interesting not only from an Egyptian point of view, but also as a time of contact between Egypt and the newly resurgent, exploratory Greek peoples. After a Dark Age following the rapid decline of the Mycenaean kingdoms, the Greeks of the seventh and sixth centuries B.C. once more traded and settled colonies abroad. One of their most important settlements was at Naucratis in the Egyptian Delta, founded in the late seventh century B.C., supposedly by people from the city of Miletus. Through this treaty port (a port designated for foreigners), the Greeks absorbed the millennia-old traditions of Egypt. As early as the time of Psamtik I, known to the Greeks as Psammetichos, the Greeks were impressed by the grandeur of Egyptian constructions. They brought back to their homeland the lessons of Egyptian architecture and the human warmth and solidity of Egyptian monumental sculpture. The sturdy stance of Thoth and Hapi was part of the inspiration for the first Greek monumental sculptures.

The reliefs were in the collection of Arthur Sambon in France before World War I. They were exhibited at the Galerie Georges Petit in May 1914. In their recent history, the reliefs were auctioned by Sotheby Parke Bernet, London, in April 1978. The Thoth relief was purchased for the DMA in 1979. Its companion relief with the Nile god Hapi was purchased by a private collector, who placed it on loan to the Museum for many years and then gave the piece to the DMA in 1991, thus once again joining two works from the same ancient object.

PUBLICATIONS: For the Thoth relief see Sotheby Parke Bernet 1978, 70, no. 297, and pl. 32; Edward H. Merrin Gallery 1978 (poster); Bromberg 1979, 63, no. 71; Bromberg 1983, 94, no. 90. For the Hapi relief see Sotheby Parke Bernet 1978, 70, no. 298, and pl. 32; DMA 1992, 6.

REFERENCES: For a relief from the Saite dynasty see Fazzini 1989, no. 73. For a discussion of Late Period art see Scott 1986, 137 ff.

4.
Coffin

Egyptian, Twenty-fifth Dynasty, c. 700 B.C.
Wood, gesso, paint, obsidian, calcite, bronze
H: 76.8 cm
Green Estate Acquisition Fund, 1994.184

IN THE EGYPTIAN CULT of the dead, the survival of the dead person's body was critically important. Not only was the body embalmed, but it was placed in one or more ornamental coffins and surrounded by an elaborate array of grave goods and tomb art, all of which served magical purposes believed essential for the afterlife. Should the actual body not survive well (embalming practices became more successful in the New Kingdom), the inscriptions, amulets, and magical imagery accompanying the corpse would ensure a long and happy life in the afterworld. From the Middle Kingdom onward, coffins were often made in the shape of a human body wrapped in the linen shrouds of burial. Fine Middle Kingdom coffins might show the deceased's features and attributes as similar to those of Osiris, lord of the dead, for Egyptian funerary beliefs involved the identification of the dead person with Osiris. Osiris is usually represented with a green face, which symbolized the green growth of vegetation, new life, and immortality.

The pure and powerful style of Middle Kingdom anthropoid coffins was succeeded by various ornamental styles that employed brightly painted funerary symbols like scarab beetles, the vulture goddess Nekhbet, the Horus hawk, and the goddess Hathor in cow form. The DMA has on display a number of examples of this type of coffin, as well as cartonnages (a plaster/gesso material molded in the form of the dead body), on long-term loan from the Museum of Fine Arts, Boston.

The DMA's Late Period coffin is a substantial work made from a single tree trunk. It is a fine example of the Twenty-fifth Dynasty's return to an earlier, classical style in Egyptian coffin design, having been made during the period when Egyptians, under Nubian rulers, attempted to revive ancient Egyptian glories. It therefore relates well to the Museum's exhibition of Nubian loan material from the Museum of Fine Arts, Boston.

The front and back of the anthropoid coffin are modeled to imitate the appearance of a mummy wrapped in its linen shroud. The painting is on a gesso ground over linen, which completely covers the body of the coffin. The colors have survived well, especially the blue and yellow on the wig and the green on the face. The main body is a warm off-white. Blue pigment appears on the inscription on the base. Because the head of the mummy identifies the dead person with Osiris, god of immortality, the face is given a startlingly lifelike appearance, achieved by sparkling eyes of calcite and obsidian set in bronze sockets. The vigorous modeling of the facial features, suggesting youth and health, add to the impression of eternal life.

This coffin was made for a high official or priest in the area near Thebes. His name, which appears in fragmentary form on the base, was Horankh. Photographs taken before the damage to the base show the whole name. The rest of the inscription is an invocation to Osiris, as Lord of Djedu. John Taylor of the British Museum suggests that the work is one of a group of coffins made in the workshops of Heracleopolis Magna, near the Fayum.

REFERENCES: *Egyptian Museum Berlin* 1990; Bourriau 1988; Dils 1991, 196, nos. 244–45; Petrie 1891; Verner 1982; Taylor 1991.

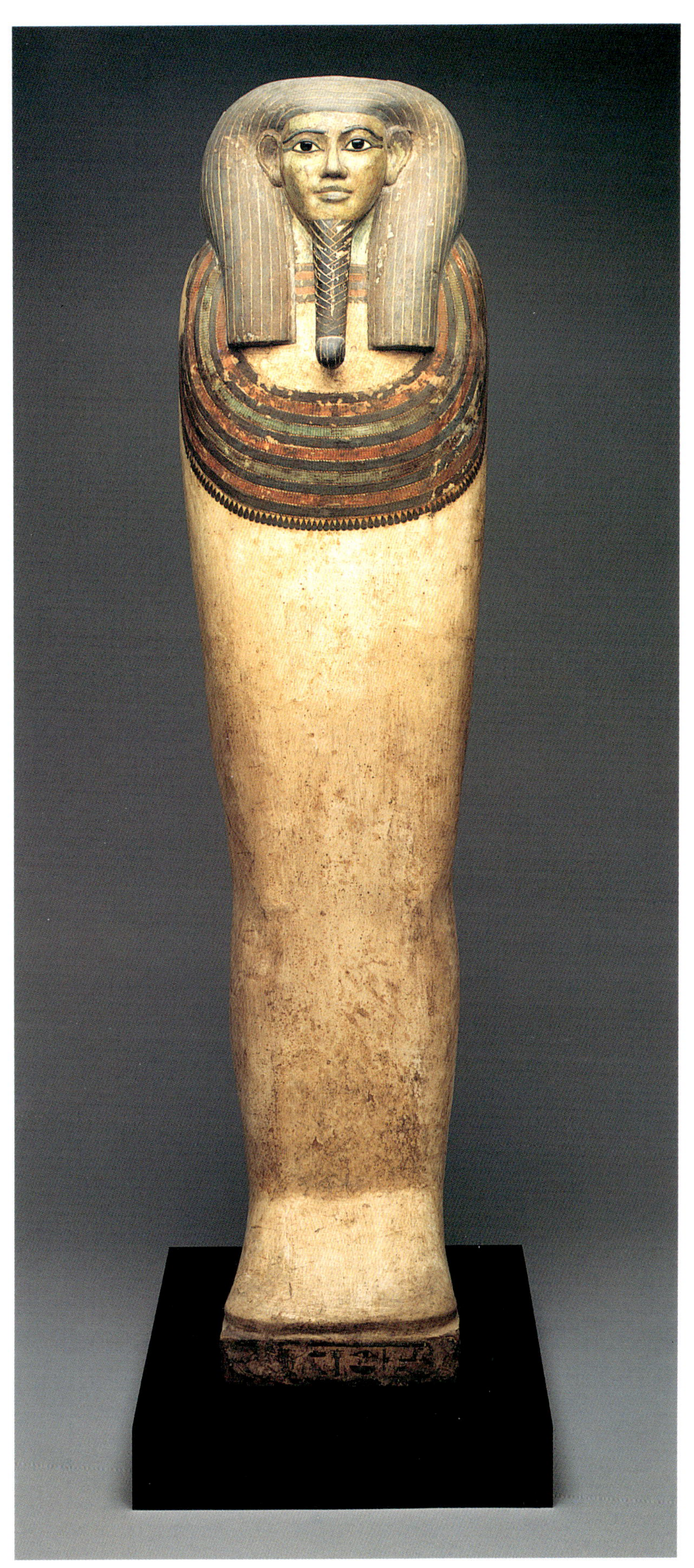

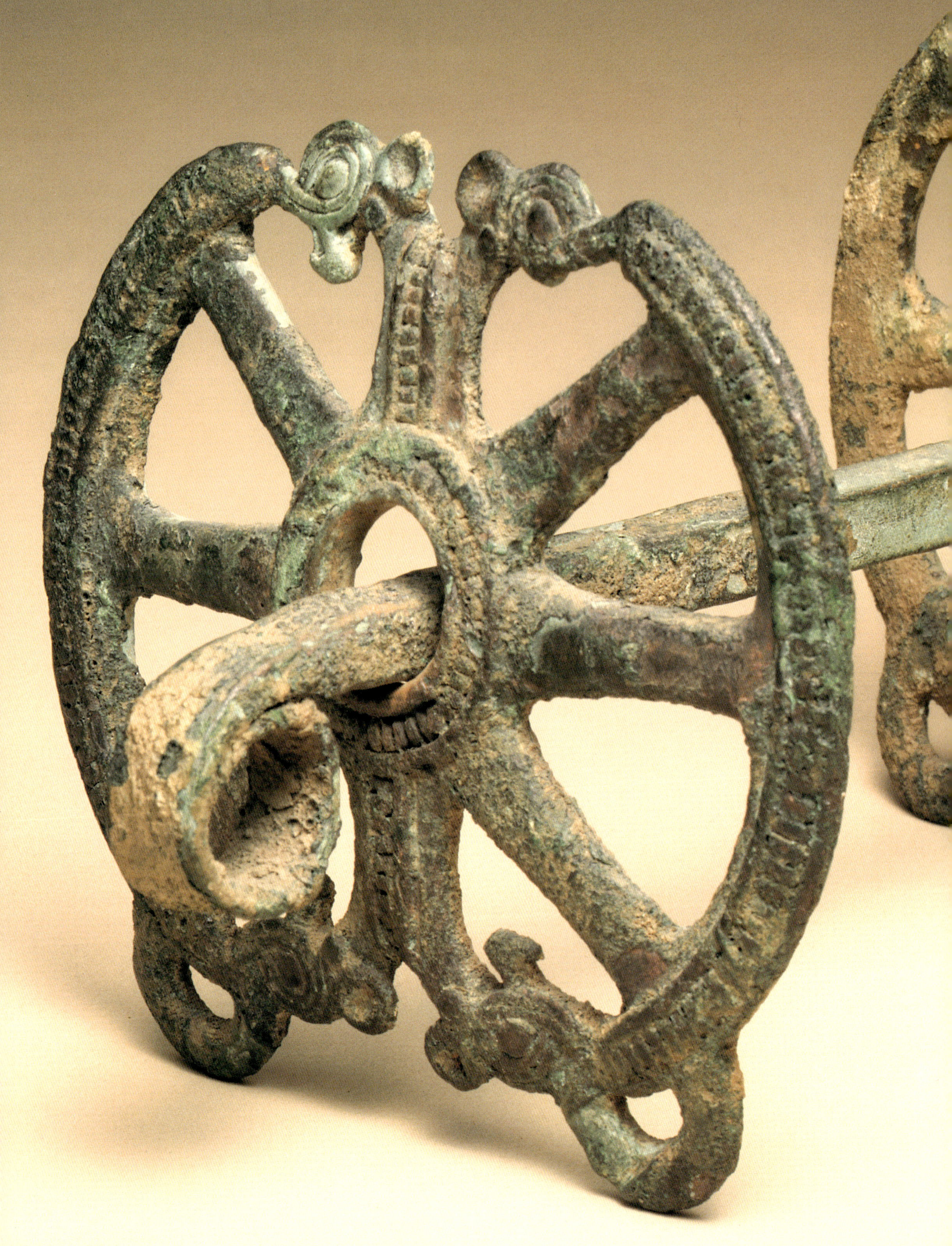

Chapter 2

The Near East: Cult and Craftsmanship

The destiny was fulfilled which the father of the gods, Enlil of the mountain, had decreed for Gilgamesh: "In nether-earth the darkness will show him a light; of mankind, all that are known, none will leave a monument for generations to come to compare with his. The heroes, the wise men, like the new moon have their waxing and waning. . . . You were given the kingship, such was your destiny, everlasting life was not your destiny."

—*The Epic of Gilgamesh*

In contrast with Egypt, favorably situated in the rich valley of the Nile River and cut off from surrounding peoples by deserts, the upper Nile rapids, and the Mediterranean and Red Seas, the Near East was a geographical and cultural crossroads for millennia. Some of the earliest experiments in the domestication of crops and animals occurred in this area, as did early forms of writing. The first city-states grew up in Mesopotamia. The Fertile Crescent, stretching from the mouth of the Tigris and Euphrates Rivers north and west to Syria and down the coast of the Levant, was an axis for the movement of peoples, crops, technology, and artistic ideas over a large area from India and the Iranian plateau westward to Anatolia, the Aegean, and North Africa. There was also a great deal of trade and interchange to the north of the Black Sea, on the plains and mountain ranges of southern Russia.

Whereas Egyptian civilization, in its great periods, represented the values of a long-lived traditional society with stable religious beliefs and formulaic conventions in art, the character of Near Eastern city-states was far more diffuse. They were true entrepôts: merchant centers for wares and ideas coming from all parts of their world. It is no accident that both the original idea of writing and the more sophisticated concept of alphabetic writing probably originated here. Priests, tax collectors, and traders needed a convenient system of tabulation for their businesses. Cylinder seals, stamps, and clay tablets were convenient tools for these early accounting systems.

This commercial society had a very high standard of craftsmanship. Bronze working, ceramics, architectural brickwork and glazed tile, monumental sculptures and reliefs and decorative work in gold, gems, and ivory all were of superb quality. What did not occur were the systematic conventions of Egyptian art; Near Eastern pieces were more varied and experimental in form.

There was also a difference in artistic development outside the great cities of the Near East. The nomadic horsemen and pastoralists of Iran, eastern Anatolia, and Scythia created a distinctive kind of portable art, often with animal imagery. In turn, this art style passed westward to the Carpathians, Thrace, and the Danube Basin, where it had an influence on early Celtic and Germanic art. The art of horse nomads was to play a very important role over the vast extent of Eurasia.

Two of the most critical developments in the rise of city-state civilization are represented in the DMA collections: the domestication of animals and grain crops, which were the basis of settled village life, and the specific domestication of horses and cattle as draft animals to draw wheeled vehicles. Farming and pastoralism are now believed to go back to at least the eighth millennium B.C. in the Near East. The fifth-millennium-B.C. Anatolian lugged vessel (cat. no. 5), representing this Neolithic village art, is the oldest work in the Museum. The rise of wheeled vehicles from sledges and runner-carts, a development that also seems to have occurred first in the Near East by the third millennium B.C., is evident in the DMA's bronze wagon drawn by oxen (cat. no. 8). This fine work represents, in elegant line, a seminal moment in human history.

The importance of wild and domesticated animals in the Near East, and the loving intensity with which artists observed antelopes, ibex, goats, horses, oxen, and birds, appear in many works in the collection. Human and animal life were so intertwined that Near Eastern deities often appear with animal-human genies, or magic servitors, and as "master/mistress of animals," in heraldic poses that suggest a union of man and nature. The DMA's ceremonial standard top with a figure (cat. no. 10), perhaps a deity or hero, supported by entwined animals is a motif with a long life. Such heraldic images were later transferred to Greek figures, like the huntress goddess Artemis, who appears as a "mistress of animals."

As in pharaonic Egypt, Near Eastern societies worshiped deities who were images of fertility and natural power. This power was implicit in animal art, but there were also more conceptual images symbolizing fertility, such as nude female figurines supporting their breasts. This design, too, was passed on to Greek goddesses like Demeter via the mother-goddesses of Anatolia, Minoan Crete, and the Aegean Islands. In this dispersal of fertility imagery, the DMA has a Syro-Hittite ceramic figurine, two Cycladic marble figurines, and Archaic Greek terracotta figures associated with the worship of Demeter and Persephone.

Only institutions such as the Bode Museum in Berlin, with its complete reconstruction of the Ishtar Gate from Babylon, or the British Museum and the Louvre, with large-scale Assyrian relief sculptures, or the archaeological site of Persepolis in Iran, with intact ceremonial architecture of the Achaemenid Persian kings, can present in monumental form the power of ancient Near Eastern art associated with architecture. Unlike in Egypt, where monumental tombs and temples were made of hard stone, most Near Eastern buildings were constructed of mud brick and decorated with glazed tiles. The grandeur of ancient Babylon is far less apparent today than the funerary grandeur of ancient Giza or Thebes (although Egyptian palaces, made of mud brick, have largely vanished, too). However, surviving small-scale examples of sculpture, jewelry, amulets, precious vessels, horse trappings, and architectural ornament do testify to thousands of years of meticulous artistry.

In Egypt, the patrons of such craftsmanship were the royal court, the nobility, local notables, and priests. In such a centralized world, the elite patronized artisans continuously for thousands of years. No Near Eastern society had such continuity: power passed from one city to another; states and empires rose and fell; and a lack of defined geographic borders led to a very fluid political situation, as it does today. Social identity was based on language, ethnic group, or religion.

At the same time, the lack of impenetrable geographical frontiers, so different from Egypt, also led to trade and to the dispersal of art far and wide. When the fifth-century-B.C. Persian king Darius designed Persepolis, his craftsmen managed to combine motifs as disparate as the Egyptian winged sun disk, Mesopotamian animal-human genie figures, Assyrian winged bulls, Persian warriors, and a realistic train of tribute bearers, who may owe something to East Greek art.

Trading communities in the Levant, more so than the inward-looking kingdom of Egypt, spread art styles and sophisticated techniques like faience, enamel, glass, inlay, gold working, ivory ornament, and decorative sculpture from the mountains and plateaus of central Eurasia to the Black Sea, Aegean Sea, and western Mediterranean Sea. While the great heritage of Egyptian art played a key role in the development of early Greek sculpture and architecture in the seventh century B.C., influence from Near Eastern art goes back to the Bronze Age. Indeed, in one sense it has never stopped. Islamic art built on a millennia-old tradition of craftsmanship in the Near East, a tradition that still exists today.

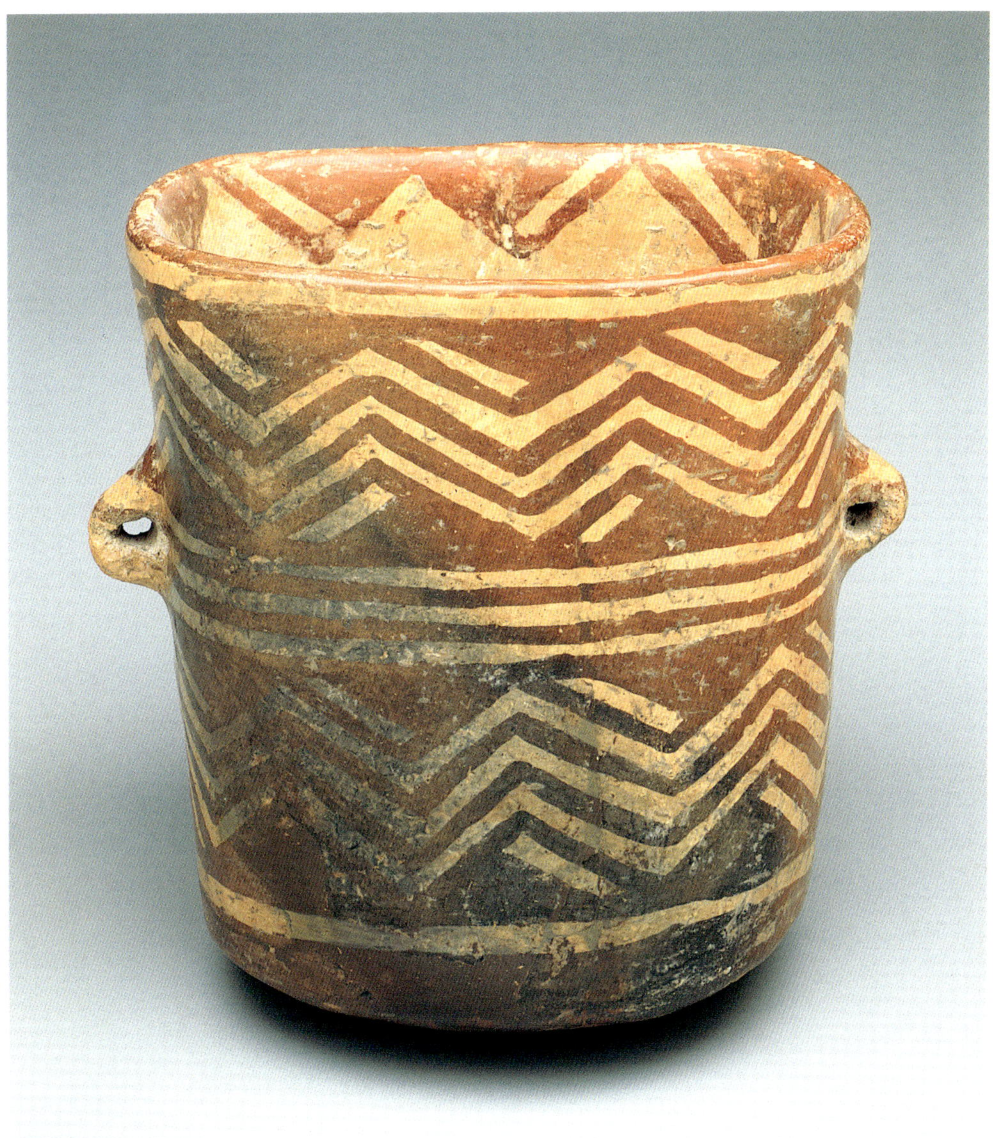

5.

Vessel with suspension lugs

Anatolia, Hacilar, Late Neolithic, fifth millennium B.C.
Painted ceramic
H. 12.7 cm, W. 13 cm, D. 10.2 cm
Foundation for the Arts Collection, gift of Mr. and Mrs. James H. Clark, 1974.79.FA

THE EARLY GROWTH of Neolithic farming communities in Anatolia is indicated by elaborate traditions of pottery going back to the sixth millennium B.C. This example of handmade pottery, painted in red over a cream-colored slip, is one of many examples of painted pottery from the Neolithic/Early Chalcolithic site of Hacilar in southwestern Anatolia. Both the shape and the decoration of such vessels vary considerably. The DMA example is an ovoid cylindrical vessel with two bands of painted chevron designs formed by reserved bands. The lip is marked by red and white bands, and there is a triangular chevron decoration inside the rim. The two chevron bands on the outside of the vessel are separated by a median band of three lines, which is level with the attached lugs on the sides. Such lugs may have been used to suspend the pot. The subtle use of single reserved lines to accent half of each chevron triangle creates a lively rhythm. This piece exemplifies the rapid growth of arts and crafts in farming villages that could amass a surplus food supply and so could support craftspeople such as potters.

REFERENCES: Muscarella 1981, 154, nos. 115–16.

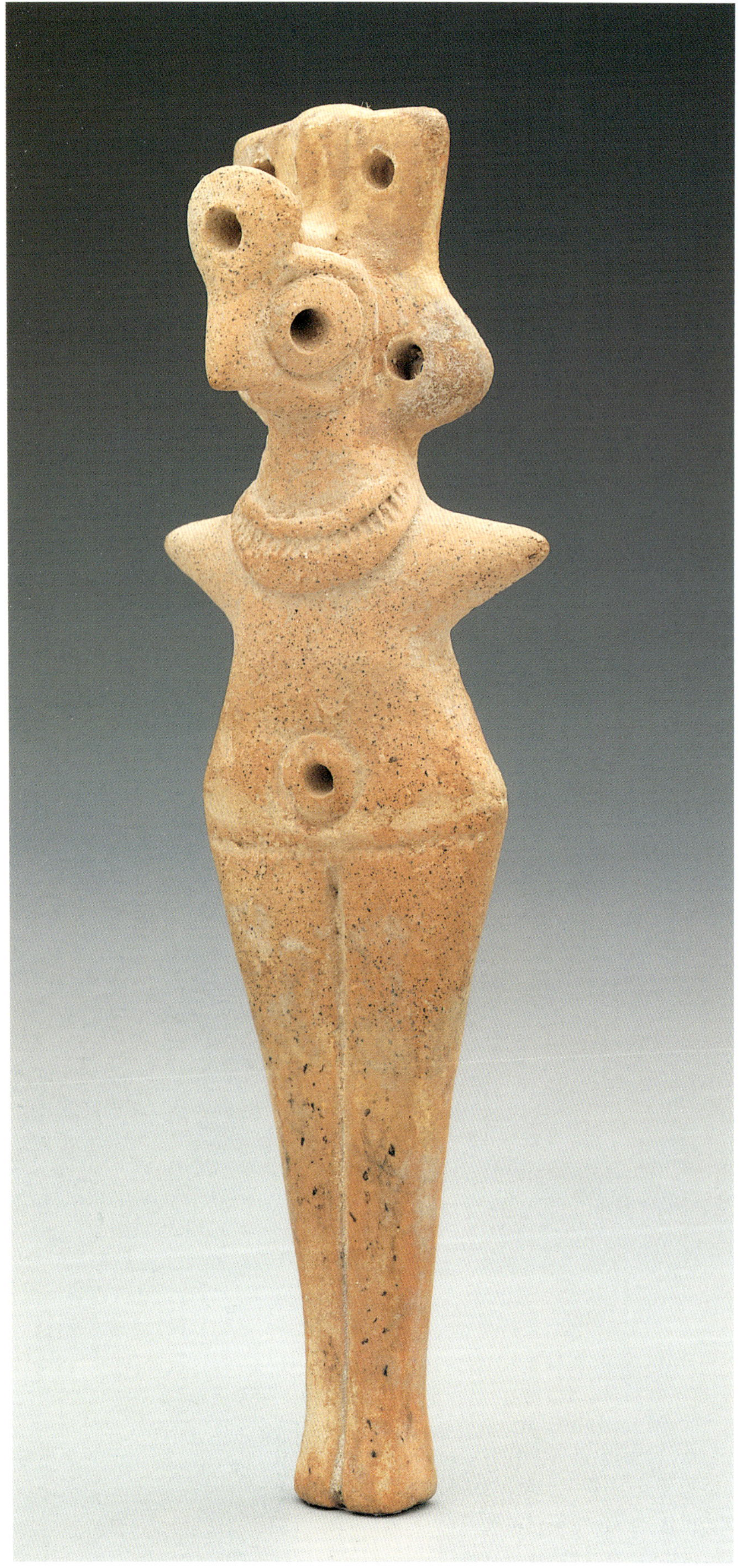

6.

Female fertility figure

Syria, Second millennium B.C.
Ceramic
H. 15.2 cm, W. 5.2 cm, D. 3 cm
Foundation for the Arts Collection, gift of Mr. and Mrs. James H. Clark, 1974.81.FA

THIS KIND OF CERAMIC female figurine was quite common in Syria during the Bronze Age. The statuettes consist of standing frontal female figures that are nude, though usually wearing ornaments and headdresses. Features like ears, eyes, and navels may be indicated by incised circles. The high headdresses are also pierced with similar circles. The DMA example has a pinched nose, a double-banded necklace, indications of a hip band or pelvic area, abbreviated triangular arms, legs separated by a groove, and slightly modeled toes. These common figurines were possibly votive offerings or amulets to a mother-goddess, and their form may have been influenced by cult statues in a temple. Many other examples indicate the nurturing female breasts more than the DMA piece does. The connections in form, and probably in meaning, between this little statuette and the DMA's two Cycladic figurines (cat. nos. 15 and 16) are apparent in the frontal pose and the strongly stylized forms of the female body.

REFERENCES: Muscarella 1981, 236–37, nos. 204–7 (esp. no. 206).

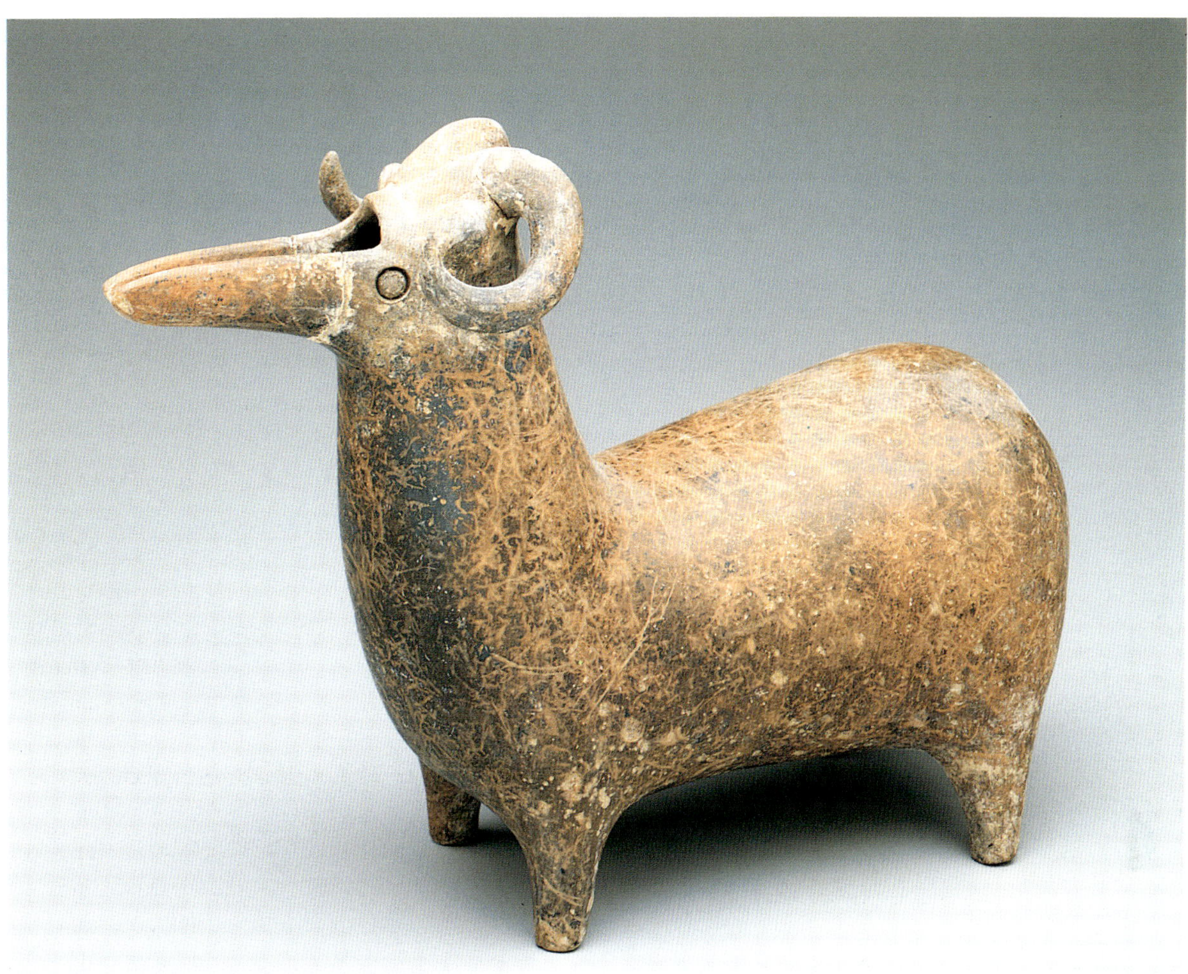

7.

Ram rhyton

Northern Iran, Marlik (Amlash), c. 1350–1000 B.C.
Ceramic
H. 9.1 cm, W. 26.7 cm, D. 10.8 cm
Dallas Art Association Purchase, 1963.26

THE RHYTON IS ANOTHER example of a common ceramic type in the early Near East. Ram-headed rhytons, or drinking vessels originally based on animal horns, are common in the arts of northern Iran during the Late Bronze Age. This culture is called Marlik, after a tomb site in northern Iran, or more generally Amlash, after the town where such rhytons were first found. There are numerous other kinds of animals represented in Amlash ceramics, including horses, bulls, camels, monkeys, mountain sheep, and antelopes. Animal art was one of the finest creations of the nomadic people inhabiting the Iranian plateau. The Marlik tombs also included fine metal drinking vessels. The DMA ceremonial clay drinking cup is related to similar sculptural vessels in bronze, silver, and gold from the Bronze Age and later; during the Achaemenid Persian period of the fifth century B.C. a number of spectacular examples occur. It is not surprising that twentieth-century abstract artists admired Amlash work when it first became widely known in Europe and America in the 1960s. The elegant linear abstraction of the DMA vessel is breathtaking. Each part of the animal seems to be formed of one continuous curving shape. The ram's muzzle is extended in a fluid curve to form the spout of the rhyton. The only other detail described is the pair of horns, which curve forward to echo the lines of the ram's body. The tail and eyes are lightly indicated by incised circles.

REFERENCES: Israel 1966 passim.

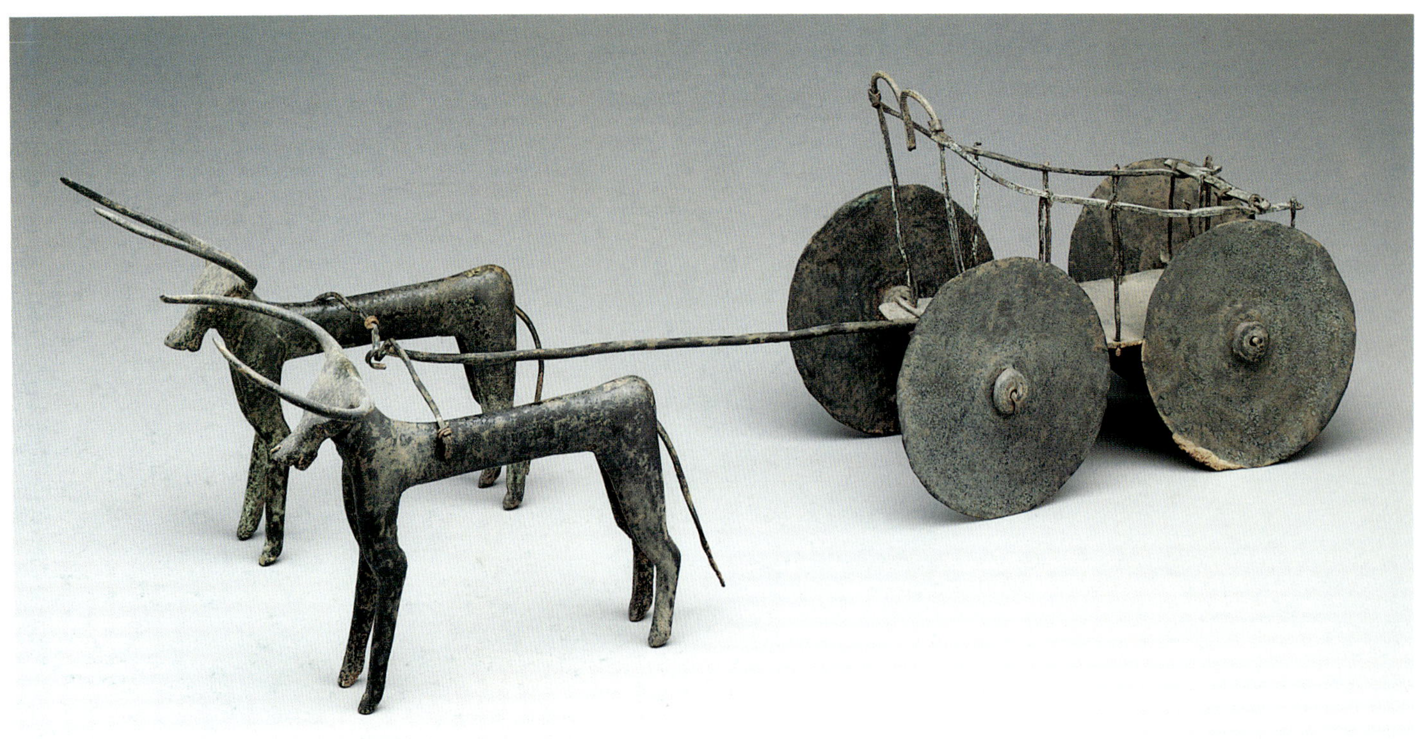

8.

Oxen and wagon

Northern Syria, Proto-Hittite, c. 2000–1800 B.C.
Bronze
Oxen: H. 14.8 cm, L. 22.2 cm, D. 10.3 cm
and H. 15.1 cm, L. 39.5 cm, D. 10.3 cm
Yoke: H. 8 cm, L. 15.6 cm, D. 0.6 cm
Wagon: H. 16.5 cm, L. 46.1 cm, D. 11.5 cm
Irvin L. and Meryl P. Levy Endowment Fund, 1972.38.a–d

OTHER EXAMPLES OF these four-wheeled bronze wagons from Mesopotamia, Syria, and Anatolia are generally attributed to the late third and early second millennia B.C. Although very few works come from controlled excavations, the large number of examples, as well as representations of wheeled vehicles in other media, like the famous Standard of Ur in the British Museum, tell us a great deal about the critical early stages of the development of wheeled transport. The Mesopotamian and Syrian examples are commonly horse-drawn and may be war chariots or royal vehicles. The Anatolian carts are generally drawn by oxen or bulls and may be farm carts used for transporting foodstuffs. The openwork structure of the Anatolian carts, as opposed to the high frontal build of the Syrian examples, also suggests a farm cart. In either case, these four-wheeled wagons were developed from sledges and two-wheeled carts. The idea of wheeled vehicles is as critical an invention for human civilization as the development of farming and pastoralism at the beginning of the Neolithic period. It made possible more far-ranging and much faster travel, transportation, trade, warfare, and farming activities. The wheel was introduced into Egypt from the Near East only after the great age of pyramid building. In the Americas, where the wheel was never used for transport in ancient times, probably because the New World lacked suitable draft animals, peoples' movements were limited to foot and llama travel.

It is difficult to overestimate the importance of this development in Eurasia. While the horse may have first been domesticated north of the Black Sea, and the largest number of representations of wheeled vehicles appeared in Eurasia, it still seems likely that the key idea of drawing four-wheeled wagons with draft animals occurred in the Near East sometime in the third millennium B.C.

The DMA oxen and wagon is an especially fine work of art. Few other examples of this type have so clean and graceful an outline. The oxen, particularly, are as handsome in their way as the Amlash ram rhyton. The ox figures were cast by the lost-wax method in bronze with a strong copper component. The animals' tails were cold-worked and mechanically attached to the bodies. Both the yoke and the cart were cold hammered. The cart has a flat floor and movable openwork sides, back, and front. The front of the cart frame has a double-curved top. The wheels are solid disks.

PUBLICATIONS: DMFA 1973; Bromberg 1983, 93–94, no. 89; Carravetta 1991, cover.

REFERENCES: Littauer and Crouwel 1979; The Metropolitan Museum of Art 1968, no. 3; Piggott 1983, 60–63; The Brooklyn Museum 1966, 29, no. 26; Terrace 1964, 56ff., fig 12; Bothmer 1990, 32, no. 19.

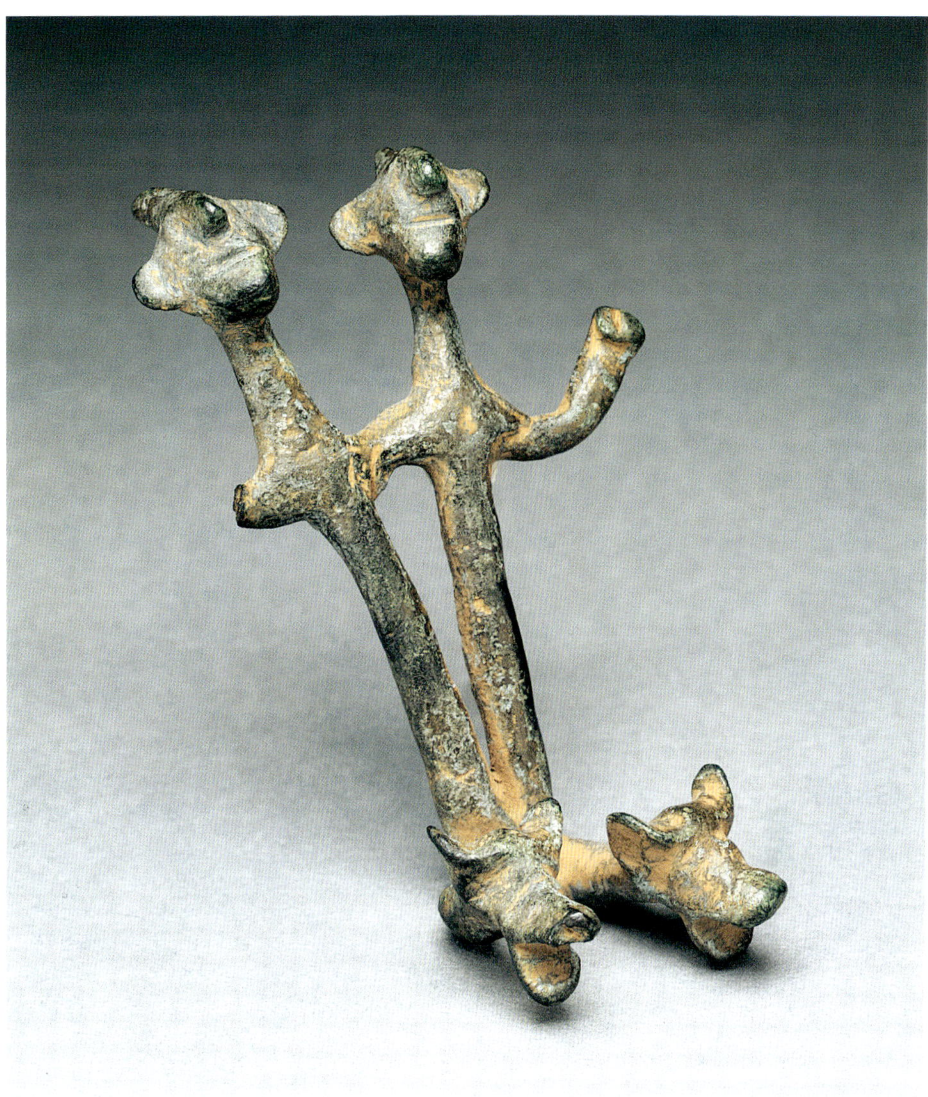

9.

Couple atop two animal heads

Northern Syria, Syro-Hittite, 1500–1000 B.C.
Bronze
H. 8.5 cm, W. 4.4 cm, D. 3.4 cm
Foundation for the Arts Collection, gift of the Wendover Foundation, 1970.21.FA

THIS APPEALING PIECE is an ornamental figure from the top of a ceremonial standard. Such objects were carried in ritual processions throughout antiquity. Processional poles in Islamic culture were surmounted by objects like the DMA Seljuk dragon finial. The image, which combines human and animal elements, may represent deities associated with fertility and the powers of weather. Similar single standing figures represent the Hittite thunder deity. The work was solid cast by the lost-wax method and is in good condition, except for a missing arm on the left-hand figure.

REFERENCES: Muscarella 1988; Doeringer 1970, 202, figs. 12–16, esp. fig. 16, a Syrian figure from the Louvre. For Luristan metalwork see Curtis 1988, 23–44.

10.
Mythological figure

Iran, Luristan, c. 1000 B.C.
Bronze
H. 20.3 cm, W. 7.3 cm, D. 2.4 cm
Dallas Art Association Purchase, 1963.21

THIS BRONZE FIGURINE, usually described as a standard finial (see cat. no. 9), consists of a composite human figure and animals. The upper part of the figure holds two mythological animals of lion-monster form in the "master of animals" position. The lower half of the figure includes a repeated human head flanked by the heads of cocks, which form the tails of the upper animals. The entire image is supported by a form resembling animal legs, which in turn rests upon a tripod-like structure with lugs. The work is solid cast in one piece.

There are a number of parallels to this figure, some quite close, such as a piece in a private collection in Brussels, illustrated by Edith Porada in *The Art of Ancient Iran* (Porada 1965, 81, pl. 19). Like the axe, animal-headed pin, and horse bit from Luristan in the DMA collections, this work is part of a large body of material from western Iran, about which there is little concrete information. Who the people of Luristan were in antiquity, what language they spoke, and whether they were nomads or sedentary villagers are unanswerable questions. Given the quality and output of their bronze work, they seem to have been at least partly settled people, and it is clear that horses played an important part in their culture. The heraldic figure in this example has been interpreted as Gilgamesh, the hero of a Mesopotamian epic. Since the "master of animals" motif occurred in Mesopotamia, this may be so, but without any written documents it is hard to know the meaning of the wealth of human and animal imagery in Luristanian art. Roman Ghirshman interpreted the figure as Sraosha, the early Iranian god of justice (Ghirshman 1964, 44ff.). Whether these figures really were carried on standard poles in processions is not clear. Some of them were buried in graves, as were other major types of Luristan bronzes.

REFERENCES: Muscarella 1988; Curtis 1988, 23–32, and pls. 2–4, 8; see also a discussion of Luristan bronzes by Muscarella in that volume, pp. 33–44; Carnegie Institute 1964, no. 25; Terrace 1962, figs. 35 and 36; Moorey 1971, pls. 34 and 35 (esp. pl. 34, no. 178); Hôtel Drouot 1972, nos. 103–8; The Brooklyn Museum 1966, 32, no. 30.

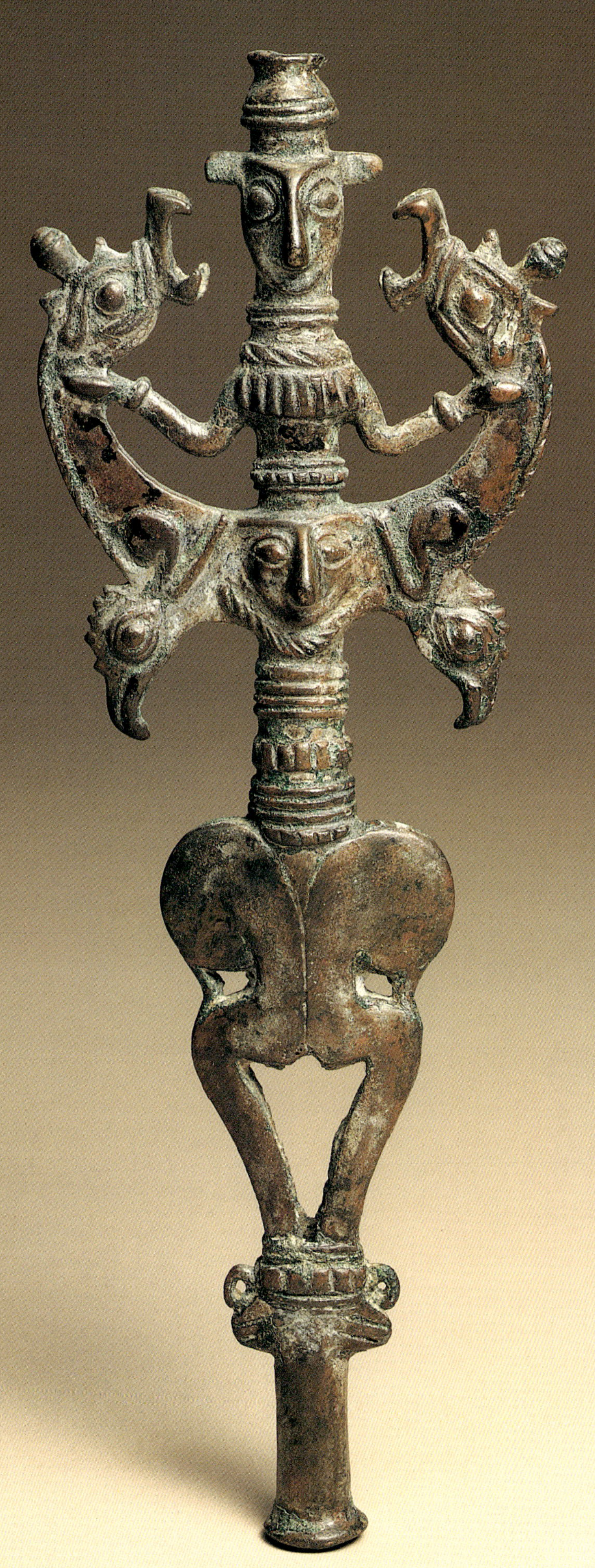

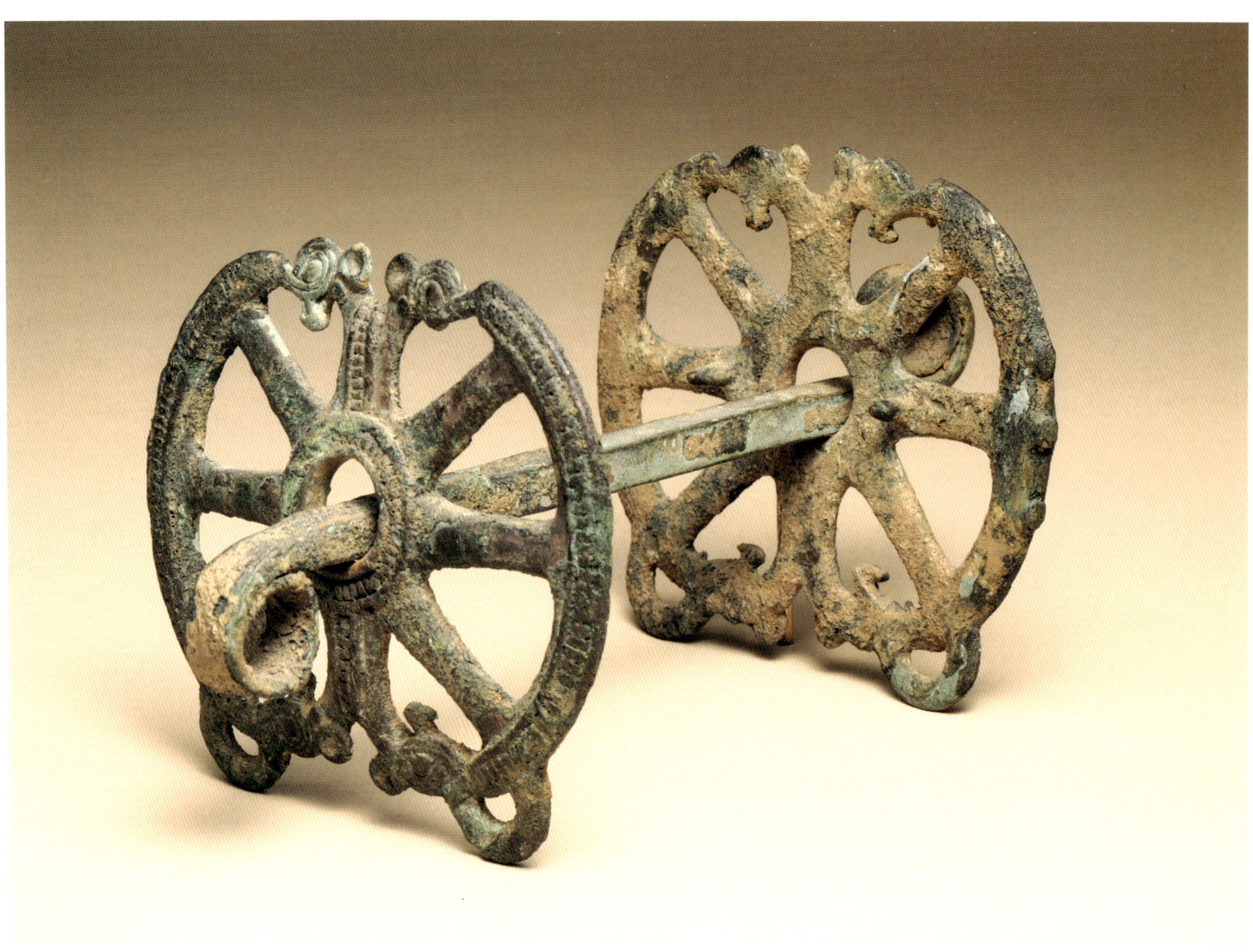

11.

Three-piece horse bit

Iran, Luristan, 800–600 B.C.
Bronze
H. 11.2 cm, W. 22.8 cm, D. 12.8 cm
Dallas Art Association Purchase, 1974.75

THE DMA'S LURISTANIAN horse bit makes an interesting comparison with the more elaborate Villanovan horse bit in the Museum collections. The Near Eastern bit combines cast cheekpieces (probably from the same bivalve mold) and a cold-worked bar, one end of which spirals up and the other down. The imaginary animal ornamentation is fairly restrained in comparison with other horse trappings from Luristan. There are monster heads facing each other on the upper part of the circular cheekpieces and bird figures facing away from each other on the monster's tails, which form the lower rim. In bits like these, the crossbar fitted in the horse's mouth and was controlled by the cheekpieces. The bit reins were attached to the rings at the bottom of the cheekpieces. There is still no agreement as to whether these elaborate kinds of bronze horse trappings were designed for burials or were used in life and buried with the dead person. Some do appear to have wear on the bar piece. Both men and women were buried with horse trappings, which indicates the vital role that riding and driving played in ancient Iran. If these people were not actually nomads, the free life of horse riders on the Iranian plateau clearly defined much of their culture.

REFERENCES: Muscarella 1988; Moorey 1971, 101–39, pl. 13, and nos. 109–11; Carnegie Institute 1964, no. 24; Godard 1965, figs. 17 and 18. For Luristanian metalwork see Curtis 1988, 23–44.

12.

Pin with animal head

Iran, Luristan, c. 800–600 B.C.
Bronze
H. 6.7 cm, L. 20.8 cm, D. 3.2 cm
Dallas Art Association Purchase, 1963.22

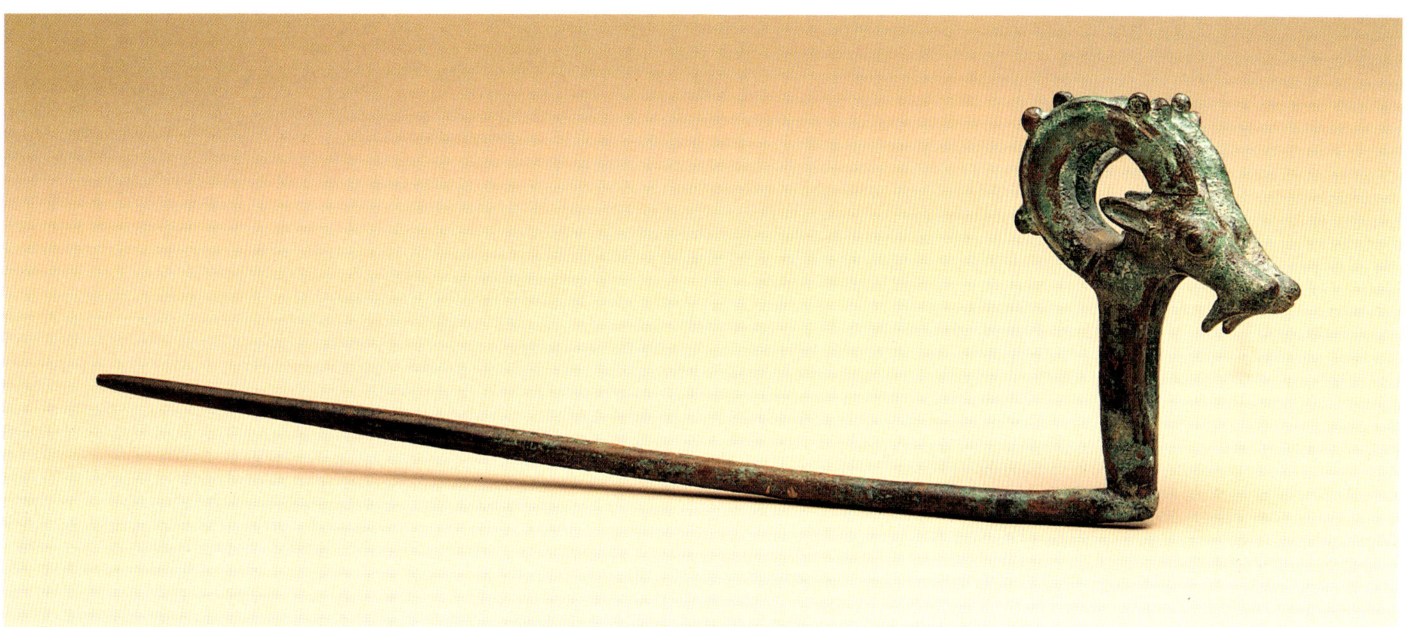

ORNAMENTAL BRONZE pins are another example of Luristanian bronze work employing animal imagery. The DMA ram-headed example was cast by the lost-wax method in five pieces (each pair of horns, each animal head, and the pin itself). Horizontal pins appear as often as vertical pins in Iranian art and were probably used to pin large sections of garments together. The double curve of the two pairs of animal horns is especially elegant.

REFERENCES: Muscarella 1988; Hôtel Drouot 1972, nos. 221, 226, and 287; Carnegie Institute 1964, no. 18, a finial with similar mouflon or ibex head; Carnegie Institute 1964, no. 23, a whetstone with similar head. For a discussion of Luristanian pins see Moorey 1971, 172–215. For Luristanian metalwork see Curtis 1988, 23–44.

13.

Tripod in the form of a man-animal

Iran, Pre-Achaemenid, seventh–sixth century B.C.
Bronze
H. 12.6 cm, W. 3.2 cm, D. 5.8 cm
Gift of Mr. and Mrs. Cecil H. Green, 1966.24

AN EXCEPTIONALLY REFINED piece, this tripod may reflect the influence of Assyrian art, with its great man-animal sculptures. The figure has the head and forelegs of a horse, but the forelegs are drawn up so as to suggest they are the arms of the rest of the figure, which is generally human in form, though with animal hocks and tail. The figure is ithyphallic and has a three-ring necklace, two-ring anklets, and a two-ring tail band as ornaments. Cross-hatching defines the figure's hide or skin. It supports a tripod-shaped structure on its head. The whole figure was presumably part of a set supporting a larger bronze tripod. Although vase and tripod supports in the shape of animals are common, this particular figure is unusual, possibly unique. The work is an exceptionally fine piece of lost-wax casting with cold-worked ornament on the surface.

REFERENCES: Ghirshman 1964, 78, no. 103, a vase handle with animal-human supports.

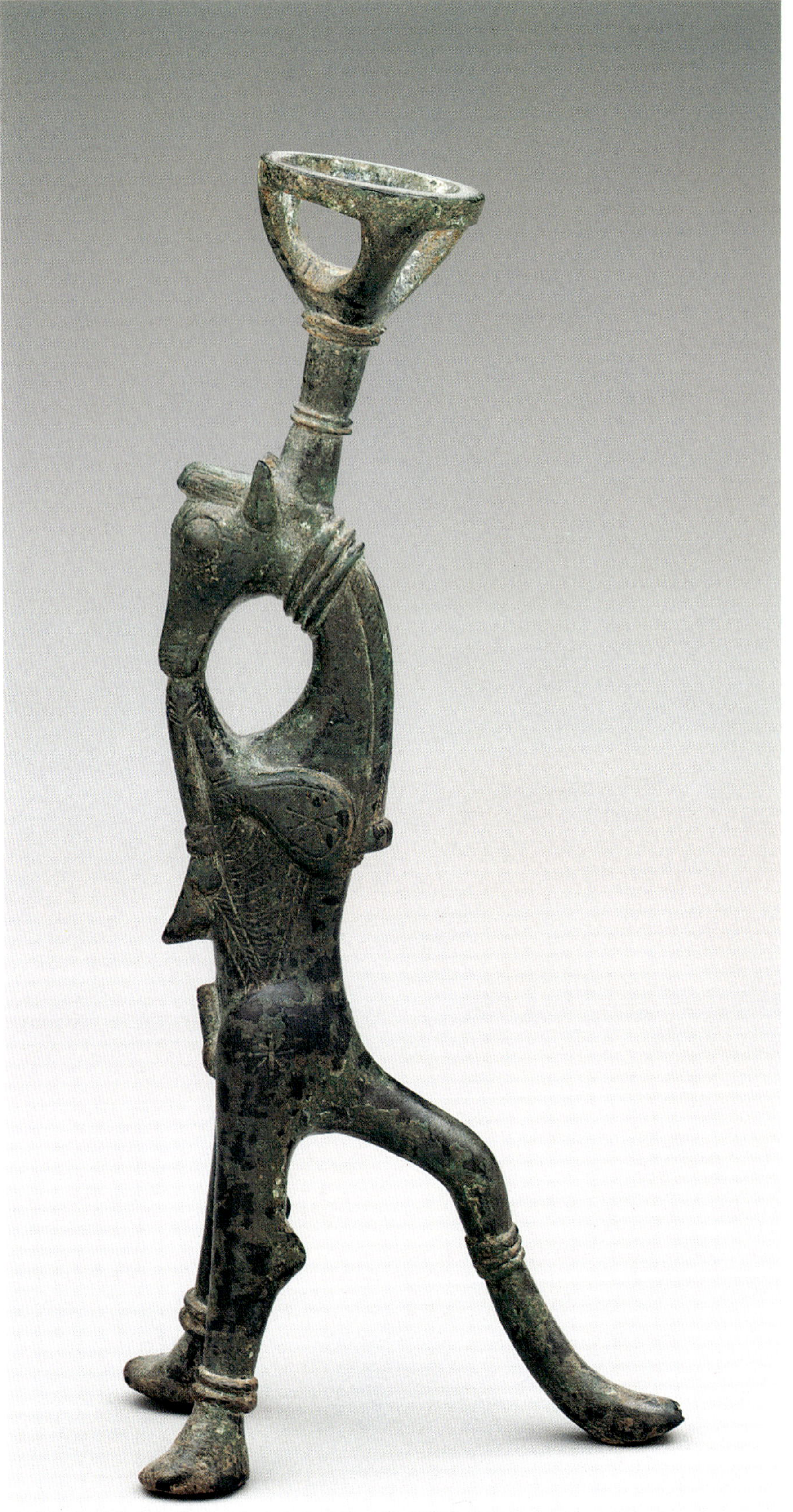

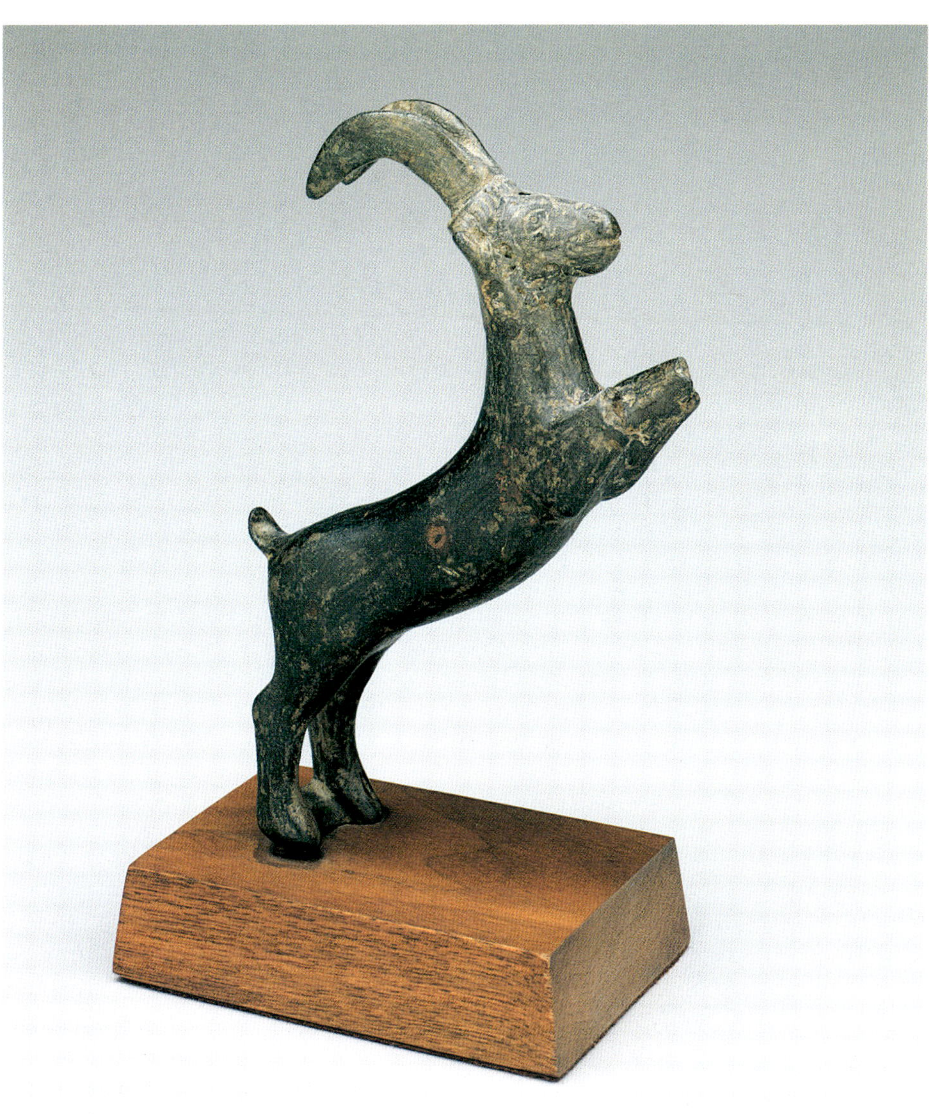

14.

Rearing ibex figure

Iran, Early Achaemenid, sixth–fifth century B.C.
Bronze
H. 13.4 cm, W. 3.1 cm, D. 8.5 cm
Gift of the Wilson Family in memory of Edward Lawrence Wilson, 1977.38

THIS FIGURE, WHICH MAY have been the support of a bronze vessel, is much more common than the previous piece. There are many striking animal support figures in Achaemenid Persian art. The ibex is shown in a rearing posture; the two front legs are largely missing. The animal's curly hair and facial features are indicated by cold-working on the surface after the body was cast by the lost-wax method. Both the naturalism and the detailed working of the surface indicate a later production date than that of the previous figure.

REFERENCES: Hoffmann 1964, no. 76; Moorey 1981, no. 658; Ghirshman 1964, 96, no. 125; Porada 1965, 169, pl. 49, and 171, pl. 50; Terrace 1962, nos. 43, 44, and 59.

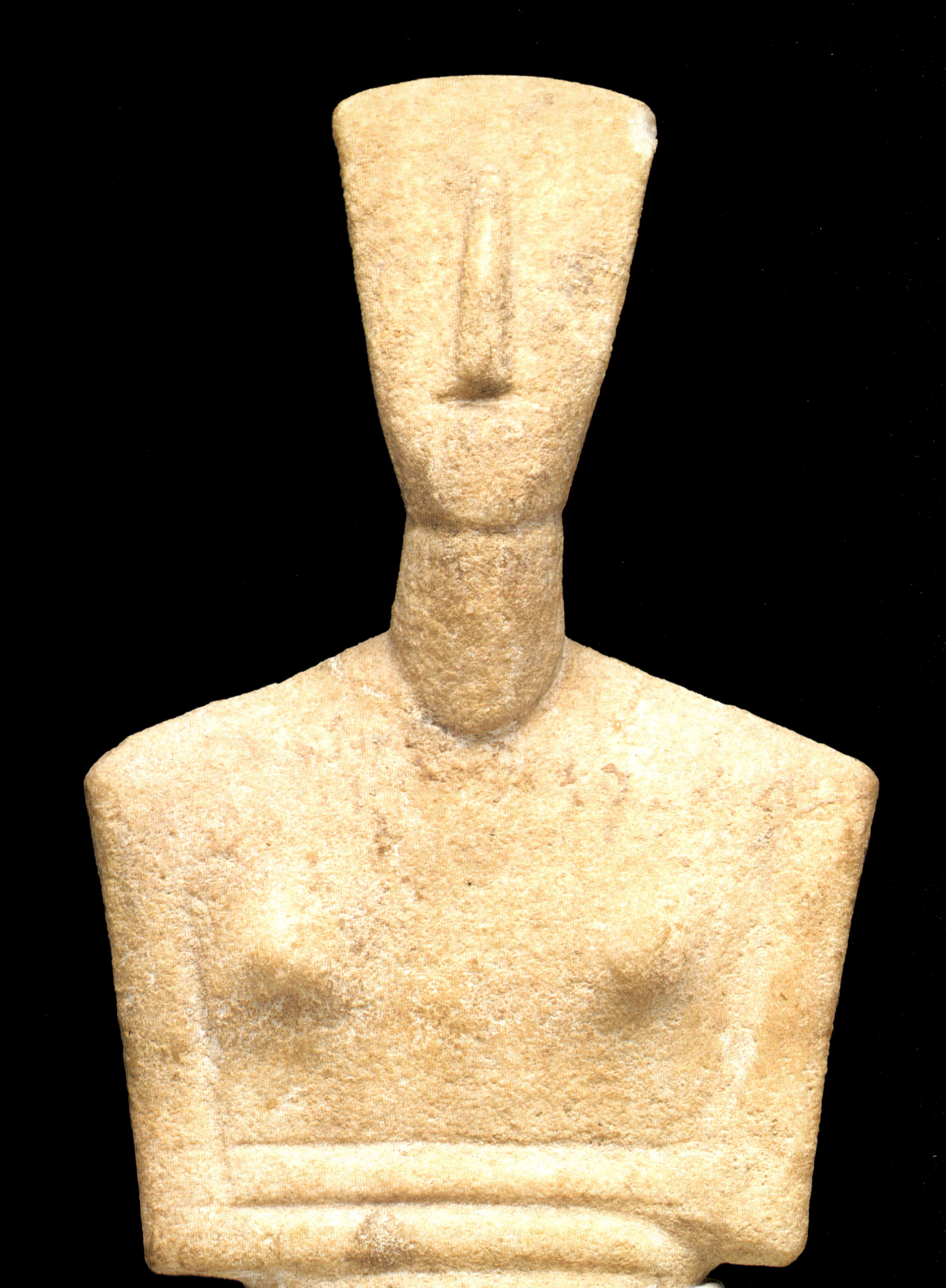

Chapter 3

Greece: Man and Nature

Nineteenth-century scholars saw classical Greece as a purely humanist culture, born, so to speak, fully formed, like Athena from the head of Zeus. This idea ignores the character of Greek cult and society, which were deeply rooted in nature. The idealist view of Greece was already challenged in the nineteenth century by anthropologists such as Sir James Frazer, whose work *The Golden Bough* tried to imagine the actual nature of Greco-Roman cults in a worldwide context. Frazer's efforts to consider Greek religion as similar to tribal or "primitive" religions were continued by Jane Harrison, who attempted to understand the ritual underpinnings of Greek myth. Today, anthropologists and classical scholars like Walter Burkett and Jean-Pierre Vernant are still trying to comprehend the peculiar character of early Greek religion, which might, in fact, best be understood from the point of view of the cults of Hinduism, a living polytheistic Indo-European religion, rather than from the viewpoint of Christian and capitalist Europe.

In the Homeric epics, the bible of the Greeks, the gods appear in human form. Nevertheless, all major Greek gods have animal attributes (Zeus's eagle, Athena's owl, Artemis's bear, Ares' boar, Dionysus's panthers, etc.), and many minor gods regularly appear in man-animal form, as did the Egyptian and Near Eastern deities (e.g., Triton, Proteus, Typhon, Pan, Nereus), while other Greek mythological characters also take hybrid shapes (e.g., centaurs, satyrs, sileni, Nereids). Then there are mythic figures who are turned into other natural forms: Io, who becomes a cow, Daphne a tree, and Clytie a sunflower. In the dark but very informative tale of Actaeon, the doomed hunter is turned into a stag by Artemis and is torn to pieces by his own dogs. A similar, highly ambiguous story concerns Hyacinthus, who was accidentally killed by his lover, the god Apollo, and was turned into the hyacinth flower. The coinage of ancient Elis, the city-state near Olympia, which was the central sacred place of Greek-speaking people, shows Zeus, the king of the gods, as a mature bearded human figure on one side and as the divine eagle of power on the other.

The Greek-speaking peoples who arrived in the Balkan peninsula late in the third millennium B.C. met populations of settled villagers with whom they mixed to form the lavish Mycenaean Bronze Age civilization. The great complexity of the Greek language testifies to this cultural blend, as does the nature of Greek mother-goddesses in historical times, with their clear connections to non-Indo-European deities of Crete, the Aegean, and the Near East. The Greeks' stories of their gods, such as Zeus's many love affairs, also imply a meeting of different kinds of societies, since the tales recount several versions or combine various characters into their fabric. A collision of Indo-European warriors and earlier farming peoples also occurred in Anatolia, as the Hittites, the Mycenaean Greeks, the Phrygians, the Lydians, the later Ionian Greeks, and the Persians periodically dominated settlements going back to Neolithic times.

It is hardly surprising to find a common symbolism of animal art and fertility deities, of the sort discussed in the Near Eastern chapter, appearing in Greek cults from the Mycenaean Age down to the Classical period. Until the balance of power in the Mediterranean shifted westward, when the Greek states (for once fighting together) defeated the Persians in the early fifth century B.C., all the great Near Eastern civilizations—Egypt, the Hittites, Assyria, Babylonia, Persia—were clearly world powers of great wealth, refined artistic craftsmanship, and organized military capacity compared to the Greeks. What is remarkable about Greek art and religion in these early stages is just how stubbornly Greek they appear to be. To the rapidly expanding Greek states of the seventh century B.C., the glories of Egyptian art were interesting, but not to be slavishly copied, and the magical powers of oriental gods were fascinating, but not awe-inspiring. In some ways, the early Greeks shared the nature-oriented cults of the Mediterranean world, but in other, more critical, ways they had a determined will toward their own idea of divine powers, a view that was canny, fatalistic, and essentially Indo-European.

Fertility cults in early Greece were part of a larger web of myths and cults associated with deities of the earth, who were especially important to people whose livelihood and wealth came from farming. Demeter, the Greek equivalent of Near Eastern mother-goddesses like Ishtar, was the protector of grain and growing crops. In the myth of her daughter, Persephone—who was carried off by Hades, the god of the underworld, and then returned to her mother for several months of the year—the annual rhythm of seedtime and harvest, summer and winter, appears in human form. The little Boeotian figurines of deities (cat. no. 19) are offertory statuettes representing Demeter and Persephone as fertility goddesses. The pomegranate necklace on one of the figures refers to the pomegranate seeds that Persephone ate in the underworld, which forced her to spend the winter months in the land of the dead. These ceramic figures are highly formalized and symbolic, were placed in graves and shrines, and are little geometric diagrams of the forces of nature.

It is not easy to disentangle the complex ways in which the early Greeks thought about the relationship of man and animals. On the one hand, Greek religious cult owed much to Near Eastern deities of fertility, who were associated with animals. Both the "Gilgamesh" figure clasping heraldic animals on the DMA's bronze standard (cat. no. 10) and the relief of the Egyptian god Thoth with an ibis head (cat. no. 3) exemplify this tradition. So do the various fertility goddess figures in the DMA collections, whose associations are with crops, immortality, and the birth of young, whether human or animal. On the other hand, the Greeks' own Indo-European tradition, militant and warlike in almost all the manifestations we can trace, meant an emphasis on the animal most important to aristocratic warriors: the horse. Horses and cattle were both important to the Greeks as signs of wealth, but horses had specific connections with nobles. It is no coincidence that an image of a horse, not a human, is the first figural form to appear in Greek painting after the collapse of the Mycenaean Bronze Age. Since the Greeks were also ardent huntsmen, boars (as on the DMA's Corinthian-Etruscan helmet, cat. no. 34) and deer (as on the DMA's Etruscan amphora, cat. no. 32) were important, too.

Not only in myth did the mysterious power of bloodshed and transformation have religious force. The central experience in Greek cult practice was blood sacrifice. To kill an animal ritually, particularly a bull, by spilling the blood from the animal's throat upon the altar and ceremonially consuming the meat, was part of all important Greek ceremonies. This communion with the physical world of nature—the horse slain at funerals, the cock whose blood was spilt as an offering to the gods, the great ox killed at major Greek festivals—was a communion with the powers of existence and also a reestablishment of the formal bonds between men and the gods and between man and man in human society.

In the *Odyssey,* Homer gives a pristine view of such a sacrifice:

> When everything was ready, Lord Nestor began the sacrifice. Holding the bowls of holy water and barley, he threw some of the ox's hair on the fire, and made a long prayer to Athena. Then, when the barley had been scattered, Thrasymedes struck the ox a mighty blow; his axe severed the tendons of its neck, and it collapsed on the ground. The watching women cried out; but the men held the ox's head while one of them cut its throat. Dark blood poured out and life left the carcass. ([trans. Rieu] 3.430–63)

15.
Figurine

Cycladic, c. 2400–2300 B.C.
Marble
H. 30.5 cm, W. 10.2 cm, D. 2.5 cm
Gift of Virginia Lucas Nick, 1992.2

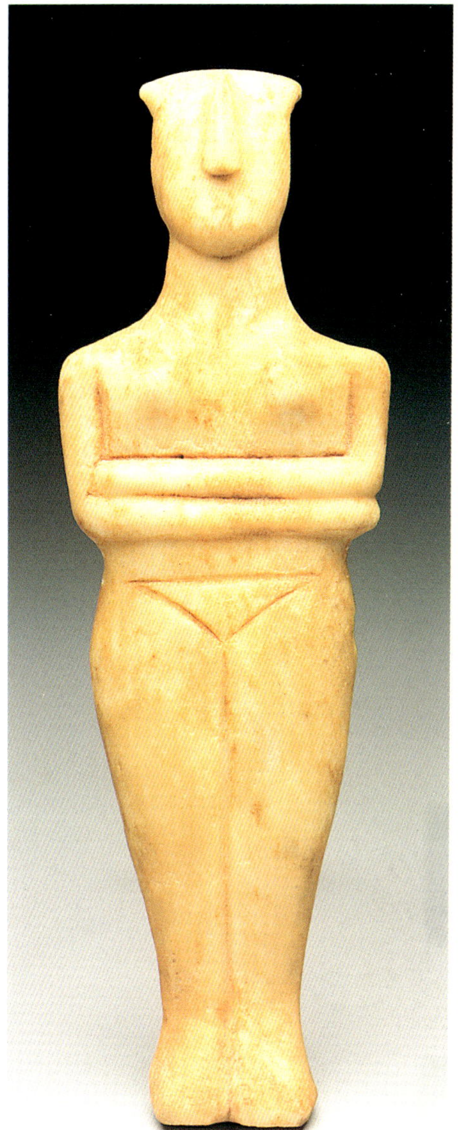

THIS ERECT FIGURE OF Greek island marble depicts a naked female in a frontal pose. This excellent example of Cycladic sculpture and others like it typify in form and subject the classic expression of the human figure in Greek island art during the third millennium B.C. The head is lyre-shaped with the crest markedly broadened. The strong vertical nose bisects the convex curvature of the face. The arms of the figure are modeled and horizontally set; no indications of fingers are present. The breasts are clearly indicated, one slightly higher than the other. The abdominal and inguinal lines form the pubic triangle. The thighs are heavy and taper without disruption at the knee into the lower legs. The feet lack indications of toes. The leg-cleft is unperforated and only slightly deeper than the incisions that form the pubic area. The leg-cleft is similar on the back of the figure, and the spine is rendered in a like manner. The buttocks are clearly modeled.

This figurine belongs to the Spedos variety of Early Cycladic marble sculpture. The lyre-shaped head, rounded chin, convex face, folded-arm pattern, and modeled waist of this example are attributes common to this group. The lack of distinction between the upper and lower legs is not a typical feature of the Spedos variety but is more common to the Dokathismata variety, which appears to overlap in date with later examples of the Spedos variety. The clear modeling of the buttocks on this figure is an unusual feature in a Cycladic marble figurine.

Although marble figurines of human form are known from the Neolithic period in the Cyclades, the best known types are from the Early Bronze Age, or the Early Cycladic period. The figurines, predominantly female, are generally upright (or reclining). They emerge in limited numbers in Early Cycladic I (EC I), reach their peak of production during EC II, are significantly reduced in number during EC III, and become virtually nonexistent by the Middle Cycladic period. Although examples of the canonical types are known in ivory, bone, shell, clay, and metal, the primary material is coarse-grained marble, which is found on most Cycladic islands and is the dominant stone of some.

The vast majority of recorded find spots are island graves, a fact that has led to a number of plausible interpretations for the figurines. They have been compared to the Egyptian *ushabtis,* magical workers who served the dead. For the Cycladic peoples, the purpose of these figurines has been considered to be of a sexual nature, given their strong fertility elements. Others regard them as substitutes for human sacrifice, toys (although none have thus far been found in children's graves), underworld guides for the dead, mythical characters, or divinities, especially the Great Mother Goddess of fertility, although a number of the figures are male. Each argument, with its strengths and weaknesses, underscores our need for more precise information about these graceful and simplistic images that have much visual appeal.

REFERENCES: Thimme 1977; Doumas 1983; Renfrew 1991.

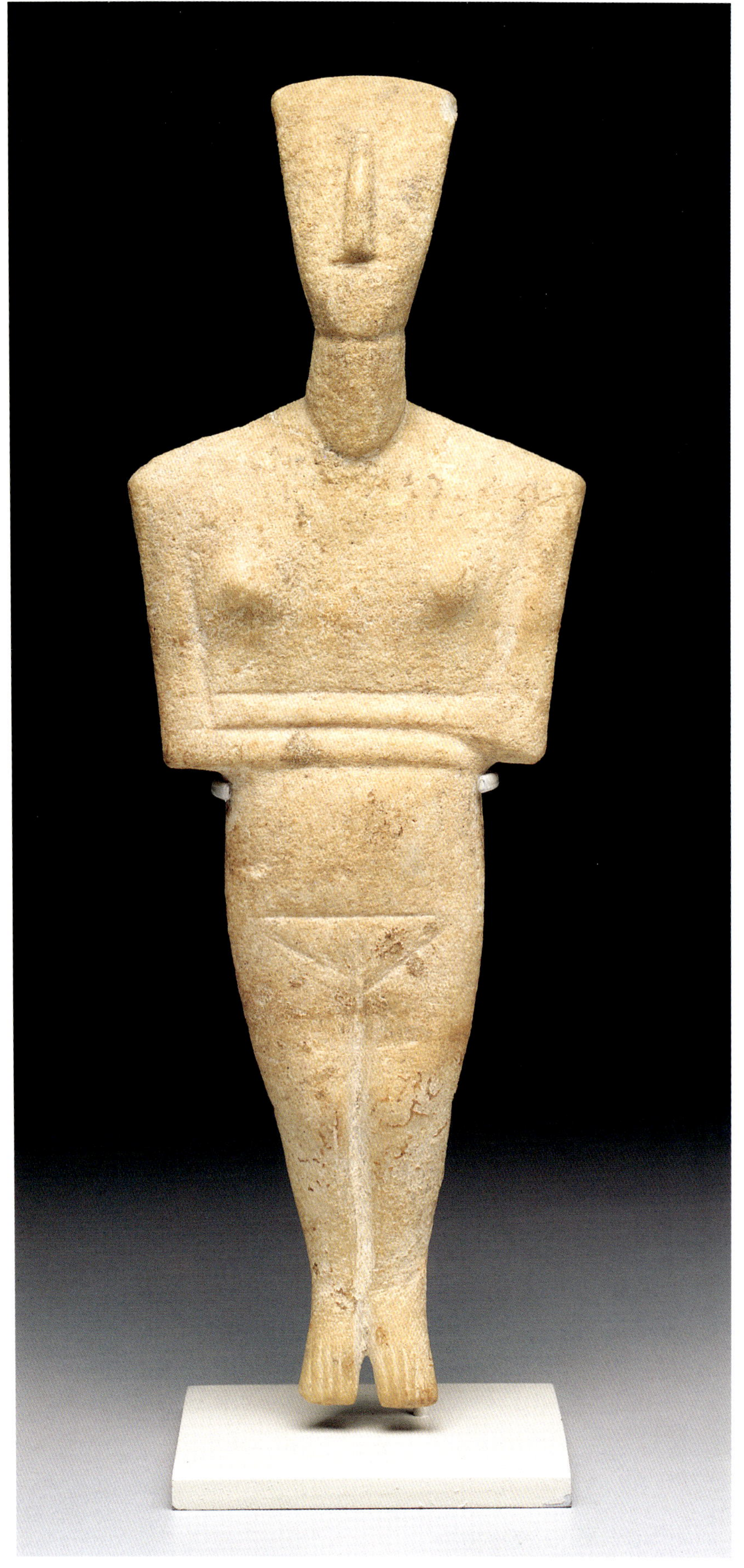

16.

Figurine

Cycladic, c. 2300 B.C.
Marble
H. 27.8 cm, W. 9.9 cm, D. 2 cm
Foundation for the Arts Collection, The Mr. and Mrs. Stanley Marcus Collection of Fertility Figures, 1982.292.FA

THIS FIGURINE IS MORE angular than the previous example and perhaps slightly later in date. The pronounced flatness of the figure and its trapezoidal face, pointed shoulders, widely spaced breasts, and shallow leg-cleft all contribute to its classification to the Dokathismata variety, named after an Early Cycladic cemetery on the island of Amorgos. As with other examples of this type, the forearms of this figure are strictly horizontal, folded at the waist, and indicated by little more than incisions. The abdomen is swollen, a feature found on other figurines in the Dokathismata variety, and is perhaps meant to indicate pregnancy. The leg-cleft, which intersects the pubic triangle, deepens below the ankles to separate the feet. On the back of this figure the neck is articulated to the torso by an incised V line. The spine and leg-cleft are indicated by separate shallow incisions. The toes have been restored.

This figurine is very close in its details and general form to a second example in Houston (Thimme 1977, no. 216) and a third in Athens (Doumas 1983, no. 178). Thimme (p. 481) believes that these two previously published figurines were carved by the same sculptor.

REFERENCES: Thimme 1977; Doumas 1983; Renfrew 1991.

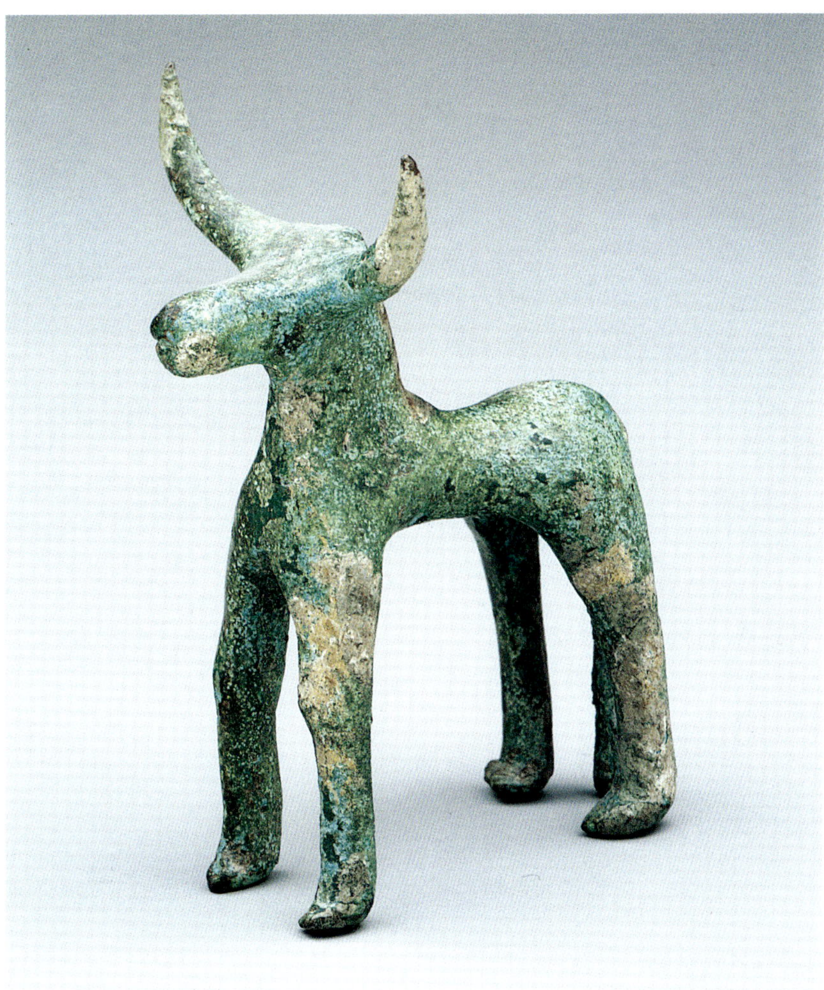

17.
Bull

Greek, Geometric period, late eighth or early seventh century B.C.
Bronze
H. 8.4 cm, W. 6.9 cm, D. 4.5 cm
Foundation for the Arts Collection, gift of Mr. and Mrs. James H. Clark, 1974.85.FA

THE BULL IS INTACT AND solid cast by the lost-wax method. The body is slightly swayed, rising gently to the rump. The tail is unusually long, more like those on Geometric period bronze horses, and descends to the ground. The legs are stiff and only slightly splayed, with spurs on the forelegs to indicate joints. The feet are flattened to provide stability since the figure lacks a base. The neck is thick and the eyes and ears are not indicated. The great horns, the primary element that distinguishes this figure from those of horses, curve out and upward from the crown of the head. A horizontal slash across the end of the cylindrical muzzle indicates the mouth.

Hundreds of bronze bull figurines have been excavated at the sanctuary of Zeus and Hera at Olympia. The bronze images were produced in such quantities, undoubtedly in the immediate area, primarily during the eighth and early seventh centuries B.C. for pilgrims to the shrine to use as votive offerings to the two divinities. Live bulls were sacrificed to Zeus at Olympia, but this was a costly exercise. The small bronze, and even terracotta, substitutes catered to the needs of the average dedicator.

Differences in style separate this bull from the general type found at Olympia, indicating that it comes from another part of Greece, perhaps Thessaly.

REFERENCES: For examples from Olympia see Furtwängler 1890, pls. 10–12; Neugebauer 1931, 55–57, nos. 143, 145, and 148–49, and 4, pl. 17; Hill 1955, 41, and pl. 30, fig. 10. An example of the typical Olympia type is in Houston, see Hoffmann 1970, 147, no. 68. A slightly later example with flattened feet is in the Bastis collection, see Hall 1987, 172, no. 87.

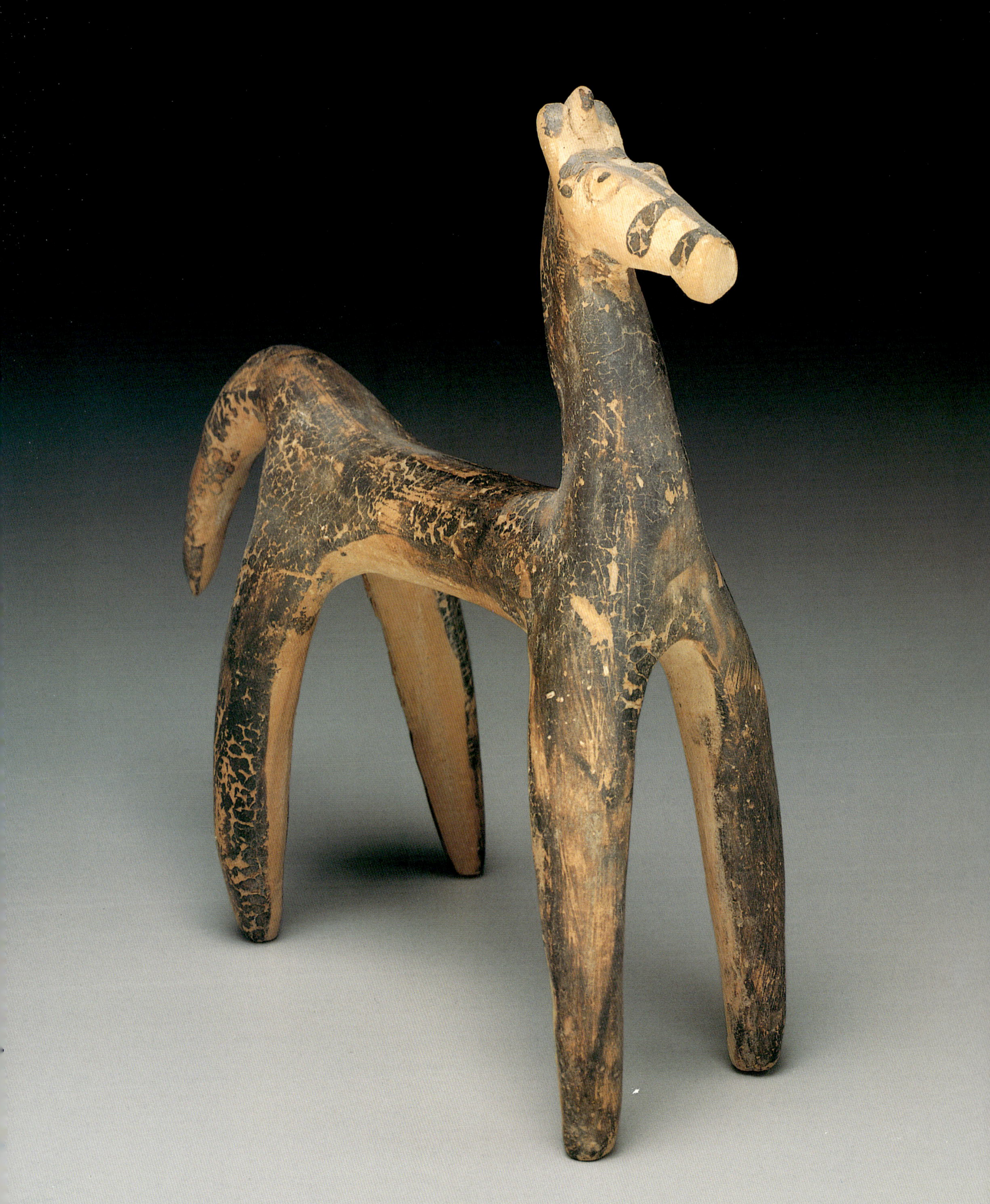

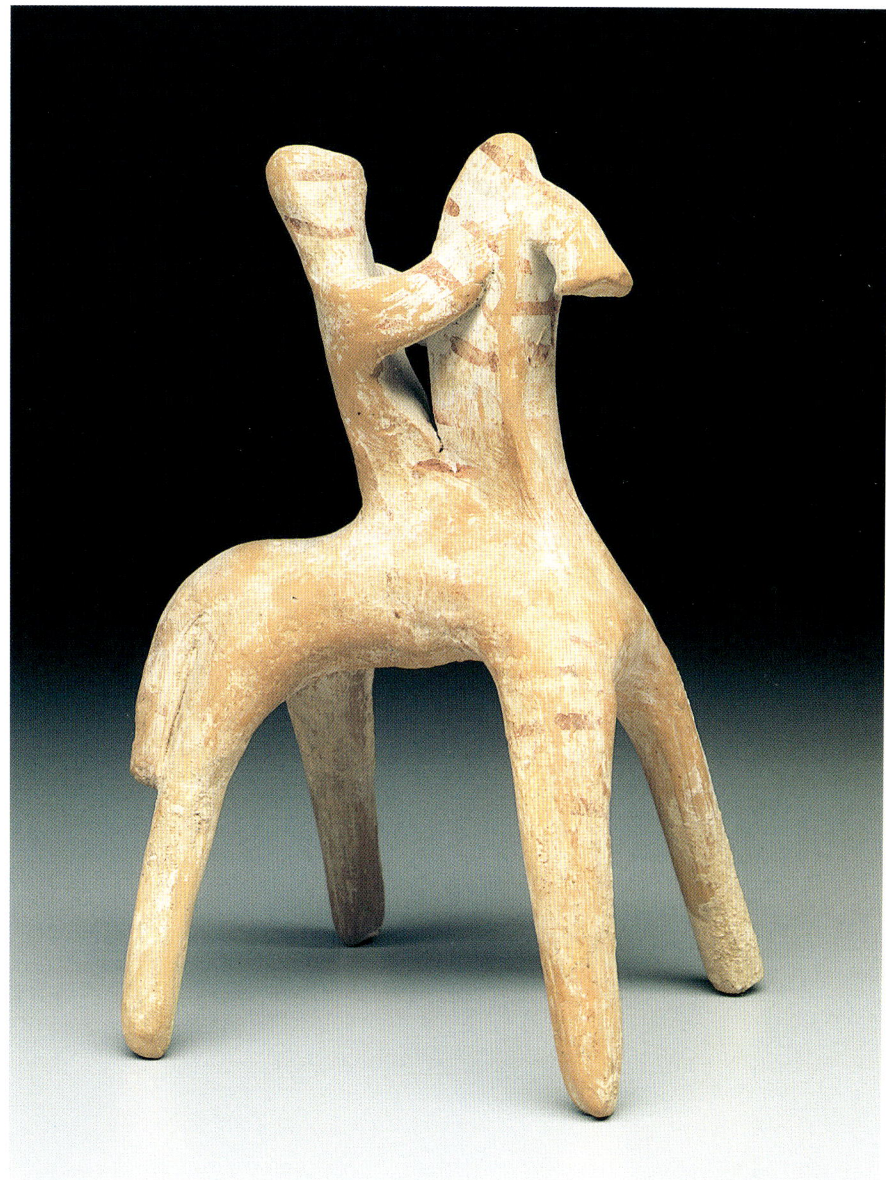

18.

Figurines: horse and horse with rider

Greek, Boeotian, sixth century B.C.
Ceramic
Horse: H. 13.3 cm, W. 12.7 cm, D. 5.1 cm
Horse with rider: H. 11.7 cm, W. 7.6 cm, D. 6.7 cm
Foundation for the Arts Collection, gift of Mr. and Mrs. James H. Clark, 1974.90.FA and 1974.91.FA

THE FIRST EXAMPLE IS A riderless horse covered in glaze except for the underside of its tail, body, legs, and head. Glazed bands on the face and muzzle might suggest a bridle. The eyes are indicated by raised areas accented with dotted circles. The tail is arched and angled away from the body.

The horse and rider are decorated with matte paint; the simple reddish brown bands over a white ground give both man and mount a zebralike appearance. The rider lacks features and clutches the neck of the creature with both arms. His legs are fused with the body of the horse beyond distinction. The legs of the animal are slightly splayed, and its neck is pulled back in coordination with the backward tilt of the horseman. The horse's pose gives the impression that it has come to a sudden stop, brought about by the body commands of the rider.

Horses were highly prized animals in Greek culture and were considered symbols of wealth and rank. Many Greek aristocrats, like Hippocrates, bore the word *hippos* (horse) in their names, and the sons of Peisistratos—Hippias and Hipparchus—were likened to the Dioscuri, the equestrian twins Castor and Pollux, who ride to mythical adventure in Greek art and literature. The overlapping imagery of the hybrid creatures known in Greek mythology as centaurs is perhaps derived from the melding of man and beast, a process seen in the horse and rider here. Homer, in a passage perhaps reflective of his own time, speaks of expert riders who could leap from horse to horse in a linked group of four abreast while in a full gallop (*Iliad* 15.679ff.).

The Boeotian plain was one of the few regions of Greece where the great swiftness of horses could be appreciated, and the Boeotian cavalry played a significant role in the Persian wars. Homer also recounts how Achilles sacrificed four strong-necked horses to the dead Patroclus (*Iliad* 23.171–72), and archaeological excavation has shown that members of Mycenaean royalty had their favorite teams of horses buried outside their tombs. Across the straits from Boeotia at nearby Eretria, horses were still sacrificed in funeral ceremonies as late as Hesiod's time, but by the sixth century B.C. they were apparently too valuable to the families of the deceased to be lost in this manner. For the Boeotians, the small terracotta grave offerings would have to substitute in the next life.

REFERENCES: For comparative horses with and without riders see Ure 1934, pls. 15 and 16; Grace 1939, figs. 47, 49, and 51; Higgins 1967, 46, and pl. 19E; Chesterman 1974, 35, fig. 23. For the horse in Greek culture see Anderson 1961. For horse burials in Greece see Coldstream 1977, 349–50.

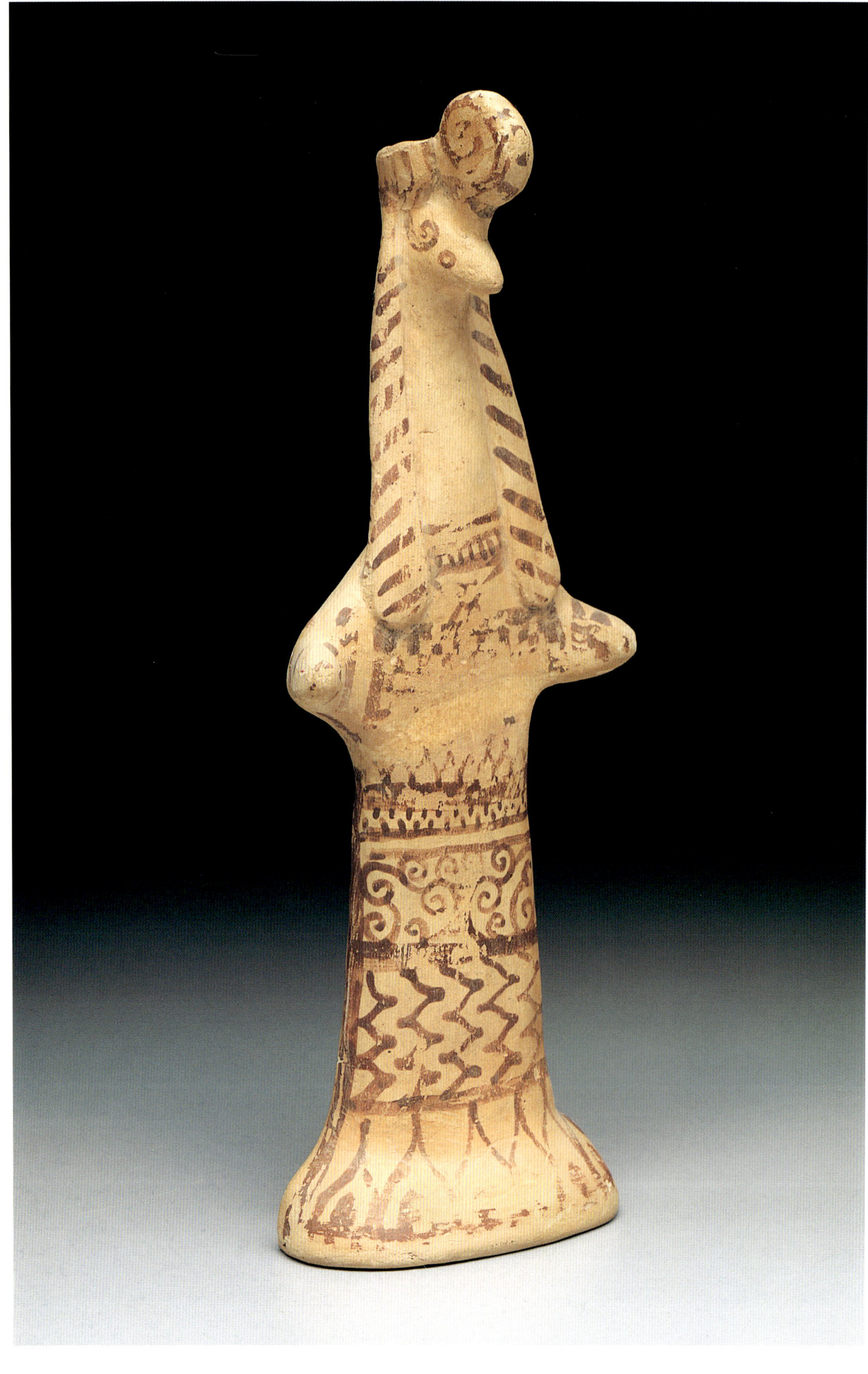

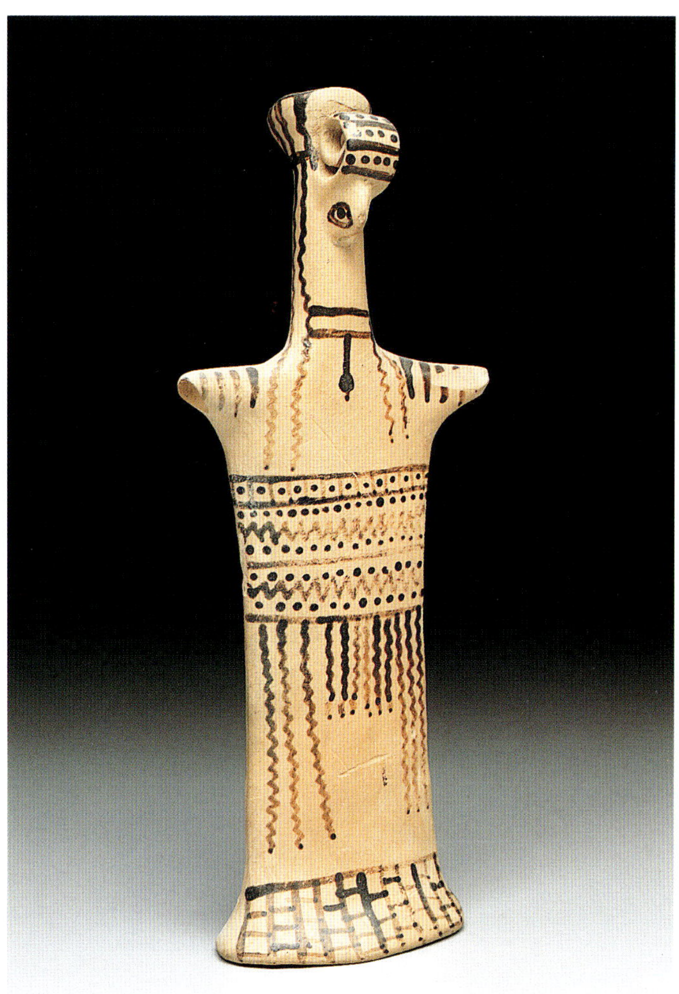

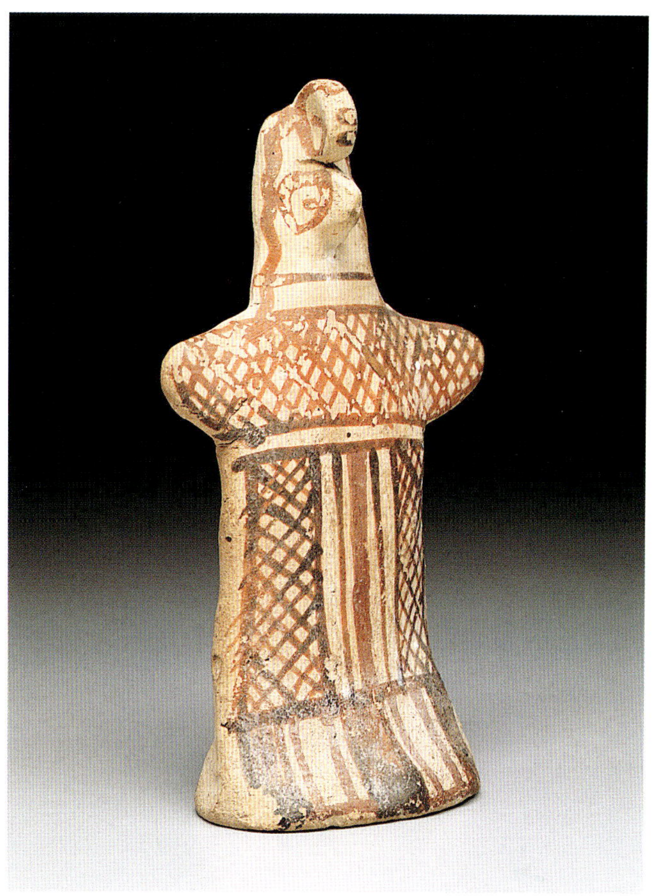

19.

Figurines: standing goddesses or women

Greek, Boeotian, sixth century B.C.
Painted terracotta
OPPOSITE: H. 21.9 cm, W. 7.9 cm, D. 3.8 cm
LEFT: H. 21 cm, W. 9.5 cm, D. 4.1 cm
RIGHT: H. 11.4 cm, W. 7 cm, D. 3.2 cm
Foundation for the Arts Collection, gift of Mr. and Mrs. James H. Clark, 1974.87.FA, 1974.88.FA, and 1974.92.FA

THE FIRST OF THESE handmade figurines (opposite) belongs to a large group of early sixth-century-B.C. examples, many of which were recovered from the ancient cemeteries at Tanagra in the last century. The cruciform figure has a flat body, a very long neck, and a mouselike head surmounted by a *polos* (cylindrical cap) with a single spiral emerging from the front. A painted curl covers each temple area, small circles indicate the eyes, and diagonal lines depict long, vertical tresses that cascade down to the shoulders. Various curvilinear and other abstract patterns decorate the front of the body. A pendant or suspended pomegranate is painted on the lower neck.

The second figurine (left) is a slightly later version of the first, datable to the mid-sixth century B.C. This type was also excavated at Tanagra and was recorded in the cemetery at neighboring Rhitsona (ancient Mycalessus) in Boeotia as well. This type differs from the former primarily in its smaller size, shorter neck, beaked face with dotted circles for the eyes, and painted (instead of modeled) hair. A clearly painted image of a pomegranate hangs from a double band on its neck, suggesting the figure is of a goddess, perhaps Demeter or Persephone (see cat. no. 20). The Boeotian plain today, as in antiquity, is a productive area for wheat, so these images of grain goddesses find a fitting place on Boeotian soil.

The third figurine (right) can be classed with the second, although its smaller size and more summary decoration might place it a few years later in date. The *polos* has all but disappeared, and the eyes have grown larger. The body is thicker and decorated with crosshatching on the front.

REFERENCES: For an example of the first type see Higgins 1967, pl. 18A–B. For the second type see Higgins 1967, pl. 18C–D; Ure 1934, pl. 13 (bottom); Grace 1939, figs. 47, 49, 51, and 62.

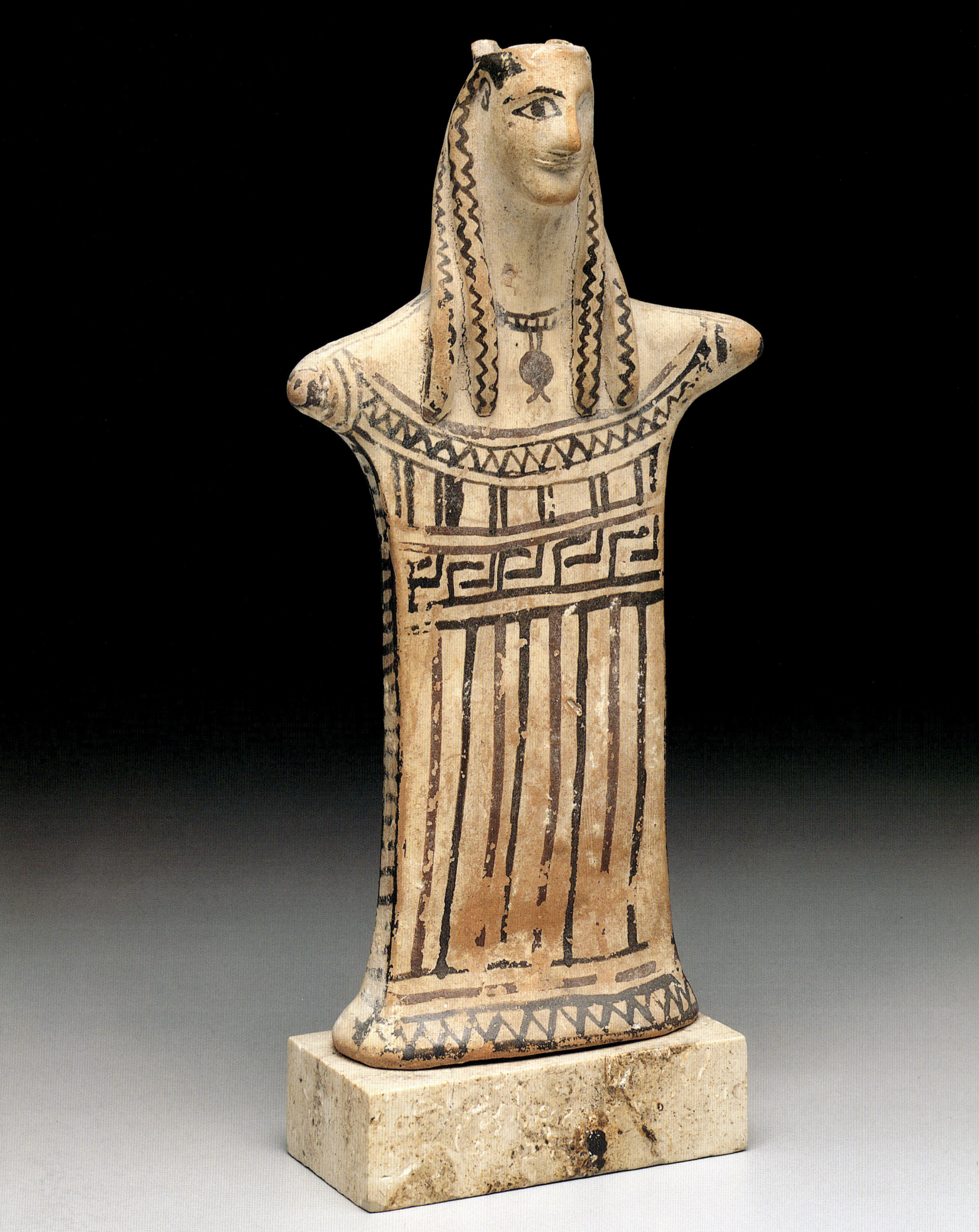

20.

Standing woman

Greek, Boeotian, first half of sixth century B.C.
Painted terracotta
H. 6.8 cm, W. 3.6 cm, D. 1.8 cm
Foundation for the Arts Collection, gift of Mr. and Mrs. James H. Clark, 1974.86.FA

THIS FEMALE FIGURE STANDS erect, facing front with her arms held out to either side. The dynamic cruciform appearance of the figure gives it power and draws our attention to its form despite its small scale. She is clad in a long gown that covers her feet and is decorated with different linear motifs. The body is flat and handmade. Her hair hangs over her shoulders and consists of long rolled strips of clay painted with a zigzag pattern in black glaze with added red. The head is far more developed than the body and is mold-made. Around her neck hangs a painted pomegranate, a sure indication that this figure is meant to represent either the goddess Demeter or her daughter, Persephone.

The cult of Demeter and Persephone centered on the renewal of life. According to Greek mythology, the pomegranate was the fruit eaten by Persephone in the underworld before her ascent back to the world of the living. The pomegranate, therefore, became the symbol for immortality. It is not surprising to find terracotta figurines like the example here in ancient Greek graves, especially those of children. The figurines were also dedicated at woodland shrines, major sanctuaries, and even at domestic altars as part of the household cult. The type of female figurine seen here, with handmade and mold-made parts, was especially popular in central Greece, particularly in Boeotia. Since these figurines were not meant for export but for local consumption, the coroplasts (Greek *koroplathos*), or modelers, often established their workshops in the immediate vicinity of a major town or sanctuary.

Terracotta figurines have a long history in Boeotia, first appearing there in the eighth century B.C. This particular example belongs to a group of Boeotian figurines in the Museum collections that display the stylistic developments of the female types from the late seventh to the mid-sixth century B.C.

PUBLICATIONS: Bromberg 1983, 95, no. 91.

REFERENCES: For Archaic Boeotian female figurines see Ure 1934, 54; Grace 1939, 27; Higgins 1967, 45–47. For grave offerings see Kurtz and Boardman 1971, esp. 209.

21.
Kerykeion (Hermes' staff)

Greek, early fifth century B.C.
Bronze
H. 12 cm, W. 10.5 cm
Gift of the Junior League of Dallas, 1969.7

TWO HERALDICALLY POISED serpents are joined in a loop supported by an Ionic capital and a thin abacus. The snakes are bearded in typical Archaic Greek fashion, and their eyes have been drilled to receive an inlay (now lost) presumably of a material other than bronze. The scales of the serpents were rendered by a punch in parallel rows from the base of the head to the beginning of the loop, which is undecorated. The spirals on the Ionic capital were also created with a punch. The underside of the capital has a hole in which a long rod was placed. Oxidized iron residue at the base of the loop indicates that the rod may have been made of iron.

The Greek *kerykeion* (Latin *caduceus*) appears in art from the Early Archaic period most often as the staff of Hermes, messenger of the gods and guide to mortals and immortals alike. It is sometimes held by Iris, another messenger of the gods (usually Hera), or by a Nike, who in this context serves as the herald of victory. Hermes, the god of herdsmen, was also known by the title Nomios (the pasturer). This office was granted to him by his half brother Apollo, who also bestowed on him a magic wand (not the *kerykeion*) to be used as a staff and symbol of his authority (*Homeric Hymn* 4.529). The origin of the *kerykeion* is not clear, but it may have its source in the ancient Near East. In his capacity as a guide, Hermes was the protector of travelers and merchants, as well as the patron of the thieves who preyed on them.

Bronze examples of the *kerykeion* are often decorated with snake heads, and in later representations the staff is sometimes depicted with snakes coiled about it. (See the caduceus on the DMA's English candelabrum, fig. 11.) These may be fanciful artistic derivatives of ribbons, which occasionally adorn the *kerykeion*. However, the snake was considered to be a communicator between the living and the dead because it spends time in the sunlight as well as underground. In this context, the reptiles make a fitting adornment to Hermes' staff, since in his capacity as Psychopompos (guide of souls) he escorted the shades of dead mortals from the world of the living to the realm of Hades.

A number of bronze *kerykeia* were found in Magna Graecia, and this example is reportedly from Segesta, Sicily. Those recovered with the rod in place often have a votive inscription and served as a dedication at a sanctuary. The DMA piece is like a number of *kerykeia* from South Italy and Sicily that also combine snake heads with an Ionic capital. The closest parallel to the DMA *kerykeion* is the example in the Bastis collection (New York), although the DMA piece is unequaled in the fine rendering of the serpents' heads and decorative scales on the bodies.

PUBLICATIONS: Hoffmann 1970, 167 no. 78; Hornbostel 1979, 48, fig. 23.

REFERENCES: For discussions on the *kerykeion* and additional examples see Boetzkes 1921, vol. 11, 330 ff.; Crome 1938–39, 117–26; Muscarella 1974, no. 28; Hall 1987, 188, no. 96. For Hermes as a guide and messenger in ancient art see *LIMC* 1990, vol. 5, pt. 1, 286–87; for the *kerykeion*, see 385.

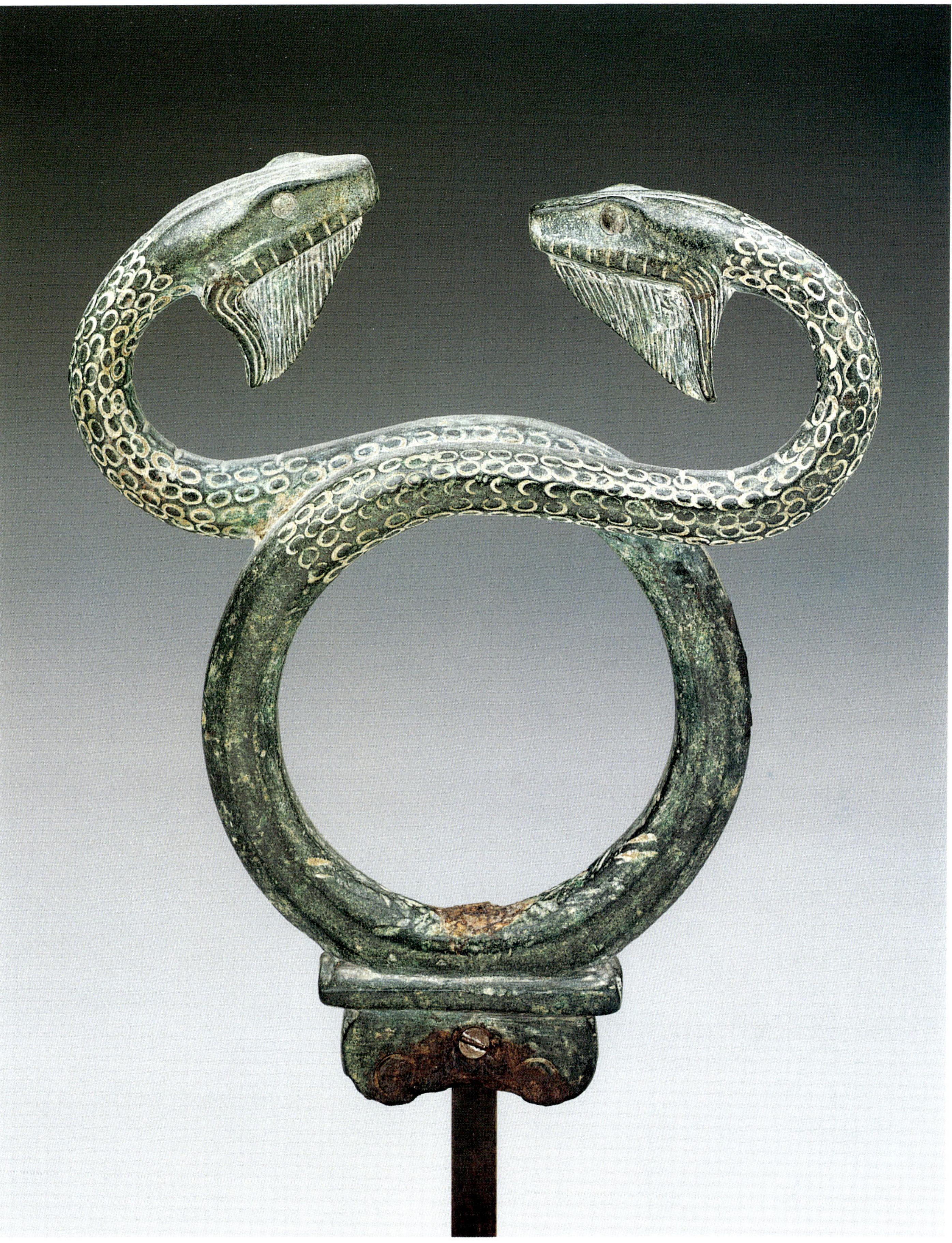

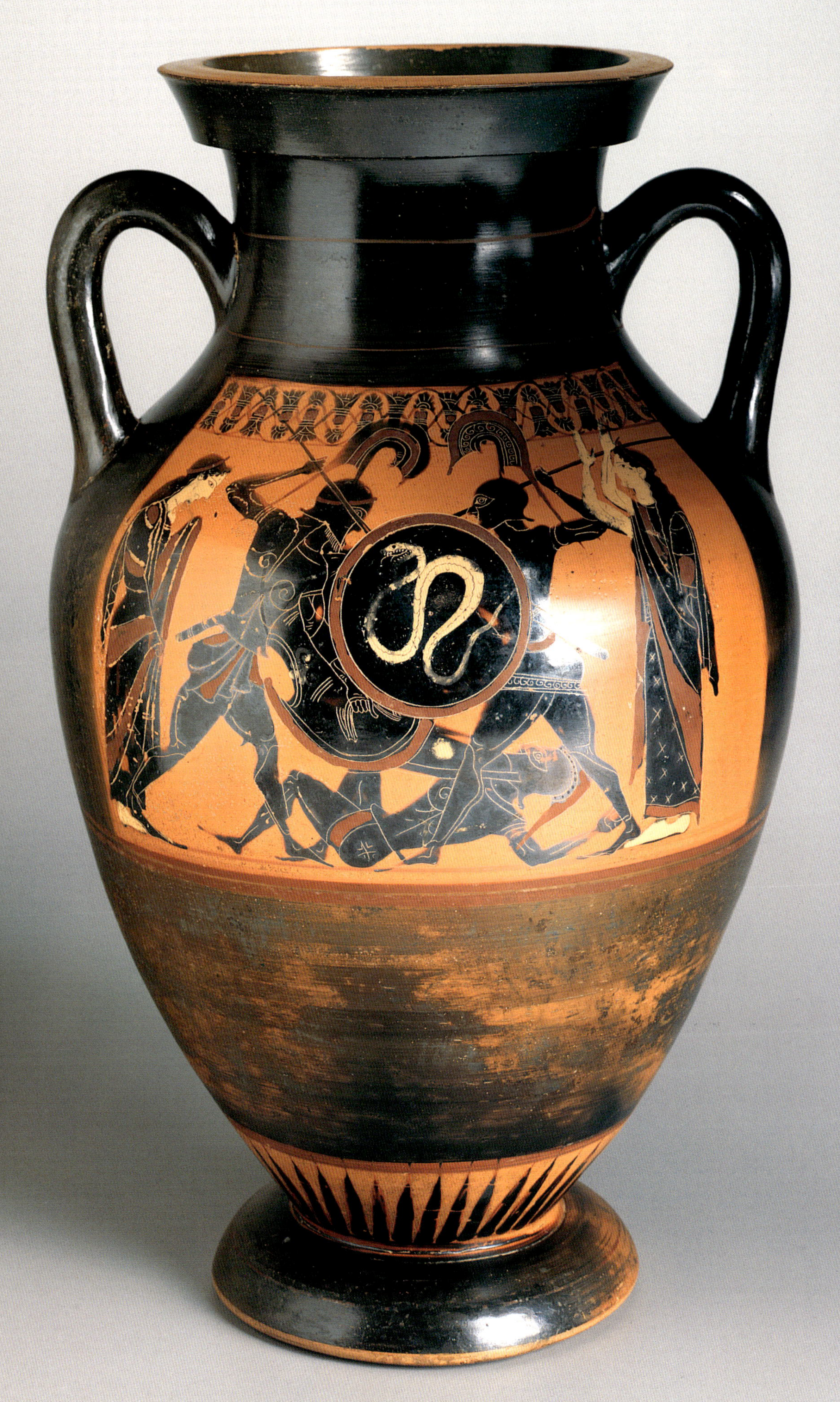

Chapter 4

Greece: The Human Image

There are many wonders in the world, but none more wonderful than man. . . . Language, thought swift as the wind, and the patterns of city life he has taught himself. . . . Only from death does he fail to contrive escape.

—Sophocles, *Antigone*

FROM THE FORMATIVE PERIOD of Greek culture represented in Homer's *Iliad*, where the gods appear in human guise, to the great creations of art and literature in fifth-century-B.C. Athens, the chief focus of Greek imagination was the human form. This essential humanism is the source of Western civilization.

The fact that mankind cannot escape death, while the gods are *athanatos* (deathless), is critical to the understanding of Greek art. Beneath the idealized, geometrically conceived forms created by Greek painters and sculptors lies the stern sense that human beauty, glory, and happiness are fleeting things. An outstandingly successful man might call down upon himself the jealousy of the gods. The poet Anacreon memorializes a fallen warrior with this sharp vision of doomed brilliance: "Here lies Timocritas: soldier: valiant in battle / Ares spares not the brave man, but the coward" (Anacreon, *Epitaph* [trans. Fitts] 7.160).

The Archaic and Classical Greek works at the Dallas Museum of Art allow one to follow the increasing confidence and skill with which Greek artists represented their central subject, the human form. In both painting and sculpture, there was a clear progression from the sixth to the fifth century B.C. in an artist's ability to create an image that was simultaneously faithful to observed visual reality and modeled in an ideal form. This creative work of imagination depended on an attempt by the artists to understand not only what human beings looked like, but what human life meant. During the Archaic period, the description of human figures is decorative: hair, clothes, jewelry, the disposition of limbs, the pattern of muscles in a nude male body—all form an ornamental design. The development of Early Classical art in the fifth century B.C., stimulated by the patriotic effort that drove the Persian invaders from Greek lands, concentrated on the inner strength, vitality, and drama in human life that go deeper than ornament. Ideal appearance and heroic mankind become one. This is still true in the later period of classicism represented by the DMA's Attic figure of a young man from a funerary relief (cat. no. 30).

Even in the ornamental art of the Archaic period, myths and religious ideas are treated with high seriousness. There is a tragic symbolism implicit in the main battle scene on the DMA's panel amphora (cat. no. 25) where both the victorious Achilles and the vanquished Memnon are doomed to death, the fate of heroes. In one of the key moments of Homeric saga, the young Achilles chooses a short and glorious life rather than a long and inglorious one. By the end of the Trojan War, he, as well as his enemies, will be dead. The heraldic scene on the panel amphora therefore implies not merely the sad loss of the youth Antilochus, whose corpse the two warriors are disputing over, but the greater tragedy of war and the briefness of human life. In this scene, Eos and Thetis, the two maternal goddesses on either side of the warriors, resemble a chorus from Greek tragedy as they lament the inevitable downfall of their heroic sons.

Although the scene on the main side of this panel amphora is strictly two-dimensional and symmetrical, many of the details are trenchantly observed. The plumed helmet, for instance, is similar to the Corinthian-style bronze helmet (cat. no. 34) in the Museum collections, and the weapons and shields would have been recognized by a Greek arms maker. Also, the stance of the warriors reflects the strain of battle, especially in the leg muscles. For Greek artists, the experimental effort to express reality went hand in hand with the will to produce formal order.

The culmination of this process may be seen in the fourth-century-B.C. funerary statue, a gentler, more sinuous version of a classical nude figure. There is a slightly sentimental cast to this vision of a boy dead at the height of youthful beauty, since the complete monument would probably have included figures of his family mourning him. Yet the heroic idealization still stands. The boy's graceful young torso includes only the minimum detail needed to make him recognizably human: the arching chest, the muscles over the pelvic bones, the plangent kneecaps and feet. There are no personal details to obtrude on the modeling of radiant youth cut down in its prime. If the head had survived, it, too, would have had this timeless, impersonal quality.

In both the panel amphora and the funerary sculpture, there is an underlying balance of opposed forces. On the vase, the warriors and the fallen corpse in schematic opposition form a triangle framed by the two goddesses; while the sculpture has an internal balance in the young man's body, formed by the S curve of his torso, as well as the balance of probable father-son figures in the complete monument. This formal compositional balance is an outward expression of a more profound sense of balance in Greek culture, in which art and the mind of man triumph over the chaotic disorder of experience by achieving ideal form. In both works, the forces of life and death, of fate and human energy, meet in an eternal balance of opposing forces. It is this vigorously resonating energy that animates the geometric severity of Greek art.

The human figure is central to the art of vase painting. From the earliest abstract decorations on proto-Geometric pottery to the splendid vase paintings of sixth- and fifth-century-B.C. Athens, vase painters developed a repertory of elegant figurative motifs, which were increasingly used to illustrate myths, events from epic poetry, religious cults, and scenes from everyday life. By the middle of the sixth century B.C., these scenes were predominantly about people; natural settings, buildings, chariots, and ships were merely subsidiary elements identifying where the human action was taking place. Since the gods were represented as human beings, marked only by attributes like Dionysus's drinking horn and vine leaf crown, religious scenes also center on the human form.

Vase painting was a commercially lucrative decorative art in antiquity, compared to the now lost art of monumental wall painting. The survival of many thousands of Greek vases in burials has had the happy result of preserving a very sophisticated art form that supplies an unparalleled picture of life in ancient Greece.

On the DMA band cup (cat. no. 26), for instance, scenes of warriors and their horses indicate that the men's families were wealthy enough to own horses. Ordinary citizens in a Greek city-state were foot soldiers; aristocrats were horsemen. As on the DMA panel amphora, the scene gives a vivid view of the importance of warfare in a society where there was no central political organization and each Greek city-state might regularly fight its neighbors, as well as foreigners like the Persians or Scythians. The cup perhaps indicates something of the shift from single feudal heroes, like the warriors in Homer's *Iliad*, to the warriors who fought as an army to defend their city. The bright, jewel-like clarity of these scenes summons a world in which young men trained regularly as athletes so they would be agile soldiers.

The balance of forces seen in these works was believed to exist in the divine, as well as in the human, world. Against the Olympian gods and the measured calm of Apollo—god of music, wisdom, and medicine and patron deity of the holy Panhellenic shrine at Delphi—was set the darker, more ambiguous cult of Dionysus, god of wine and fertility. His orgiastic rituals supplied a release for irrational emotions to his followers, who believed themselves "possessed" by the god, as a modern voodoo worshiper might be. Dionysus, too, had his period of rule at Delphi. His presence in a shrine dominated by his half brother Apollo was an acknowledgment by the Greeks of balance between order and chaos in the cosmos. Dionysus's name means "son of Zeus," indicating in part that the Dionysiac rites were seen as part of the Olympian order.

Since some of the most popular Greek vessels were the wine cups, mixing bowls, and coolers used for wine parties, or symposia, it is natural that the many fine vase paintings decorating such wares featured Dionysus and his attendant satyrs (man-animals) and maenads (crazed women). The rituals of Dionysus were a fundamental source of artistic energy and imagination in ancient Athens. Both comic and tragic drama were part of the recitals and performances at the yearly Dionysia festivals. The earlier padded dancers, called *komasts*, were also associated with Dionysus and shared in this creative saturnalia.

The DMA column krater (cat. no. 24) has a large-scale depiction of Dionysus and his followers. The god appears majestic and upright, an unmoved mover of the tumultuous dance and riot around him. His maenad followers represent a release of feminine emotions rarely allowed in the highly formal and restrictive life led by respectable Greek women, who were generally confined to their homes except during religious festivals. The Greeks recognized the importance of female deities, however, and in social life they respected the female followers of Dionysus. As Queen Agave in Euripides' play *The Bacchae* indicates, maenads might belong to the highest ranks of

Greek society. Alexander the Great's mother, Queen Olympias, performed as a maenad. The image of Dionysus as a distinguished middle-aged bearded man, who both embodies and commands the forces of disorder, reappears in the bearded faces on the shoulders of the krater.

In addition to the Dionysiac scene on the krater, there is a beautiful Archaic antefix (cat. no. 29) with Dionysiac connections. This Etruscan architectural ornament, which stems from Greek prototypes, probably represents a maenad. The calm, idealized female beauty, with its faint Archaic smile, has no suggestion of madness or ecstatic possession. The emotional turbulence of Dionysus's followers becomes part of a greater harmony, like the idea of heroic death in the panel amphora. The fundamental Greek concept of "nothing in excess" could absorb excess itself.

The ritual enactment of disturbing emotions appears even more strikingly resolved by art in the Museum's *kothon,* or tripod vase (cat. no. 22). In the three scenes on the legs of the vessel, there are figures more or less closely connected with Dionysus, but also with highly valued pastimes like athletics. There are *komast* dancers, fighting boxers, and two male figures apparently involved in a homosexual affair. The exclusively male side of Greek society, with its emphasis on contest through war and sports and its unofficial acceptance of male lovers, appears in a context that is both realistic and ritualized. There is nothing really comic on the vase, even with the *komast* dancers; the scenes are a celebration of energy released in physical action, and the taut, muscular outlines of the figures underline this exuberant vitality.

Two fine vases illustrate the contrast between the earlier black-figure style of painting and the mid-fifth-century-B.C. red-figure style. The black-figure eye cup (cat. no. 23) and the red-figure *pyxis* (cat. no. 27) present the powerful contrast that existed between male and female life in ancient Athens. There is a similar contrast between the values assigned to both sexes by the Greeks, yet there are subtle hints of interactions between the two worlds.

The eye cup is so-called because there are pairs of eyes on the exterior of the cup to ward off evil. Since the vase is a *kylix,* or drinking cup, one might think that the evil to be averted is drunkenness or that one is more subject to harm while intoxicated. The drinking theme reappears in the scene on the lip, where a satyr pours wine for the reclining hero Heracles, and in the bunches of grapes around the handles. The two lip scenes are a distillation of male Greek life: heroic warfare (Heracles reaching for his sword) and the pleasures of male drinking parties (Heracles seated enjoying his wine). In the crisp elegance of the figurative scenes, the ornamental details, and the architecture of the vase, this vessel crystallizes the sensuous and sophisticated courtly society of Archaic Greece.

Inside the cup, however, is another protective image, the Gorgoneion, or Medusa head. This female demon, whose face could turn men to stone, was adopted by civilized Greek society, and it became a powerful apotropaic device—so much so that the goddess Athena was depicted wearing the Gorgon head on her breastplate. Mortal soldiers might wear it, too. As in the cult of Dionysus, what Greek men found disturbing or uncontrollable was objectified and controlled by artistic imagery. The demons of female sexuality or violence, like the Furies in Aeschylus's tragedy *The Oresteia,* were placated for men's purposes. The Gorgon here is ornamental, treated in a lighthearted way. As one drains the wine from the cup over and over, the consumer is slowly but surely altered by the drink, if not by the Gorgon head.

In contrast, the *pyxis* wholly represents the internal world of women and the family, within the shelter of a Greek home. The vessel is a cosmetic pot, ornamented with scenes of women, children, servants, and pet birds. Perhaps a wedding gift, the handsome vessel illustrates the elegance, warmth, and charm of Greek family life. There are hints of a more ritual character to the scenes, which may depict ceremonies prior to marriage. To the Greek artist, women's lives, whether threatening or welcome, belonged to another realm of existence. What joins this *pyxis* with the panel amphora (cat. no. 25) and the funerary statue (cat. no. 30) is the double implication of the door: the gateway to married life in the bridegroom's house and the gate of death, since *pyxides* were often left in women's graves as offerings for the dead. In the words of a Greek epitaph: "At the bride bed of star-crossed Petale / Hades, not Hymen, stood" (Antiphanes the Macedonian, *Epitaph* [trans. Fitts] 9.245).

Although the classical Greeks did not imagine a consoling life after death, death defined the meaning of life. Facing the end of light and happiness unflinchingly, Greek artists expressed the heartfelt pathos of man, the most glorious of creatures, who cannot avert the darkness.

22.

Black-figure tripod *kothon*:
komasts, athletes, and animals

Attributed to the Boeotian Dancers Group (Kilinski)
Greek, Boeotian, c. 570–560 B.C.
Ceramic
H. 13.6 cm, W. 18.4 cm
Anonymous gift in memory of Edward Marcus,
1981.170

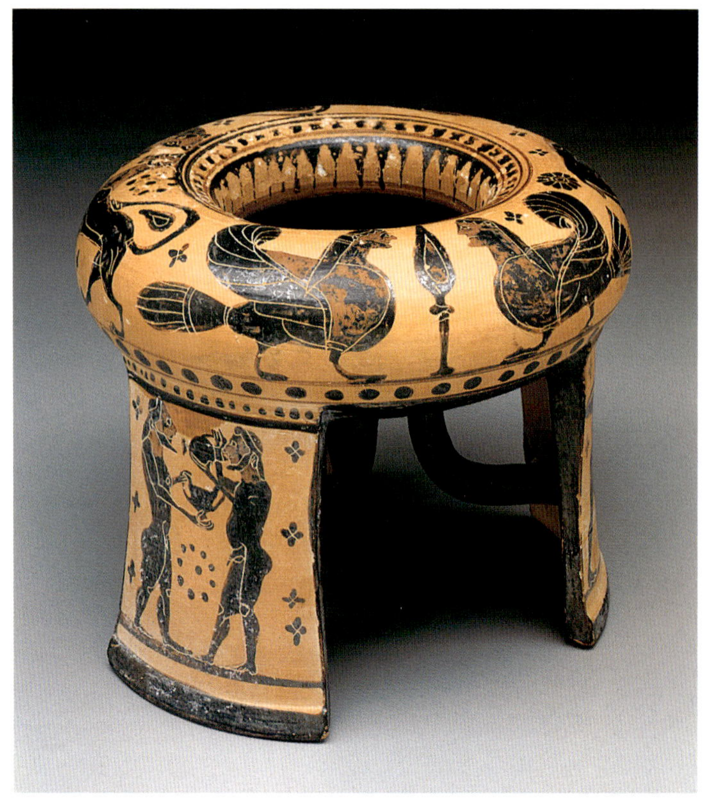

SIX NUDE MALE FIGURES ARE disposed in pairs on the three leg panels of this vase. Each set of characters is intently involved in different activities relating to the favorite pastime of Greek revelers, the consumption of wine. In the scene on the tripod leg above, the eager drinker on the right raises a wine pitcher directly to his lips. Sparing no time for the formalities of proper table manners, he steadies the hefty container with both hands while draining its contents. The disapproving expression on his partner's face and the anticipative air in his pose indicate his dismay, since the high-handled wine cup he extends toward the pitcher may well be empty.

Drinking, dancing, singing, and lively conversation were all part of revelry in ancient times as they are today, and no other participants were more attracted to these activities than the *komasts*. These comic dancers with few cares and large appetites were bent on making mischief at every opportunity, and their boisterous gusto is unequaled in scenes depicted on Greek vases. In the next scene on the vase, another pair of *komasts* frolic in a heated dance. Each dancer has an incised line across his left bicep, creating the impression of a short-sleeved garment. This indicates that members of this tribe of revelers were once clad in padded costumes, as witnessed on earlier scenes of Athenian and Corinthian *komos* vases from which these Boeotian *komasts* derive. In this scene, the heavier *komast* gingerly raises an inviting hand to the chin of his companion in hopes of obtaining an even more intimate response. Homosexual activity is frequently depicted in scenes on Greek vases and especially among the ranks of *komasts*.

The third leg panel displays not *komasts* but athletes. Here a vigorous boxing match is in progress between a paunchy, bearded figure on the left and a somewhat slimmer youth, or beardless athlete, on the right.

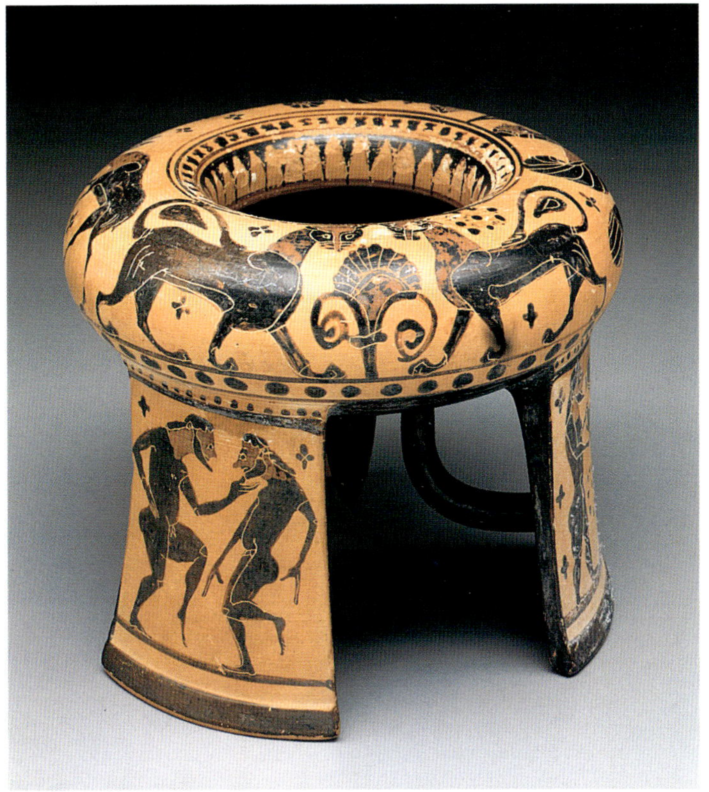

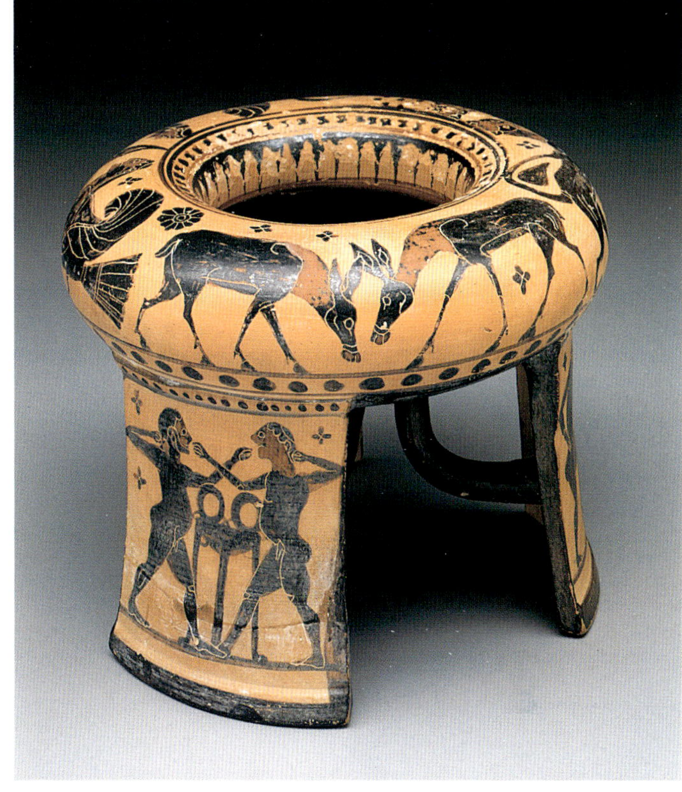

Immediately behind the boxers stands a tripod, the contested prize and no doubt an inspiration to the contenders' enthusiasm. The tripod recalls the vessel on which this scene is actually painted; however, the type depicted has tall, slender legs and large ring handles and was meant to be constructed of bronze. According to Greek tradition, the god Apollo invented the sport of boxing. Whatever its mythical origins, boxing was an old, established sport in Greece, and visual evidence for it goes back to prehistoric Aegean art.

Animated subjects, such as revelry and athletics as seen here, were favored during the Greek Archaic period by artists drawn to action scenes in an era that in general lacked artistic allowance for displays of feelings and mood through facial expression. The artists, absorbed in the interplay of pose and form of the body, were readily inspired by the animated poses of the human figure exhibited in the daily life of Greek culture. Scenes of athletic activity in the gymnasium, as well as festival performances and street scenes of revelry, provided the vibrant content from which the artists drew inspiration.

The tubular body of the vase is decorated with three pairs of heraldically placed panthers, deer, and Sirens, real and fantastic creatures from a long-established iconographical tradition in Greek art. In contrast to the animated humans, the six creatures appear lifeless, serving merely as decorative objects, and provide us with a clear indication as to where the painter's interests lay.

The shape of the tripod *kothon* is designed for maximum stability. Its relatively small size indicates that it contained scented oils, a substance too precious to be wasted by tipping over a vase. A lid, now lost, would have curtailed evaporation. The central spike under the bowl and the struts attached to the back of the legs are ceramic, but they reflect the construction of metal prototypes.

PUBLICATIONS: Muscarella 1974, no. 53; Kilinski 1981a, no. 55; Bromberg 1983, 98, no. 94; Kilinski 1990, pl. 11, no. 1.

REFERENCES: For other depictions of *komasts* see Greifenhagen 1929; Seeberg 1971. For homosexuality in Greece see Dover 1978. On the subject of dancing see Lawler 1964; Webster 1972, 114ff. On Greek athletics see Harris 1964; Sweet 1987. For the Boeotian Dancers Group see Kilinski 1978, 173–91.

23.
Black-figure eye cup

Attributed to the Group of Walters 48.42 (Kilinski)
Greek, Attic, c. 520–510 B.C.
Ceramic
H. 12.3 cm, W. (without handles) 31.7 cm
Gift of Mr. and Mrs. Cecil H. Green, 1972.5

ON ONE SIDE of the cup, Heracles reclines against a rock, holding a *phiale,* a footless bowl without handles, in his left hand. A soft cloak is casually draped over his left shoulder and arm. His traditional lion skin, taken from the mythical Nemean lion, hangs magically behind him from the vase rim. His weapons, a sheathed sword with shoulder strap, bow, and arrow-filled quiver, also hang above him. The hero has been distracted from his contemplative mood by something behind him. While his powerful body remains in repose, his head snaps about in the direction of the disturbance, and his right hand instinctively grasps his sword hilt.

The scene on the other side is more tranquil. Heracles reclines once again on a rock, his weapons suspended above him. Clad in an elegant mantle, he extends a *kantharos,* a high-handled wine cup, toward an obliging satyr who obediently fills his vessel from a wineskin. The satyr is smaller in scale, denoting his secondary status to that of Heracles, and is distinguished by his equine ears and tail. In Attic vase painting, satyrs are partial to drink and are frequent companions to Dionysus, god of wine. The lack of furniture and the rocky setting create an out-of-doors atmosphere to which the satyr—a semi-divine spirit representing various aspects of nature—and the grapevines growing around the vase handles add a fitting touch.

Heracles was the most popular of heroes in Classical art and his cult was venerated throughout Greece. He was born of the mortal Alcmene, queen of Thebes, and sired by the father of the gods, Zeus, who appeared to the queen in the guise of her husband, King Amphitryon. During his life, Heracles accomplished many heroic feats (including the killing of the Nemean lion) and upon his death was apotheosized to join the gods on Mount Olympus. It is perhaps in this setting that we see him on the eye cup, in repose after his labors. Perhaps because of his own divine status, the images of the god Dionysus appear in like repose on Athenian vases during the last quarter of the sixth century B.C. The analogies extend to the reclining pose; the head twisting about; the attendant satyr; the presence of grapevines; the *phiale,* which denotes a ceremonial or ritual occasion; and the *kantharos,* which became a regular attribute of Dionysus before becoming that of Heracles in Athenian vase painting.

Flanking each scene of Heracles are large almond-shaped "female" eyes, with eyebrows but without extended tear ducts. Such eyes were thought to avert evil from the bearer. When the cup was raised to the lips, the fertile imagination of one's drinking companions saw a comical face with cup handles serving as ears and the open, hollow foot as the mouth. The cup interior holds a Gorgoneion, also an apotropaic image, derived from the severed head of the Gorgon Medusa. Here one senses the humor of the vase painter in placing this motif so that the drinker comes nose to nose with this demonic image each time he drains the cup.

PUBLICATIONS: Bromberg 1979, 64, no. 73; Kilinski 1981b, no. 28; Shapiro 1981, 3; Bromberg 1983, 98, no. 95.

REFERENCES: For Heracles in Classical art see *LIMC* 1988, vol. 4, pt. 1, 728–838, and *LIMC* 1990, vol. 5, pt. 1, 5–262; for Heracles reclining with satyrs, see *LIMC* 1988, vol. 4, pt. 1, 819, and pt. 2, cf. pl. 546, n. 1511. For parallels in Heraclean and Dionysiac imagery see Carpenter 1986, 112 ff. For Athenian eye cups see Boardman 1974, 107; Kraiker 1930, 167–69. On the Group of Walters 48.42 see Beazley 1956, 205–7; Beazley 1971, 94–97.

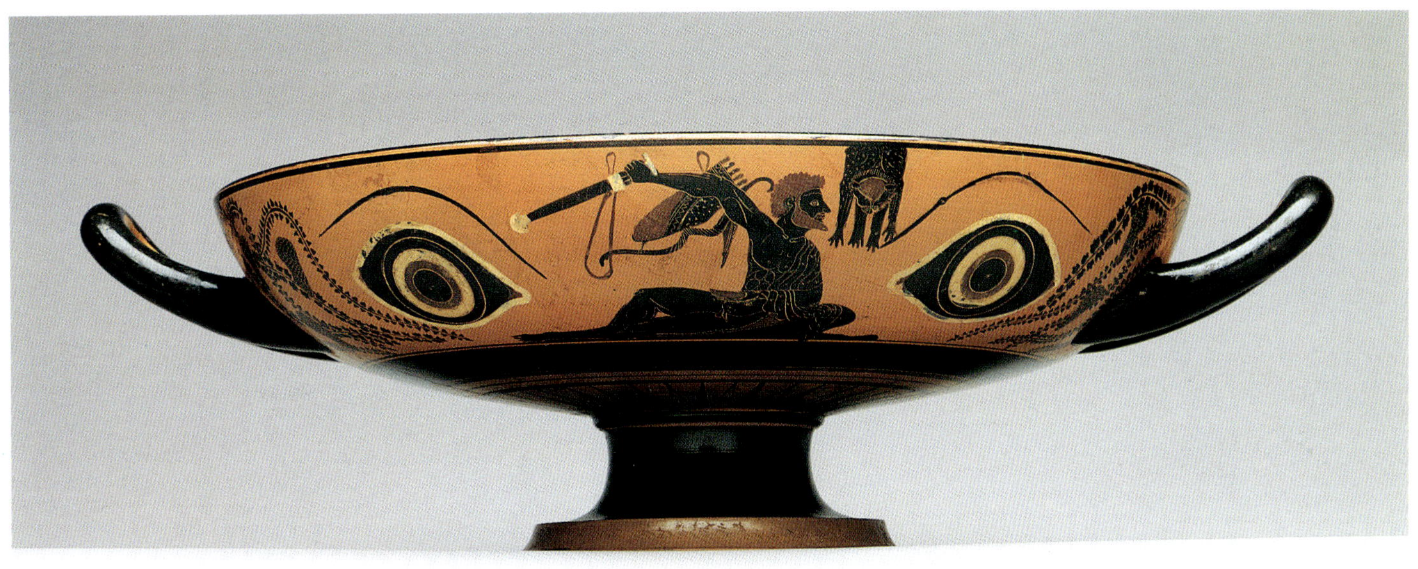

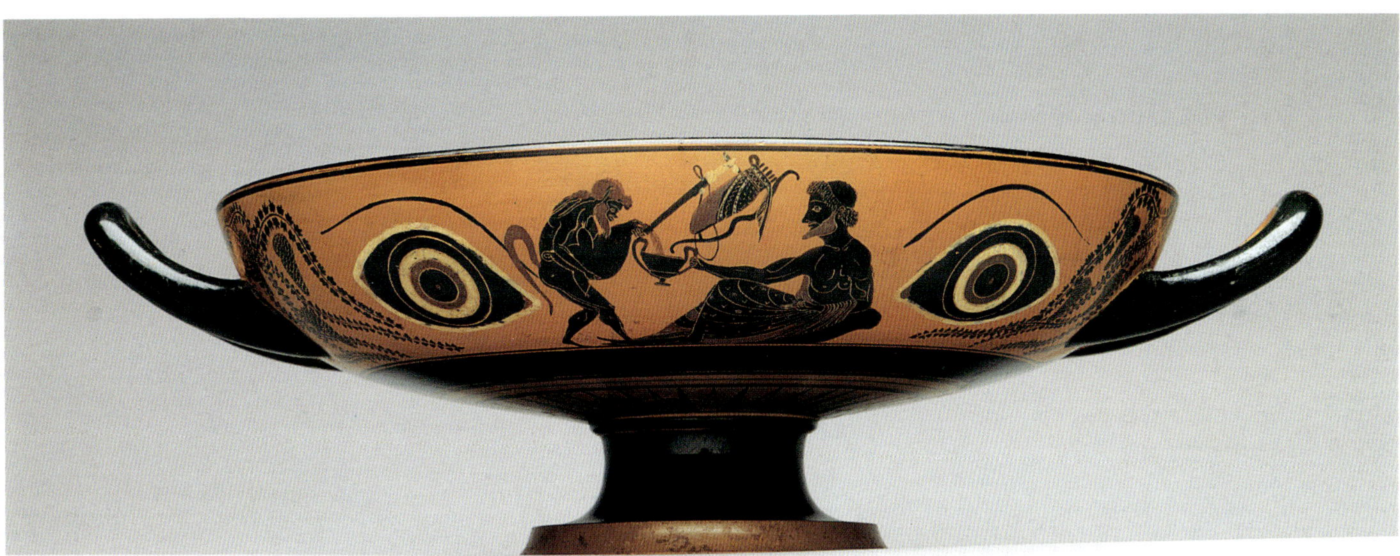

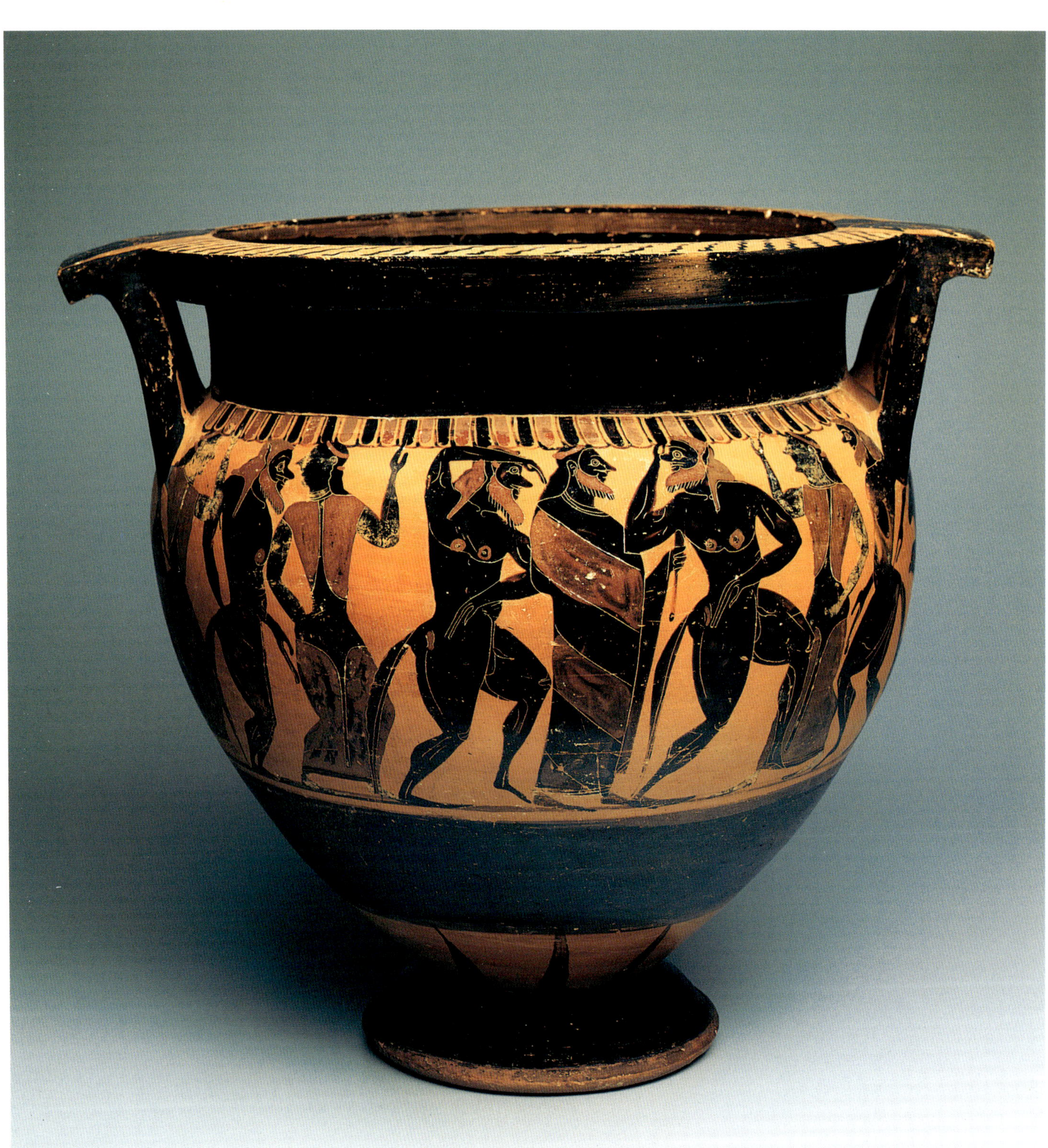

24.

Black-figure column krater

Attributed to the Painter of Louvre F 6 (Kurtz)
Greek, Attic, c. 560–550 B.C.
Ceramic
H. 44 cm, W. 53 cm
Gift of the Jonsson Foundation and Mr. and Mrs. Frederick M. Mayer, 1972.22

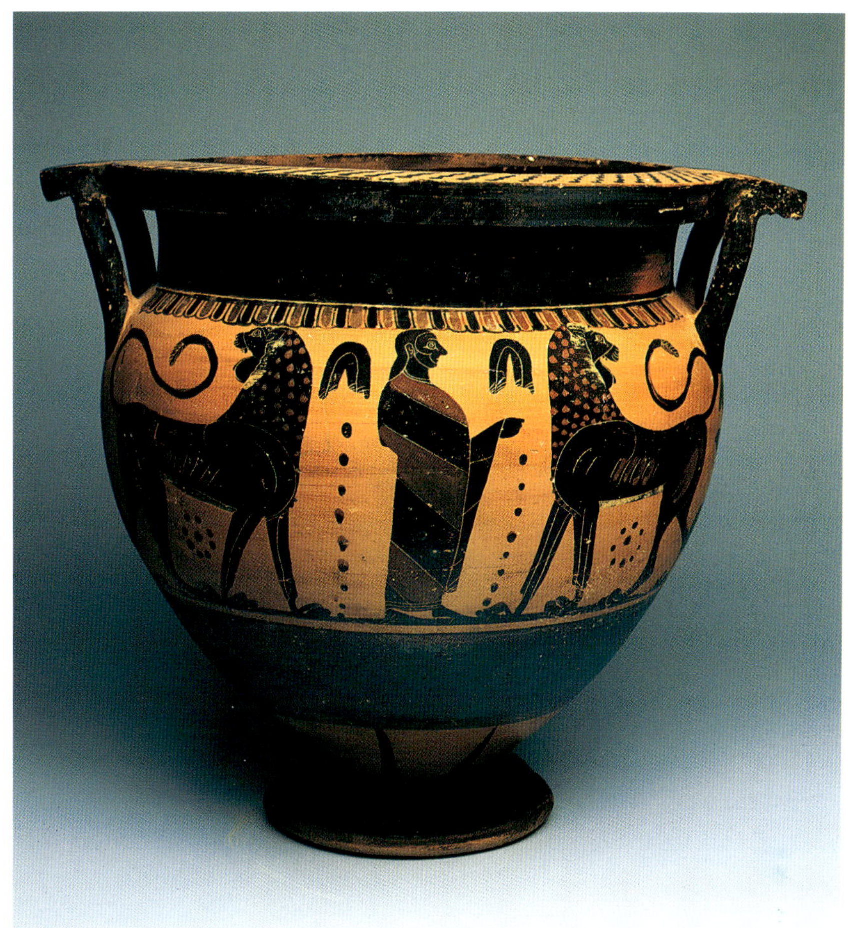

THE PRIMARY SCENE (opposite) is of a boisterous group of dancing satyrs and maenads who cluster about a single bearded male figure. These wildly gesticulating revelers are the companions of Dionysus, who is recognizable as the central figure, clad in a long robe and holding a drinking horn in his left hand. Dionysus was a latecomer to the Olympic pantheon, yet he was especially favored by Athenian vase painters from about 580 B.C. Dionysiac revelry was a popular subject in Greek art soon after this date. Satyrs, with their equine ears and tails, are uninhibited creatures with strong tastes for wine, women, and song. Maenads are "crazed women" who draw the inspiration for their ecstatic mood from Dionysus, the god of ecstasy and abandonment of the rational. The frenzied state of the revelers, however, is contrasted with the sedate and restrained pose of Dionysus himself, as seen on this vase. The direction of Dionysus's slow pace indicates a movement of the group to the right with the god in the center of his fold. Such scenes on Athenian vases are sometimes expanded to include the returning outcast Hephaestus, god of crafts and magic, being led back to Olympus by Dionysus, who intoxicated his half brother with wine.

The reverse of this column krater (above) does not include an image of Hephaestus but simply a single bearded male figure clad in a robe similar to that of Dionysus. He is flanked by two pieces of cloth, which seem to float mystically in midair but are actually draped over pegs on the wall, and in turn by two heraldically placed lions with flicking tails and reversed heads. The man has been segregated from the lions by vertical rows of black dots, thereby excluding any narrative theme and leaving the lions with little more than a decorative function. The two sides of the krater are separated from one another by a great bird in flight under each handle. Bearded male heads adorn the handle-plates on the vase rim, which is decorated with wavy lines that recall the rippling action created by stirring the vase's contents.

The Painter of Louvre F 6, named for a *hydria*, or water jar, in Paris that is also decorated with a Dionysiac revelry, was a companion of the master painter Lydos. The choice and arrangement of subjects on the column krater, including the snarling lions on the reverse and the soaring birds under the handles, as well as the vase shape itself, are all familiar traits of Lydos's work.

PUBLICATIONS: *Gazette des beaux-arts* 1973, 103, pl. 367; *On View* 1974, vol. 8, 79, pl. 247; Kilinski 1981c, no. 11; Shapiro 1981, 5, fig. E; Kurtz 1983, 220.

REFERENCES: For Dionysus and his companions see Carpenter 1986, chap. 5. For Lydos and his companions see Beazley 1951, 38–49; Tiverios 1976; Tiverios 1981.

25.
Black-figure panel amphora

Attributed to the Painter of the Medea Group (Bothmer)
Greek, Attic, c. 520–510 B.C.
Ceramic
H. 46.4 cm, W. 19.7 cm
Munger Fund, 1965.29.M

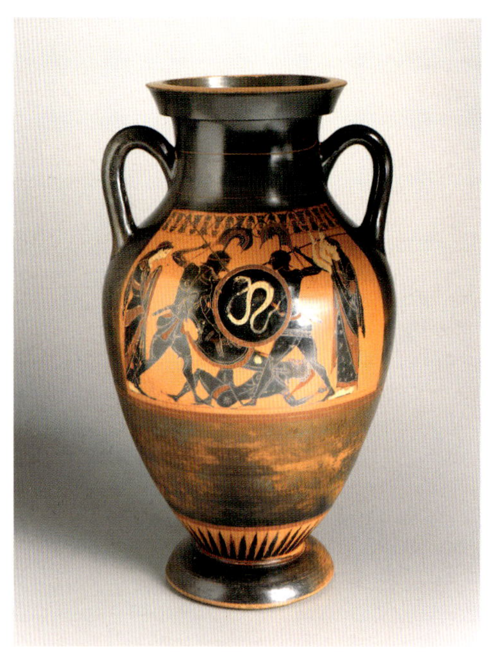

IN THE SCENE ON the obverse of the vase (above), two armed warriors engage in battle over the fallen body of a third. The combatants wear high-plumed Corinthian helmets, cuirasses over short tunics to cover their torsos, and greaves to protect their lower legs. They engage each other with shields and spears, their swords still in their sheaths held in place by red-painted baldrics. The warrior at right holds a round shield of Boeotian shape decorated with a serpent. The fallen warrior is also in full armor, although lacking weapons, and wears a low-crested helmet. Flanking this trio are two female figures wearing red headbands and mantles over long woolen garments *(peploi)*. There are no inscriptions to identify these characters, but other vases with similar arrangements of figures are inscribed. There the warriors are identified as Achilles and Memnon, who fight over the fallen Antilochus—all of whom are renowned fighters in the Trojan War. The female onlookers must be Thetis and Eos, the divine mothers of the two combatants.

The scene on the reverse side of the vase (opposite) is similar to that on the obverse with some important exceptions. Here the warrior at left, who now wears a low-crested helmet and holds a round shield with white dot decoration, clearly has the advantage over his opponent, who stumbles to the ground. This fallen figure holds his shield, now with an ivy pattern, to protect himself as he falls. The body of the third warrior is not present, and the female at right turns to depart, looking back over her shoulder.

The duel between Achilles and Memnon occurs not in Homer's *Iliad*, but in the *Aethiopis*, an epic poem by Homer or Arctinus of Miletus, of which only fragments survive. Part of the Epic Cycle, this poem is the continuation of the Trojan saga following the *Iliad*. King Memnon of Ethiopia, the son of Eos, goddess of the dawn, joins the Trojan War against the Greeks and takes the life of Antilochus, Nestor's son, in battle. Despite his armor made by Hephaestus, Memnon is then killed by the heroic Achilles, son of the sea nymph Thetis, who takes revenge for Antilochus's death.

Determining which of the combatants is the ill-fated Memnon and which one is Achilles is not always possible without inscriptions, since either opponent can appear on either side of the scene. In the obverse scene on the amphora, the raised arms of the goddess at right may be interpreted as encouragement for the warrior in front of her; the downward glance of the goddess at left may be the ominous pose of a mother about to lose her son. This would place Achilles and Thetis on the right and Memnon and Eos on the left. It is also possible that the female at right is meant to be gesticulating wildly out of desperation at her impending loss, while the one at left is more calm, confident of her son's victory. The artist has painted a red band around the helmet of the warrior at left, but it is unclear whether this signifies the impending victory of the wearer or is simply an expression of decorative fancy on the part of the painter. In the reverse scene, the outcome of the duel and therefore the identification of the combatants seems certain. However, we cannot automatically equate one scene with another even on the same vase. The very fact that the body of Antilochus is entirely missing from this scene casts the identification of all of the participants into question. It is probable, though, that the artist still had the Homeric heroes in mind while painting this scene and reduced the number of figures to create a more simplistic composition for the back side of the vase.

PUBLICATIONS: Hoffmann 1970, 365, no. 172; Bromberg 1979, 64, no. 72; Bromberg 1983, 101, no. 96.

REFERENCES: For Achilles and Memnon in Greek art see *LIMC* 1981, vol. 1, pt. 1, 175–81; Brommer 1973, 348–52. For the Medea Group see Beazley 1956, 321; Beazley 1971, 141. For the attribution by Bothmer see Bothmer 1965.

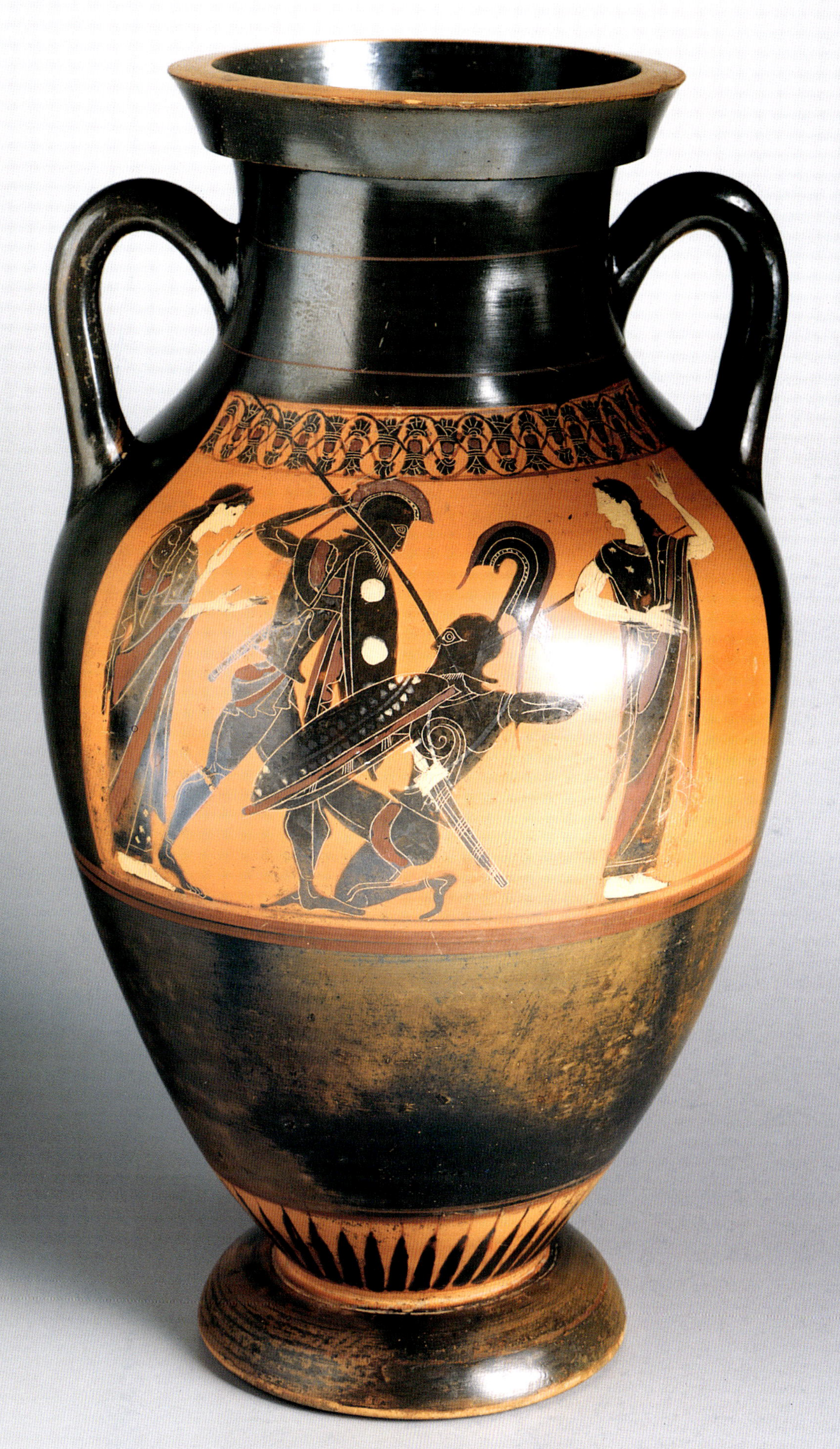

26.

Black-figure band cup

Greek, Attic, c. 540–530 B.C.
Ceramic
H. 18.4 cm, W. (without handles) 11.8 cm
Gift of the Dallas Foundation, 1968.2

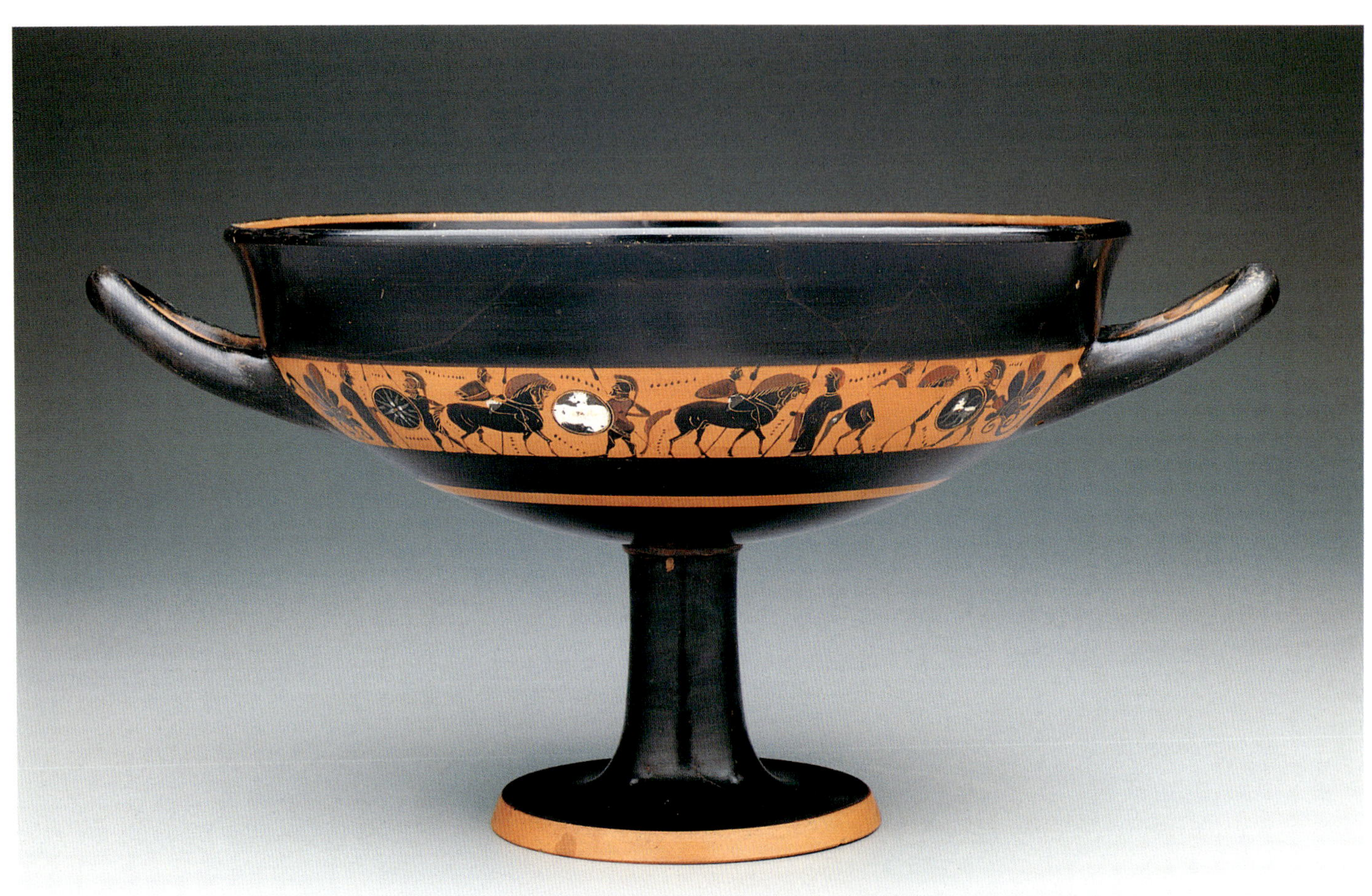

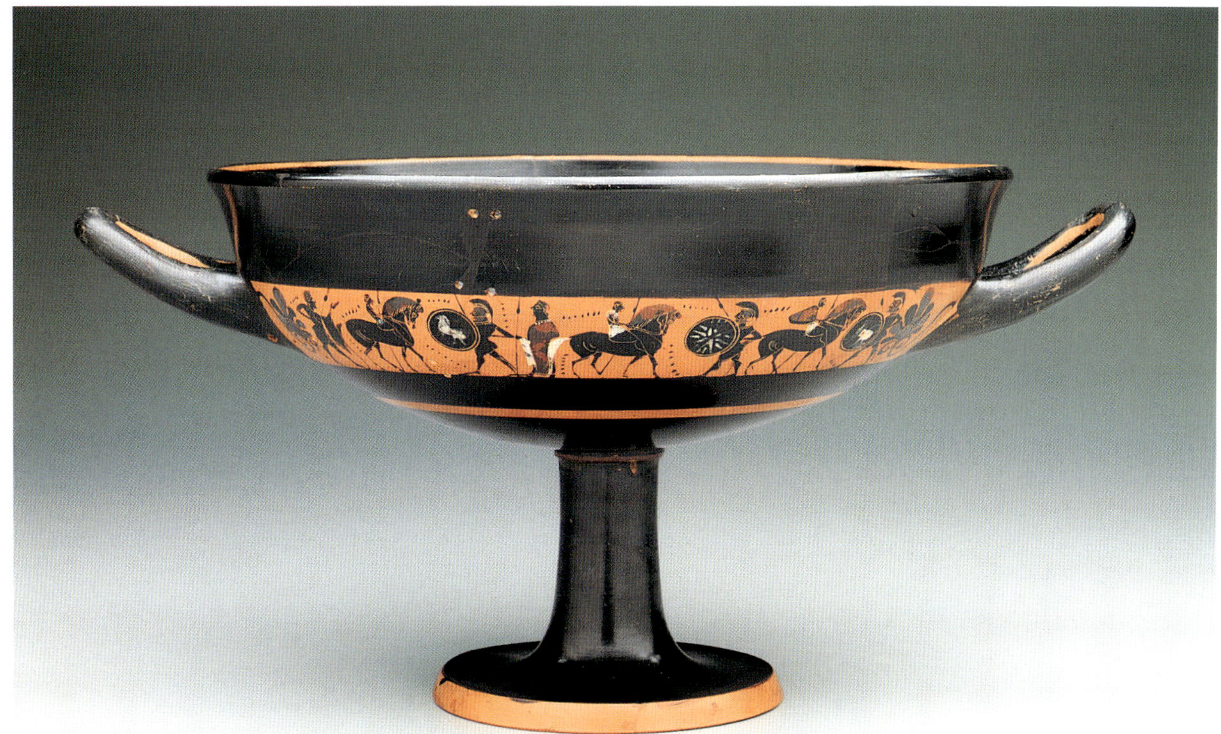

THE COMPOSITIONS ON both sides of the vase are set between stylized palmettes and resemble each other quite closely. Each frieze of armed men contains three horsemen holding spears and wearing short white tunics and, except for a figure in the center of one side (above), cloaks. Interspersed around the horsemen are three warriors in armor, all with spears, and two men wearing or holding cloaks. The warriors wear low-crested helmets and greaves and hold round shields. These last vary in decoration: a ram, a starburst, and a lion for shield blazons on one side (above), and a starburst and a lion on the other (opposite), with the middle shield once covered with white paint. The rows of dots in the field around the figures give the semblance of letters in inscriptions, often without meaning, that regularly contribute to the subsidiary decoration of a figured scene.

The subjects of war and fighting were common to ancient Greek culture and are frequently found in Greek art. In the scenes on this cup, the artist seems less interested in depicting actual combat than in rendering different types of combatants. They are not engaged with one another but simply put on display as miniature studies. Band cups belong to the category of "Little Master Cups" and were popularized in Athens from the 550s to about 520 B.C. The reserved strip between the handles accounts for the name and carries the figure decoration. Painters of these cups preferred a miniature scale for the figures, and the cup pictured here displays the artist's ability to design his scenes with a multitude of characters with appropriate detail and still allow for adequate spacing. The crowded scenes on the band cup filled with warriors and artificial inscriptions recall those in the Group of Louvre F 81.

PUBLICATIONS: Hoffmann 1970, 352, no. 167.

REFERENCES: For Greek armor and warfare see Snodgrass 1967; Adcock 1967; Greenhalgh 1973. For the Group of Louvre F 81 see Beazley 1956, 191.

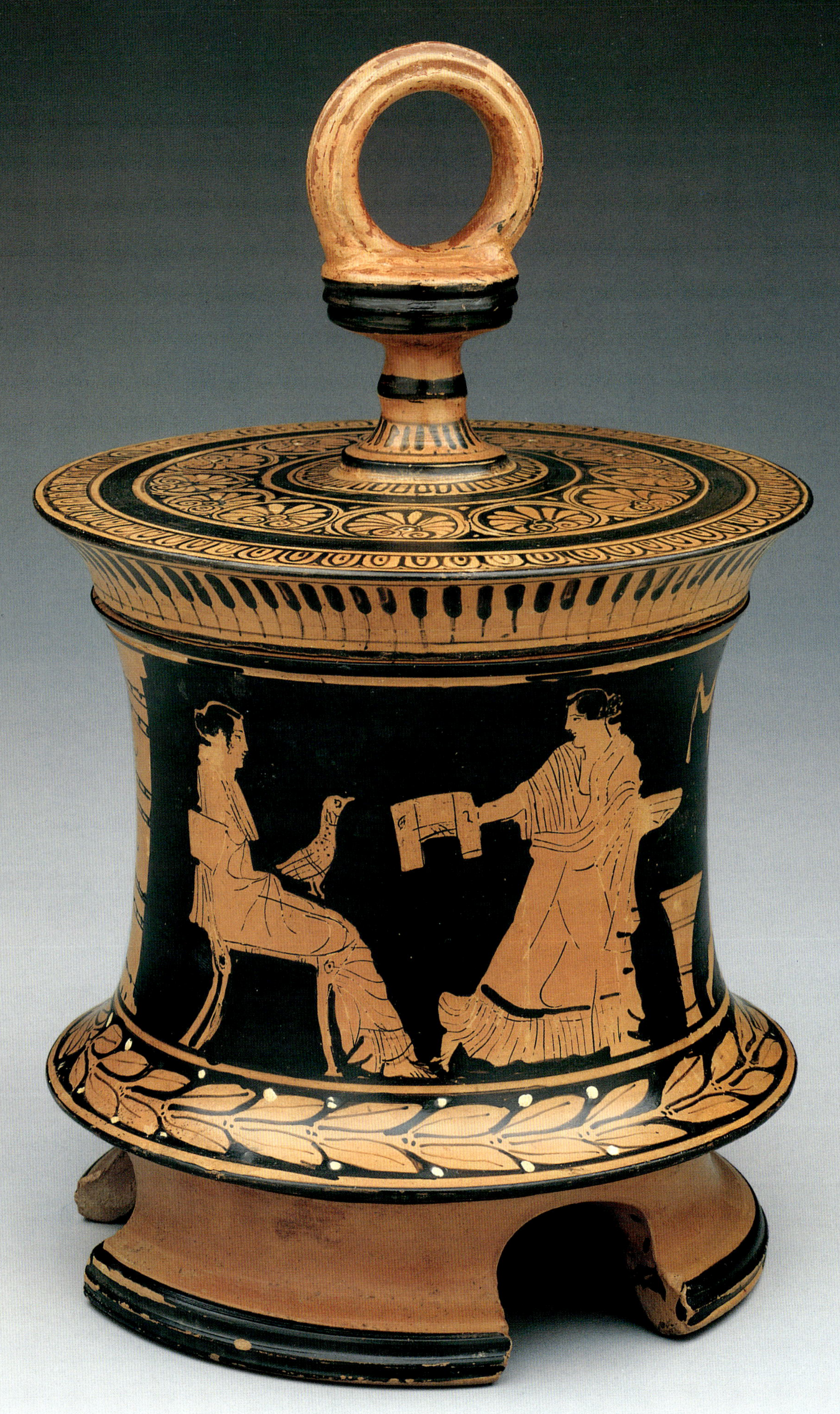

27.
Red-figure *pyxis* with lid: women's quarters

Assigned to the Penthesilea Workshop (?)
Greek, Attic, c. 450 B.C.
Ceramic
H. 23.9 cm, W. 13.8 cm
Gift of the Junior League of Dallas, 1968.28.a–b

SIX FIGURES OCCUPY the scene, which is wrapped around the concave body of this elegant container. A woman sits at ease in a chair, facing right with a pet bird in her lap (opposite). Before her another woman holds out a box or chest in her right hand, offering it to her seated companion. She holds a bowl or basket in her left hand as she rapidly moves off to the right while looking back. A wicker wool basket *(kalathos)* stands on the floor below a cloth hung on the wall by pegs. Next, a nude young boy with outstretched arms runs toward a woman, his mother or nurse, who holds a hoop or basket against her right thigh (overleaf). Behind her stands another woman in quiet tranquility, a pet bird resting on her extended right arm. Last is a woman who rushes toward a closed door with a box or small chest at her side. She holds up part of her drapery with her right hand to facilitate her rapid motion and swings her head about as if to catch a fleeting glimpse or spoken word from behind (page 71).

The *gynaikeia*, or women's quarters, was a subject growing in popularity among Athenian vase painters during the last half of the fifth century B.C. Indeed, the subject of women in Athenian art and literature during this period has a much greater profile than ever before in Greek culture. That the artist, like several others decorating this vase shape, has depicted a domestic scene of women interacting on a *pyxis* is certainly appropriate, since this shape functioned as a container for jewelry, incense, medicine, and cosmetics. The composition of the figures in this scene is deceivingly casual. In fact, the artist has carefully arranged the figures into three pairs, each focused inward and containing both animated and tranquil characters.

The closed door might signify only that this scene takes place inside, an interpretation supported by the presence of the cloth on the wall. The role of women in fifth-century-B.C. Athens was largely indoors. Yet the door may have one or more symbolic meanings worthy of note. The *pyxis* was commonly decorated with scenes relating to and focusing on marriage. The seated woman depicted on the DMA vase here may be a bride about to receive a chest from which she will take items to prepare herself for the marriage ceremony. A seated figure among other standing ones often denotes special importance in Classical Greek art, and the artist responsible for this scene has bestowed on her a contemplative mood befitting one about to engage in marriage. The presence of the young boy in this scene also alludes to marriage and family life. Socrates is quoted as stating that the procreation of children was the primary purpose of marriage (Xenophon, *Memorabilia* 2.2.4).

Wedding processions represented on sixth-century-B.C. Greek vases make their way toward the house of the bridegroom, where the newlyweds will reside. By the middle of the fifth century B.C., depictions of the wedding party show that the bride-

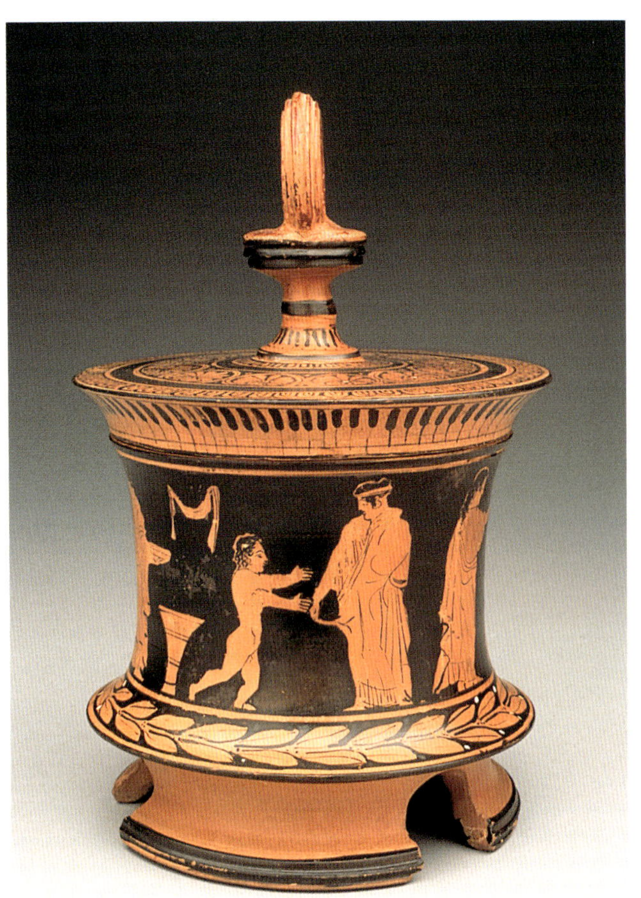

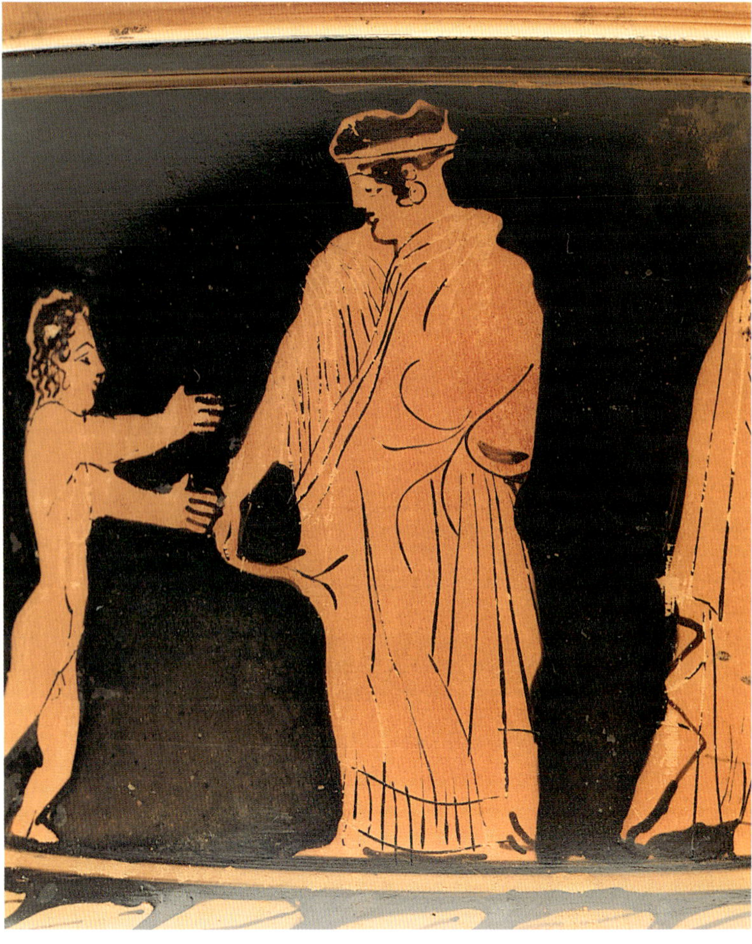

groom's house has been reduced to double doors symbolizing not only the threshold of the family homestead, but the portal of transition for the bride from maid to matron. Contemporary Athenian literature supports this interpretation. In the play by Euripides, *Alcestis* (914–25), Alcestis's husband, Admetus, addresses the door of their house after returning from her funeral. His lament includes references to their wedding day, when they first entered the house through the very same door out of which Alcestis was carried to her grave. Euripides' double meaning was intentional. The joys of life are always only one step away from death. That *pyxides* were frequent grave offerings reminds us that the closed doors on this vase may also allude to the portal separating this world from the next, a symbol found elsewhere in Greek and Etruscan art.

This *pyxis* is unusual in that it has a fluted ring handle instead of the canonical disk knob with crowning button. Examples with ring handles are rare and later in date, perhaps imitating ceramic *pyxides* with bronze ring handles from the later fifth century B.C. Hoffmann associated this vase with the style of the Aberdeen Painter (Hoffmann 1970, no. 191), but this analogy does not appear to be correct. Closer in style is the work of another member of the Penthesilea Workshop whose *pyxis* in Manchester (Roberts 1978, 50, no. 16, pl. 31, fig. 2) is listed by Beazley as near the Painter of Brussels R 330 (Beazley 1963, 931, no. 2).

PUBLICATIONS: Hoffmann 1970, 420, no. 191; Reeder 1995, 204–5.

REFERENCES: For women in Classical Athens see Lacey 1968, chaps. 4 and 6; Pomeroy 1975; Cameron and Kuhrt 1983; Fantham 1994, chap. 4; Webster 1972, 226ff. On the Penthesilea Workshop see Roberts 1978, esp. 45–60; on wedding iconography see 178ff. and Oakley 1993. On the Manchester *pyxis* see Beazley 1963, 931, no. 2.

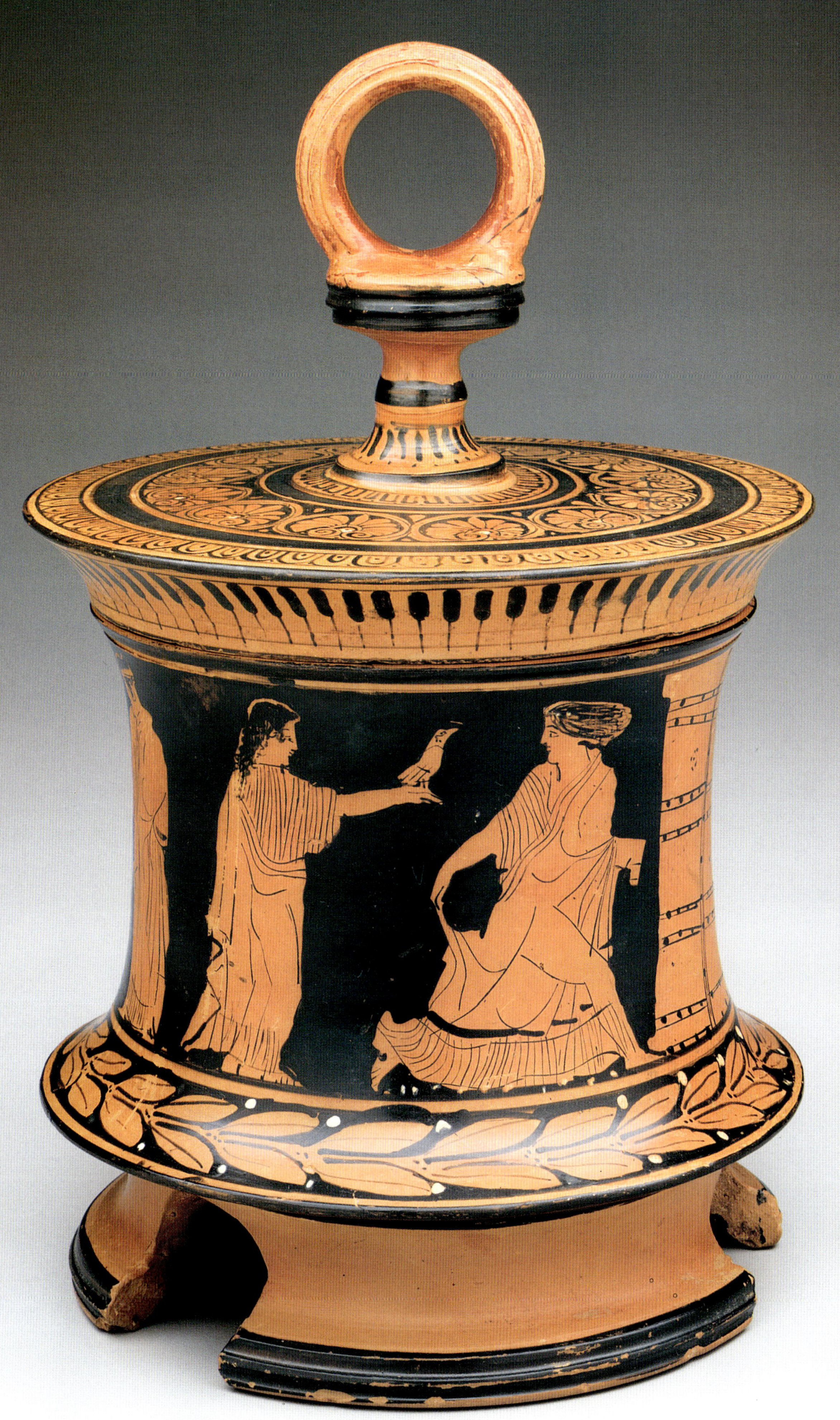

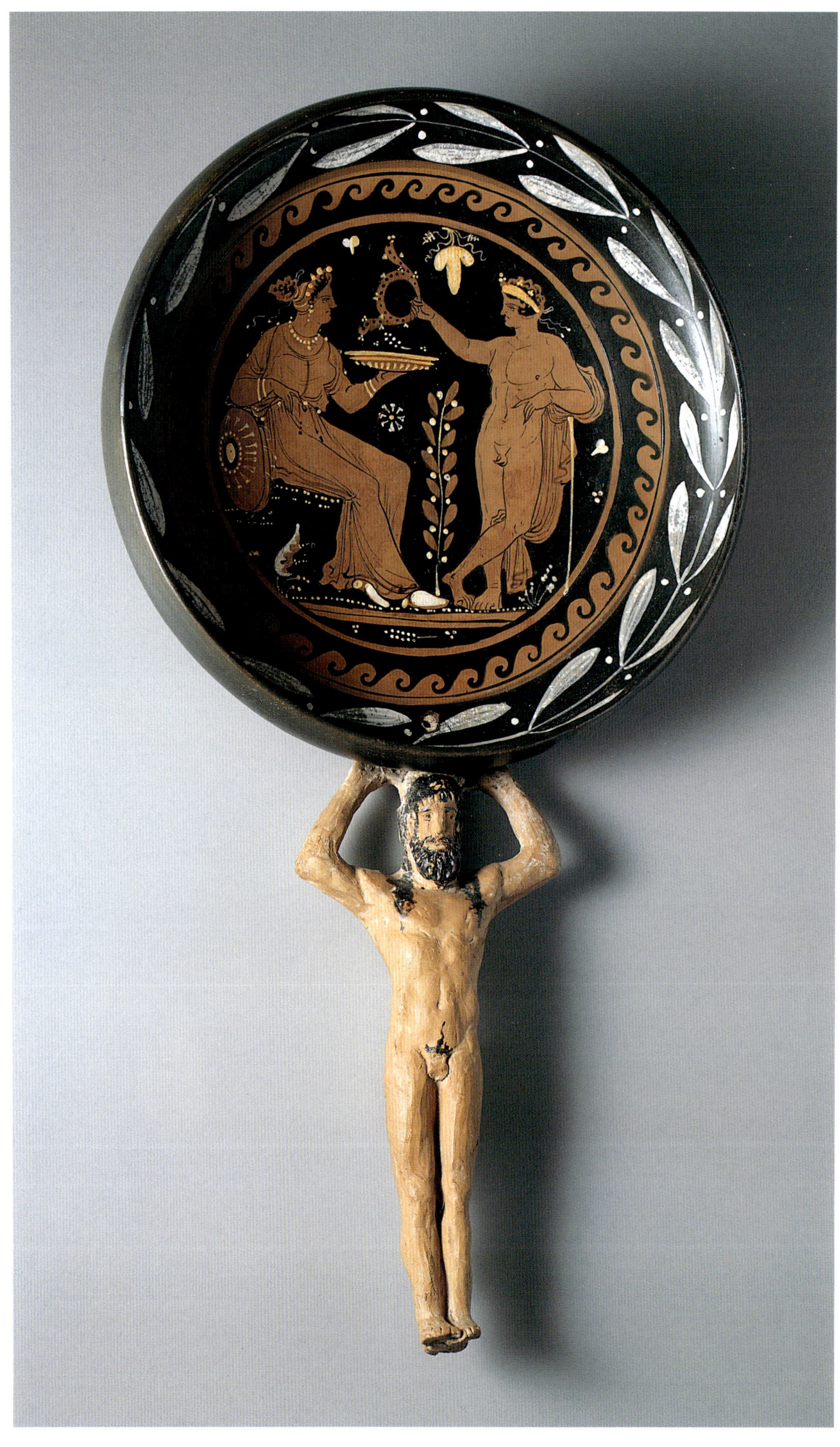

28.

Red-figure *patera* with Atlas handle

Attributed to the Painter of Louvre MNB 1148 (Trendall)
Greek, South Italian, Apulian, last third of the fourth century B.C.
Terracotta
H. (with handle) 40.3 cm, W. (at rim) 22.9 cm
Gift of the Junior Associates, acquired 1996

THIS *PATERA* IS THE FIRST example of Greek ceramics from the city-states of South Italy to enter the DMA collections. It nicely complements the Museum's extensive collection of gold jewelry from South Italy, especially since the figures depicted inside the bowl are wearing types of ornament from the fourth century B.C. The Greek cities of Italy were often wealthier than the older states on the mainland and thus were able to commission lavish decorative arts.

This handsome *patera*, or offering bowl, is unusual because the handle is terracotta instead of bronze. The handle was mold-made in two parts, from front and back molds. The two halves were then joined with clay and fired, after which they were attached to the bowl, possibly with bronze pins. The two pairs of holes for the attachment match and include identical cementlike material, though there are no metal traces.

Such vessels were used for pouring libations to the dead. The scene in the interior of the bowl shows a seated woman holding a *phiale*, a libation dish, in her left hand. She reclines against a tambourine on her right. On the right is a nude youth holding out a wreath in his right hand while supporting himself with a staff on his left. Between them is a laurel plant. Other flower motifs and bunches of grapes decorate the background. Around the rim of the tondo are an outer laurel wreath pattern and an inner wave decoration. The woman wears bracelets, a necklace, earrings, and a crown, while the youth wears a diadem. Such scenes have been interpreted as having Dionysiac or Orphic meaning, related to religious mystery cults popular in South Italy. Whatever the precise meaning of the figures, they probably do have funerary connotations as well as intimations of the revival of life, indicated by the plants. The association of the new growth of green plants in the springtime with personal immortality for initiates was common in Dionysiac cult.

The unusual handle is in the form of a mature, muscular nude man with a beard. He upholds the disk of the bowl in his upstretched hands. The figure probably refers to the mythological character Atlas, a giant who carries the heavens on his shoulders. In the stories of Heracles' labors, the giant Titan and the hero exchange roles, but Heracles tricks Atlas into taking over the burden of the sky again. In some versions of the myth, Atlas was turned to stone by looking at the Medusa head. The handle may refer to the great sculptural Atlantid figures that decorated the Temple of Zeus at Acragas (modern Agrigento) in Sicily. Only a handful of such Atlantid figures used as *patera* handles have survived.

The piece is a handsome combination of figural sculpture in the handle and refined vase painting in the tondo scene. It provides an impressive glimpse into the sacrificial rites of Greek religion, as well as into the imaginative world of Greek mythology.

PUBLICATIONS: Leipen 1994, 342, fig. 4. For further information on the Painter of Louvre MNB 1148 see Trendall and Cambitoglou 1982; Trendall 1985, 142–44.

REFERENCES: Smith 1976.

29.

Antefix in the shape of a female head

Etruscan, c. 500 B.C.
Painted terracotta
H. 22.9 cm, W. 14.3 cm, D. 13.2 cm
Anonymous gift in honor of Melba D. Whatley,
1982.93.FA

THIS MOLD-MADE HEAD IS approximately life size and exemplifies the beauty of female youth. It was the primary element of an architectural antefix designed to cover one of the end-tiles along the eaves of a roof. Originally the head was crowned with a diadem, now lost, and large Etruscan disk-shaped earrings were once attached to the ears. The hair over the brow and flanking the face has been molded in a rippling pattern enhanced by undulating lines of black paint to create a wavy effect. Large, staring eyes, accented by raised eyebrows and enhanced with blue paint (now a dull lavender), contribute significantly to the motionless frontality of the head. The double iris of each eye testifies to the artist's preoccupation with decoration over total naturalism. The intensity of the powerful gaze is muted by a subtle smile and the soft modeling of the face, with its delicately rendered nose and fleshy cheeks. An uninhibited use of bright colors, typical of Etruscan painting, contrasts with the powdery white face to create a conscious vitality and an appealing freshness nearly as effective today as it must have been in antiquity. The high brow appears to offset the balance of the face but would not have had this effect when seen at a sharp angle from far below the roofline in its original setting.

Antefixes with female heads were generally arranged alternately with those having the heads of satyrs, the promiscuous companions of Dionysus, god of wine, drama, and ecstasy. The female images represented maenads, "crazed women" taken with the spirit of Dionysus, who normally cavorted with satyrs in Classical mythology. The mixing of male and female elements in the imagery of the antefixes alludes to the dynamic forces of nature from which Dionysus's power emanates. The Etruscans, continuously responsive to Greek artistic influences, became familiar with the cult of Dionysus and the motifs of satyrs and maenads through the Greek colonies of Campania in southern Italy. They would have considered the satyr and maenad heads as guardians, protective devices projecting from the roofline to ward off evil from the confines of the building.

The exact provenance of this head is unknown, but there is evidence to support the belief that it may have been made in Caere (modern Cerveteri). Etruscan Caere was located a short distance northwest of Rome. Although a number of Etruscan towns manufactured terracotta sculpture, Caere was renowned for its abundant and aesthetically pleasing architectural terracottas. A rapid building program in southern Etruria during the latter half of the sixth century B.C. was met by an outpouring of Caeretan architectural terracotta sculptures. Terracotta sculptural decoration on Etruscan buildings included several forms, among which were antefixes, *acroteria* (roof ridge-line decor), gable decoration, and continuous figured friezes. The invention of the antefix head, however, is generally believed to have occurred in Corinth. Greeks from Corinth are known to have settled in Tarquinia, north of Caere, in the seventh century B.C., and Corinthian trade dominated the Etruscan market during this time. The primary port city of Caere, Pyrgi (modern Santa Severa), has a Greek name and was perhaps founded by Greeks, who called it Agylla. This Etruscan town was wealthy enough to establish a treasury at Delphi and enjoyed the prosperity gained by exploiting the metal deposits in the nearby Tolfa region. This affluence is substantiated by the opulent tumulus burials outside the city. The abundant wealth of Caere supported an active terracotta industry that was highly receptive to Greek artistic influence.

PUBLICATIONS: Kilinski 1983, cover and 1–2; Bromberg 1983, 101, no. 98.

REFERENCES: On Etruscan architectural terracottas see Andrén 1940; Richardson 1964, esp. 98–103; Brendel 1978, esp. 232–48; and in general Pallottino 1975.

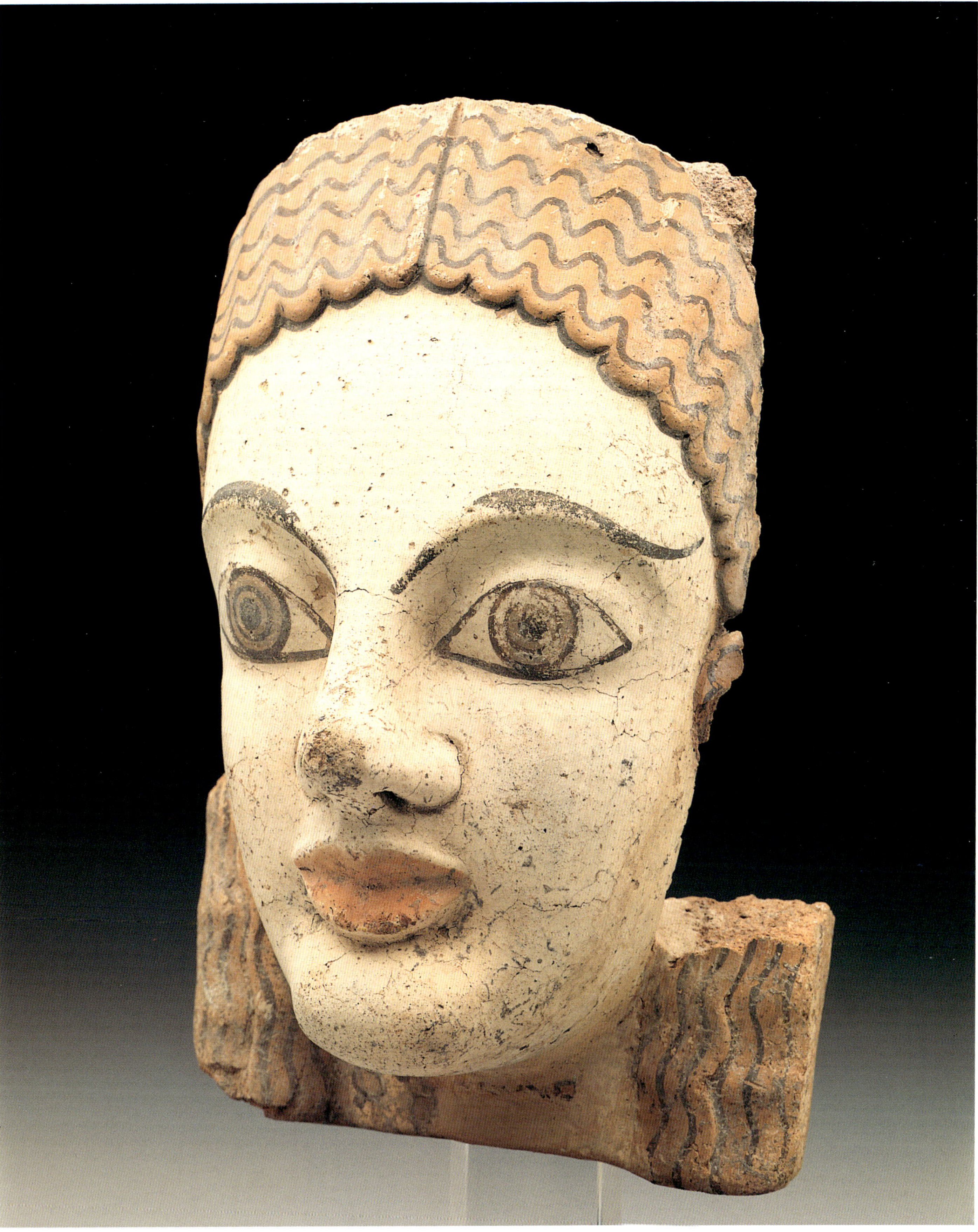

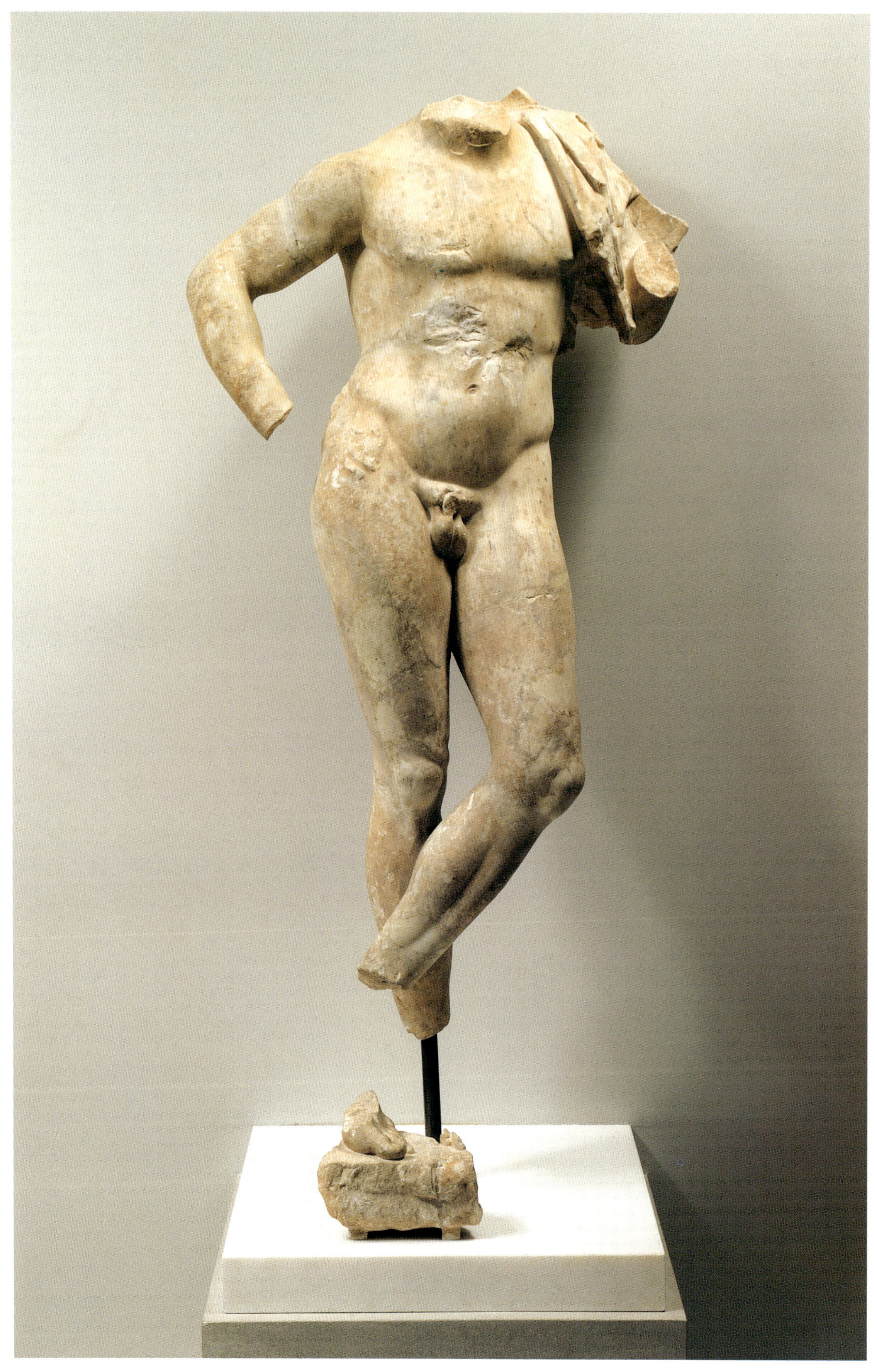

30.
Figure of a young man from a funerary relief

Greek, Attic, c. 330 B.C.
Marble
H. 161.3 cm, W. 78.1 cm, D. 47.6 cm
Gift of Mr. and Mrs. Cecil H. Green, 1966.26

THIS FIGURE OF A YOUNG MAN is made of pentelic marble and stands in a relaxed pose with the left leg crossed over the right. His right hand rests on his hip, creating a distinctive pose often associated with military commanders. A cloak draped over his left shoulder is the only apparel on his otherwise nude body. The athletic strength of the figure, as well as his nude youthful form, adds to the belief that the man represented here has been heroized in death. The figure was once part of a funerary relief and was set into a gabled tomb facade that is commonly found among Athenian grave monuments of the fourth century B.C. The head, right hand, and feet, as well as parts of the left arm, are lost. However, the angle of the upper left arm indicates that the figure was gesturing or holding something out to his left. The man's torso is turned slightly in that direction, and the neck muscles indicate that the head was as well.

These are almost certain indicators that a second figure of equal stature stood next to the young man. This could have been a man or a woman, father or wife, who has survived the young man. The presence of such a figure was an integral part of the original composition and was designed to symbolize the dramatic contrast between life and death. An excellent parallel to such a scene is found on the contemporary Ilissos monument (see fig.) in Athens in which an old man faces a nude youth, whose pose is strikingly similar to that of the DMA figure. The old man in the Ilissos monument is in lower relief than the youth before him and gestures in a contemplative manner, perhaps expressing a father's loss of a son. The supposed second figure in the DMA monument would perhaps have been carved in shallower relief as well, a practice that gives greater importance to the figure in high relief and suggests further that he is the deceased.

Although the DMA figure in its original form was not meant to be a portrait, it did represent an individual of Athens whose life was spent in a society substantially changed from that of the preceding century. Athenian art of the fourth century B.C. reflects this change, and it is manifested in the DMA monument. The placement of two figures, one living and one deceased, within the gabled frame of the funerary relief does more than focus attention on the symbolic contrast between life and death; it underscores the finality of death on a personal level by depicting individual characters in a family setting. The death of the individual is felt most keenly by the family survivors, and it is they who confront the image of the deceased in a symbolic final farewell. This glimpse into personal tragedy is reflective of Late Classical society and far removed from that of the polis in fifth-century-B.C. Athens when tragedies were measured at the state level. There is no greater contrast between fourth-century-B.C. individualism and fifth-century-B.C. solidarity than that exemplified by the personalized spirit expressed in Late Classical grave markers and Pericles' funeral oration of 430 B.C., in which the state losses were commemorated as a group.

PUBLICATIONS: Clairmont 1993, 813–21; Vermeule 1969, 648–50, pl. 234, figs. 1–2; Ternbach 1969, 651 ff., pls. 238–42; Hoffmann 1970, 12, no. 4; Vermeule and Ternbach 1972, 216–21; Vermeule 1981, 114, no. 85; Bromberg 1979, 67, no. 77; Bromberg 1983, 101, no. 97. For a different view of the DMA sculpture and reliefs at Brauron see Stupperich 1994, 61.

REFERENCES: Stewart 1990, 180. For Athenian funerary monuments in general see Diepolder 1931; Friis Johansen 1951; Robertson 1975, 363 ff. For the spirit of fourth-century-B.C. sculpture see Brown 1973.

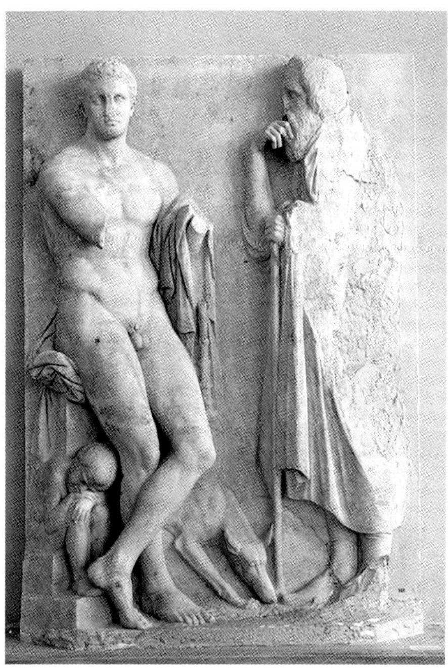

Grave relief of a young hunter, from the river Ilissos, Athens, c. 330 B.C. Marble, 1.68 m. National Museum, Athens, 869. Photo: Hirmer Fotoarchiv 561.0458.

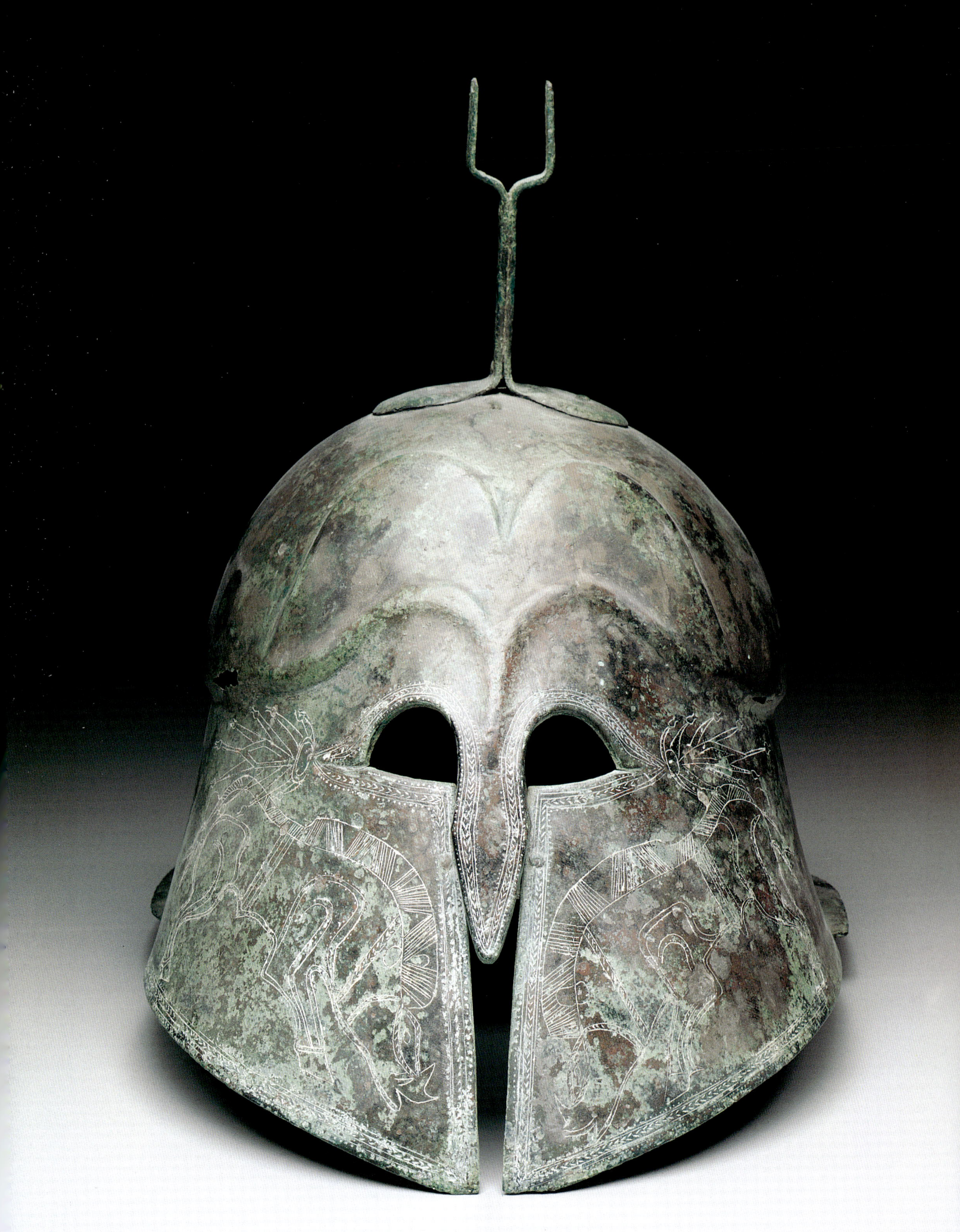

Chapter 5

Etruria: Mastery of Metalwork

Alas, old Veii, you too were once a kingdom, and the throne of gold was set in your marketplace. Now, in your walls, the only sound is the shepherd's horn, and they reap the wheatfields over your people's bones.

—Propertius, *Elegies*

That the Etruscans remain a somewhat enigmatic people in the eyes of the modern world is due in part to the conflicting opinions about their origins; to a less than adequate understanding of their language, religion, and rituals; and to the eclectic style of their art. Hypotheses about the Etruscans were recorded as early as the Etruscans themselves. Herodotus (1.94) and Virgil (*Aeneid* 8.47 ff.) recounted that the Etruscans derived from ancient Lydia, while Strabo (5.2.4) informs us of their origins with the Pelasgians in the eastern Mediterranean. Disregarding these theories, Dionysius of Halicarnassus (*Antiquitates Romanae* 1.30) expressed his belief that the Etruscans were autochthonous, native to Italy from the earliest times. A Renaissance fancy had the Etruscans descended directly from Noah and the twelve tribes of Israel, which were related to the twelve cities of Etruria. In the eighteenth century, the belief was advanced that the Etruscans were related to central European peoples and had migrated to central Italy over Alpine passes. Actually, either through stylistic similarities in art forms or cultural practices in burial customs, certain contacts with Anatolian cultures, as well as with central European and Danubian peoples, can be identified, but not necessarily explained with complete satisfaction. What is certain is that by the end of the ninth century B.C. a culture in northern Italy—named Villanovan, after a mid-nineteenth-century discovery at Villanova near Bologna—began to prosper, grow in population, excel in artistic expression (especially metalwork), establish foreign contacts, and create social distinctions within its settlements as reflected in the cemeteries. The emergence of this society as a major force in the Mediterranean world led to the establishment of Etruscan culture.

The Etruscans—known as Rasenna in Etruscan, Tyrrhenoi in Greek, Turskus to the ancient Umbrians, and Tusci or Etrusci in Latin—grew to prominence in cities primarily in Tuscany on Villanovan sites. Although Etruscan settlements are known along the Po valley to the north and in Campania to the south, the great cities of Etruria are bounded in a triangle by the Arno River, the Tiber River, and the Tyrrhenian Sea. The Etruscans were accomplished engineers, using great walls to enhance naturally defended sites for their cities. They surveyed and cut roads through hills, built bridges over streams, and reclaimed fields through the excavation of subterranean drainage canals. The Etruscans were also successful herdsmen and productive farmers as witnessed in scenes from their earliest examples of figural art. Cultivating olives and grapes imported from Greece, the Etruscans developed their agricultural industries and were able to export olive oil and wine from inland centers such as Chiusi to distant trading partners such as Gaul. Salt was mined near Veii, and the wooded hillsides of Tuscany supplied lumber for construction and fuel. Rich in minerals, the regions around Volterra, Arezzo, the Tolfa Mountains, and the island of Elba across from Populonia provided iron, copper, tin, lead, silver, and alum, all essential elements to the renowned Etruscan metal industry. Flourishing and prosperous in the eighth and seventh centuries B.C., Etruria was understandably attractive to migrant peoples of Asia Minor, the Aegean, other parts of Italy, and North Africa. This explains in part the many stylistic features of other Mediterranean art forms reflected in Etruscan crafts and designs. It is also plausible that skilled craftsmen from these foreign lands, many displaced by Assyrian and then Persian conquests, settled in Etruria to continue their trades and become part of the Etruscan ethos, as they certainly came from Corinth and East Greece in the seventh century B.C. The elaborate horse bit (cat. no. 31) exemplifies the often baroque ornamentation of the Etruscan decorative style (as opposed to a more functional design in Greek art), and also exhibits a similarity in form and function to examples in far away Luristan, where horse breeding was a supreme art. In addition, during the eighth and seventh centuries B.C., handicraft traits from Egypt, Syria, Phoenicia, Assyria, and Cyprus appeared in Etruscan art, contributing to its highly eclectic nature. Such Etruscan artworks often appear in tombs side by side with exotic imports such as ivory, ostrich eggs, faience, glass, and amber.

Along with Near Eastern influences, which are readily detectable in early Etruscan art, Greek motifs, techniques, and subjects also appear from a very early stage. Early in the eighth century B.C., Euboean Greeks with Near Eastern peoples among them settled in the Bay of Naples, where they traded with Etruscan coastal towns and provided their hosts with ideas and imagery already formulated in the eastern Mediterranean. It is after this initial period of contact with the Greeks that the geometricized designs of Early Iron Age art in Italy are replaced with figural images, the potter's wheel is introduced, painted decoration appears on Etruscan vases, and Greek pottery appears in Etruscan tombs. The animal style flourished far and wide in Etruscan art; creatures both real and fantastic were especially used as components of ostentatious decoration on objects for the affluent upper class. They are seen devoid of context on vases, inscribed on armor, adorning furniture or vessels, and embedded in the design of other objects. But the Etruscans did not always employ only minor-scale imagery in their art. It is undoubtedly through contacts with Greeks, who were establishing colonies in southern Italy and Sicily, that monumental art first emerged in Etruria during the seventh century B.C. Rock-hewn, vaulted tombs became the final resting places for prominent Etruscan families. Large-scale stone and terracotta funerary sculpture occurred near Caere and Vetulonia, while the earliest painted tombs are found at Veii and Caere. Contact with foreign sailors, as well as the export of raw materials, produce, and artworks, created a lively commerce for the Etruscans, whose port towns of Pyrgi, Graviscae, and Regae in the major centers of Caere, Tarquinia, and Vulci began to flourish. The Tyrrhenian Sea, at first of great importance to the Phoenicians and the Greeks, became an Etruscan domain by the sixth century B.C., and Greek accusations of Etruscan piracy may reflect this shift in maritime power. Evidence for Etruscan commerce beyond its territorial waters is provided by numerous finds of their gleaming black pottery *(bucchero)* in Greece, North Africa, Spain, and France.

In the struggle for trade and territorial expansion the Etruscans adapted much from Greek military tactics and their technology for production of arms. The DMA's magnificent Corinthian-inspired helmet (cat. no. 34) is a testament to the mastery of the Etruscan metalsmith, as well as a silent commentary on the fact that real power in Etruscan society rested with a warrior aristocracy. This elite class, which supported the arms industry, participated in funerary games and other religious ceremonies in which armor was worn and ultimately placed in tombs to honor the heroic character of those who had pursued a military life. The often violent nature of Etruscan funerary cult, which may originally have included human sacrifice, involved athletic activities in which armed combatants maimed or even killed one another, a practice that is echoed in the gladiatorial events of the Roman arena centuries later.

Women experienced a great deal of social freedom in Etruscan culture, participating in rituals and ceremonies and having substantial influence in public affairs. Such privileged activity was not common in the Mediterranean world and was certainly unlike the secluded lives led by women in Greece. Highborn women are depicted in Etruscan art wearing fine clothes and elaborately wrought jewelry, all made of expensive materials and denoting their aristocratic position. They are sometimes seen with their servants in attendance, assuring their comforts and elite status. Women are present at great banquets and participate side by side with men at symposia. The Etruscans were fond of music and dance, in which both males and females performed, either together or alone. Singing, so much a part of Greek entertainment, was apparently uncommon in Etruria, where it seems to have been a means of expression reserved for priests and prophets. Dance groups were usually led by young women, and Livy (*History of Rome* 7.2) tells us that they performed with grace to the accompaniment of the pipes. Descriptive scenes such as this literally materialize before our eyes with the elegant dancer and pipe player on the DMA's Etruscan mirror (cat. no. 36). The charm and merriment depicted here is expressive of both women's tastes and their central status in Etruscan society. The wealth placed in their tombs matches that associated with men and even contains objects more often restricted to male burials in other cultures, such as the trappings for horses and carriages. The family was central to Etruscan society, and men, women, and children are often depicted in domestic settings. It was here in the privacy of their homes that women utilized the many bronze utensils made for their delight: *cista* to hold their toilet objects, candelabra to illuminate their quarters, and mirrors for their fancy. Each of these often had elaborate decoration in the form of mortal or mythical characters, sometimes with accompanying inscriptions. The frequent references to characters in Greek tragedy indicate that

Etruscan women were literate, knowledgeable about theater, and able to appreciate the romantic sagas that were designed to cater to their tastes. There are many instances of women depicted on mirrors holding or reading scrolls or tablets, implying that they were educated.

Artists maintained an elevated status in Etruscan culture. Supported by a wealthy aristocracy at home and appreciated for their technological expertise and ornate craftsmanship abroad, Etruscan artists enjoyed great renown in their own time by people who sought their wares from as far away as Cyprus and the Levant, Greece, the Crimea, central Europe, and the Iberian Peninsula. Whether as bronze workers, coroplasts, goldsmiths, or potters, they combined an acute knowledge of the technological limitations inherent in their materials with an enormous aptitude for adopting or adapting foreign shapes and designs from imports to produce their own works of art. Their acquired wealth and respected status led to the establishment of a strong middle class in Etruscan society. It is little wonder that foreign merchants and craftsmen joined their number during the prosperous years of the Archaic period. Dionysius of Halicarnassus (*Antiquitates Romanae* 3.46), Livy (*History of Rome* 1.34), and Pliny (*Natural History* 35.43.152) inform us of an aristocratic merchant, Demaratus, who was expelled from his native Corinth by the local tyrant Cypselus and settled with his retinue of craftsmen at Tarquinia in the middle of the seventh century B.C. His marriage to an Etruscan noblewoman produced a son, Lucius Tarquinius Priscus (subsequently known as Tarquin), who, upon the urging of his wife, Tanaquil, migrated to Rome and became the founder of a monarchy that lasted a century before Roman rule.

Monumental terracotta sculpture is an Etruscan trademark. Among the major centers of production were Caere and Veii, both close to Greek colonies in the south where inspiration for sculptural form and function was sought. In addition to funerary and cult images, architectural terracottas were crafted by Etruscan coroplasts who decorated temples and shrines with brightly painted pedimental sculpture, ridge figures, and antefixes, like the DMA's beautiful female head (cat. no. 29). Probably invented in Corinth, the head antefix may have reached Etruscan craftsmen by way of the Greek colonies. The paint preserved on this example testifies to the colorful nature of architectural decoration, as well as to the bright and cheerful freshness of the Etruscan style. The vivacious, youthful face is perhaps that of a maenad, a follower of the god Dionysus, whose orgiastic rituals assumed a more staid form in the decoration of religious buildings. When set in alternating numbers with the heads of satyrs along the roofline, the outwardly turned faces of the maenads were believed to ward off evil from the confines of the building. Perhaps, however, with her elaborate hairdo and earrings (now lost) she represents one of the social elite among Etruscan women, a constant reflection of the elevated status of feminine beauty and grace.

Next to terracotta, bronze was the material crafted most often by Etruscan artists. Mined in the ore-rich regions of central Italy and fired with charcoal made from local forests, bronze was hammered and shaped by specialized craftsmen into statues, statuettes, vessels of various shape and ornament, utensils in abundance, weapons, armor, and jewelry. Bronze is an alloy of copper and tin, with the latter being less than fifteen percent of the whole. The Etruscans added some lead to the mixture to enhance its pliability. Artists produced many different vessels and armor by cold-working the bronze; this technique involves hammering ingots or disks into sheets and shaping them into the desired form. The exquisite DMA helmet was rendered in this manner. Raised relief work was accomplished through the techniques of chasing from above and repoussé from behind the bronze sheet to obtain the desired pattern or image. Different parts of an object were usually attached by hammering overlapping pieces together, known as crimping, or by means of bronze rivets, such as those that join the crest-mount to the helmet here. Cast bronze works like the charming lion appliqués (cat. no. 33) were solid and therefore small, for economy of labor and material. Larger works, more than six or seven inches high, were hollow. The intricate horse bit (cat. no. 31) was cast in interlinking parts and testifies to the maker's adroitness with both the material and the design. Molds for solid-cast items could be of wood or clay, but also of stone, as were those for mirrors, to withstand extensive reuse. Hollow-cast objects were created by the lost-wax casting method. A solid core of clay was suspended within the mold and a thin layer of wax was placed between the two surfaces. Details were formed in the pliable wax before the outer clay mold was applied. Metal pins held the core and the mold at the desired distance once the wax was heated and drained out through holes, allowing the molten bronze to replace it. For larger objects and statues, this process was generally done in parts. After the outer mold was removed, the exposed bronze surface of the object could be enhanced with images or designs by tracing, engraving, or stamping, and was finally polished with either pumice or cuttlebone.

Etruscan metalsmiths also produced exquisite gold jewelry and decorative pieces, many examples of which adorned their owners in life and ultimately accompanied them to the tomb. Starting in the eighth century B.C., Etruscan jewelers crafted several varieties of pins and pendants, earrings, hair spirals, fibulae (latched pins), fine rings, and bracelets, some reflecting Phoenician influence, others simply embellished versions in gold of established Villanovan bronze types. Throughout the Archaic period, Greek influence was the dominant foreign element, although this manifests itself more through adaptations of subsidiary ornament than in outright imitation; thus Etruscan gold work has its own distinctive quality apart from Greek jewelry. Of the various techniques employed in crafting ancient jewelry, the Etruscans perfected those of filigree (soldered wire patterns) and its derivative, granulation (soldered beads), beyond that achieved by any other culture. In the finest examples of Etruscan gold work, the individual grains measure less than .15 millimeters in diameter, and thousands of beads were sometimes used to ornament a single piece of jewelry. The complex amalgamation of various types of filigree wire can be appreciated in the magnificent pair of Late Archaic earrings (cat. no. 45), while granulation is employed to accent other methods of decoration in the stunning pair of Late Classical earrings with tiny human faces and rosettes. Both examples provide excellent representations of the distinctive and ornate Etruscan style.

Etruscan artists rarely signed their work, and those that did, beginning about 650 B.C., were generally potters. By the end of the eighth century B.C., Euboean colonists in the Bay of Naples had introduced the Greek alphabet to the Etruscans, who modified these letters to devise a system of writing expressive of their own language. The earliest Archaic inscriptions reveal a diversity of letter forms, perhaps indicating different dialects among the Etruscan centers. The oldest graffiti appear on pottery and precious commodities, which suggests that at first only the wealthy upper class was literate. As literacy spread through the social strata, a number of inscriptions emerge, although these are primarily votive or funerary, revealing limited information such as the names of divinities, dedicators, or the deceased—sometimes with references to parentage and rank—and occasionally identification of the object offered. A significant element in the inscriptions, divulging much about the Etruscan social order, is the use of two personal names. The praenomen, or personal name, was followed by the cognomen, or family name, specifying to which group of people the individual was bound, such as Lars Porsenna or Tanaquil Fulnia. The few ritual and legal texts that survive have yet to be fully understood and are only the remnants of a profusion of treatises on Etruscan religion, historical events, and drama that are now lost but alluded to in Roman literature. Etruscan religion, which appears to have permeated nearly every aspect of public and private life, had a profound effect on Roman culture. By the time of Augustus, however, and the establishment of the Roman Empire, the world of the Etruscans had been irreversibly altered and absorbed into the sphere of Rome. The Roman emperor Claudius I was married to a woman of Etruscan blood, Plautia Urgulanilla; had command of the Etruscan language; and, according to Suetonius (*Divus Claudius* 42.2), wrote a voluminous history of the people. Born out of a sense of nostalgia and antiquarian curiosity, this work, like the Etruscans themselves, has slipped from our grasp. Fortunately, however, Etruscan culture remains mirrored in the accounts of others and is reflected in the lively and intricate creations its people left behind.

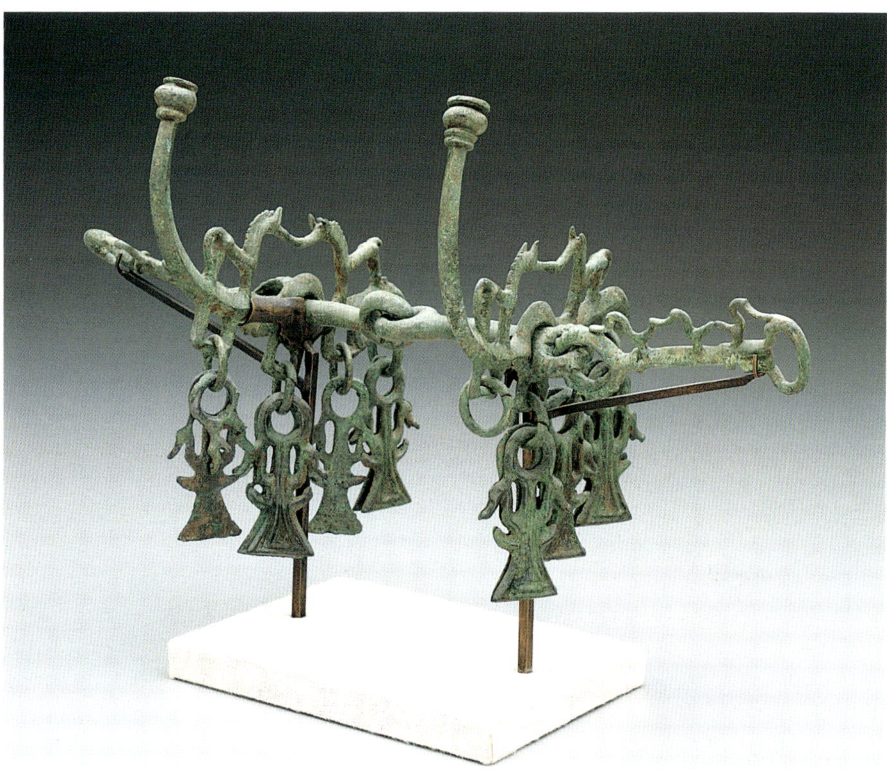

31.
Horse bit

Villanovan, late eighth–seventh century B.C.
Bronze
H. 19 cm, L. 33 cm, D. 14.5 cm
Gift of Mrs. John Leddy Jones, 1969.6

THE VILLANOVAN CULTURE of Italy represents the Early Iron Age of the Etruscans and received its name from the site of Villanova near Bologna, discovered in 1853. A remarkable number of bronze horse bits have been recovered from Villanovan sites, and this example is a particularly elaborate one. The mouthpiece is jointed by interlocking rings. The high, curving cheekpieces terminate in ornamental knobs. A pair of horses placed muzzle to muzzle decorate the cheekpieces and could have served to check the headstall straps that probably passed through the space beneath their joined noses. The horses stand erect with ears alert, their hogged manes scalloped, and their tails anchored in the space behind their rear hooves. Extending from each cheekpiece and attached to the mouthpiece by interlocking rings is a mobile bar to the end of which the reins would have been fastened. Three stylized bird-shaped ornaments are mounted on each of these bars in a design that links each set together, tail to tail or tail to beak. Dangling on rings from each of the cheekpieces are four pairs of bird-headed pendants decorated on their outer faces and set back to back. These not only added to the decorative effect of the bit, but jingled when the horse was moving.

Villanovan horse bits have been recovered from several tombs, both male and female, in northern and central Italy and were apparently meant to indicate the affluent social position of those who could afford horses and horse-drawn vehicles. The bits are often found in pairs, and occasionally in context with wagon or chariot parts. This indicates that these ornate devices were made in pairs for a team of horses and not just for an individual mount. A horse bit nearly identical to the one discussed here is in the Ashmolean Museum in Oxford. It is analogous in nearly every detail except that the horses' manes are not scalloped. Neither of these two bits has a known provenance, but whether or not they were made for the same team of horses, it seems likely that they were crafted in the same workshop.

Bronze horse bits of the same period and functioning in a similar manner were produced in Luristan (western Persia). However, the cheekpieces of those bits are decorated with fantastic, winged creatures, positioned so that the bar of the mouthpiece passes through their bodies. They are quite different in decoration and style from the types of animals on the Villanovan examples. That cheekpieces decorated with animals are almost unknown in Greece would seem to exclude this otherwise acceptable intermediary as a source of influence.

PUBLICATIONS: Hoffmann 1970, 183, no. 85; DMFA 1970.

REFERENCES: For the Oxford example see Brown 1972, 398, fig. 63, and 400. For additional examples of similar design see Mitten and Doeringer 1967, 155–56, nos. 153–54; Dörig 1975, no. 115; and especially Hase 1969. For comparisons with examples from Luristan see Anderson 1961, 47 and 65; Herrmann 1968, 1–38.

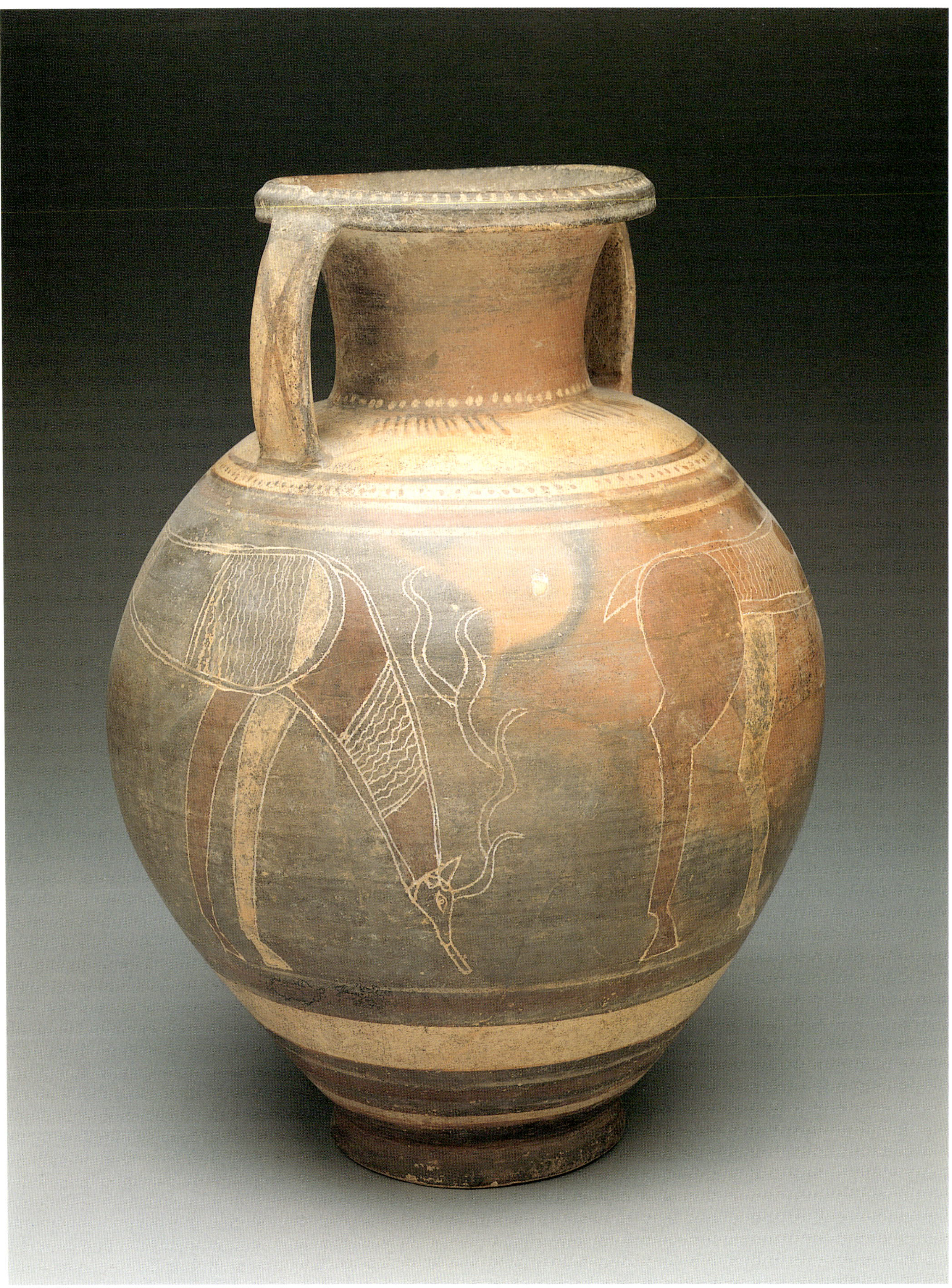

32.

Neck amphora: grazing stags and a snake

Etrusco-Corinthian, sixth century B.C.
Ceramic
H. 36.8 cm, W. 16.5 cm
Gift of Mr. and Mrs. Cecil H. Green, 1966.23

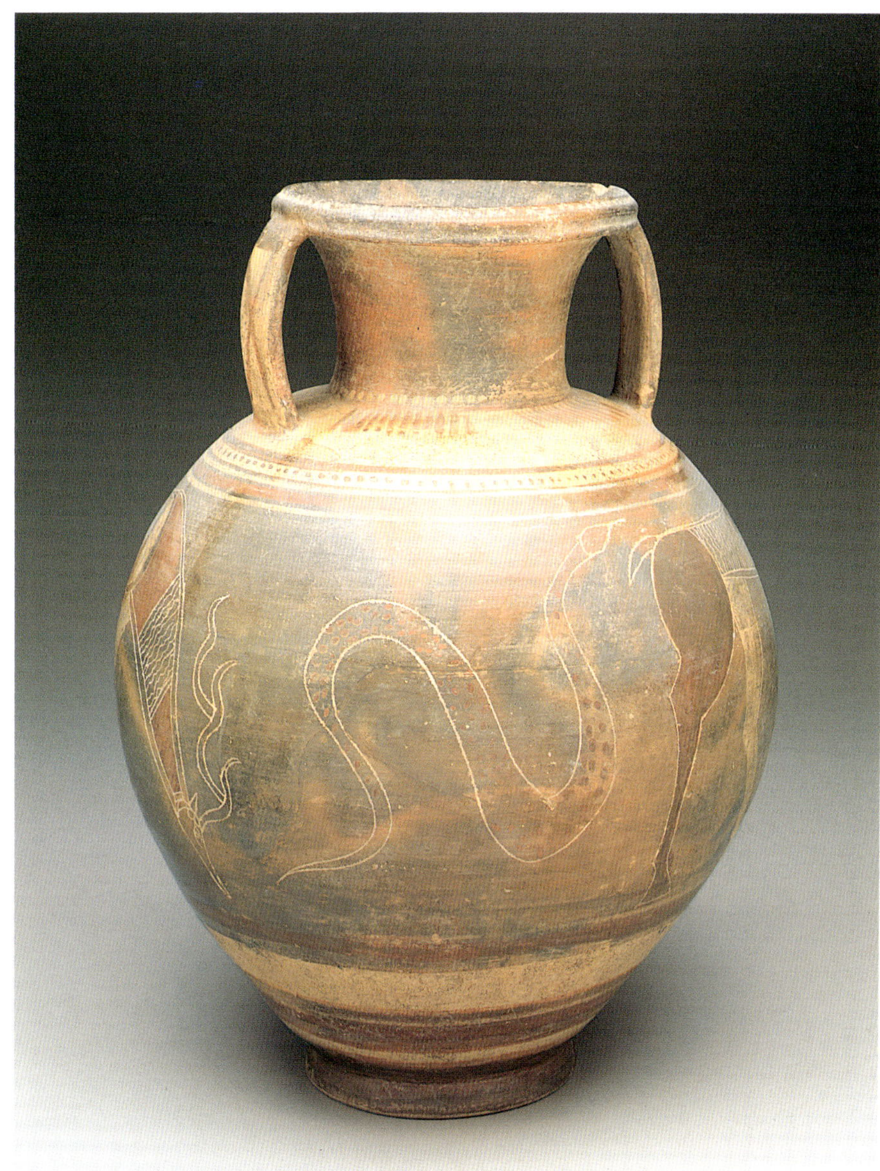

TWO STIFF-LEGGED STAGS with elaborate antlers graze with their heads to the ground (opposite). A third figure, that of a snake, follows the stags and like them is pointed to the right (right). There are no ornaments in the figured scene, but colored bands of white and red decorate the surfaces below the frieze, and rows of dots in white and black, in addition to black tongues, are painted above it. An X motif appears on the outside of the concave strap handles.

The amphora belongs to the Polychrome Group of Etruscan vases first studied by Georg Karo in 1896 and treated more completely since then by János Szilágyi. The technique of incising figures onto a black background and the animal style that dominates the vases in the Polychrome Group were probably derived from Corinth. However, the incising technique was also certainly related to the long-established line of Etruscan *bucchero* vases. Certain aspects of the animal style are also found on the later polychrome vases from the Group workshops. The figures are incised directly onto a black glazed field with added white and red paint applied to various body parts in order to enhance the overall appearance of the animals. The creation of the animals solely by the means of incision on the dark background has an interesting visual parallel with similar images incised on bronze, such as the wild boars on the Apulian-Corinthian helmet (cat. no. 34) in the DMA collections.

An amphora of the Polychrome Group now in the Louvre and listed by Szilágyi is decorated with animals nearly identical in type, pose, and placement to those on the DMA vase, except that the artist has included a lion between the grazing stags. Herbert Hoffmann has noted another Polychrome amphora on the Swiss art market and believes it to be by the same hand that decorated the DMA vase.

PUBLICATIONS: Hoffmann 1970, 320, no. 154; Bromberg 1979, 66, no. 76; Bromberg 1983, 103, no. 99.

REFERENCES: For the study by Szilágyi see Szilágyi 1967, 543–53, and see 550, no. 11, for the Louvre amphora no. D. 158 noted above. For additional studies of the Etrusco-Corinthian Polychrome Group see Amyx 1965, 7–10; Szilágyi 1975, 25–30; Szilágyi 1976, 185–86. For comments on the origin of the Polychrome Group see Brown 1960, 58–59; Amyx 1988, 688–90.

33.
Appliqués: two couchant lions

Etruscan, late sixth or early fifth century B.C.
Bronze
Lion 1: H. 2.2 cm, L. 3.9 cm, D. 0.9 cm
Lion 2: H. 2.2 cm, L. 3.8 cm, D. 0.9 cm
Gift of Dr. Elie Borowski, 1967.6.1 and 1967.6.2

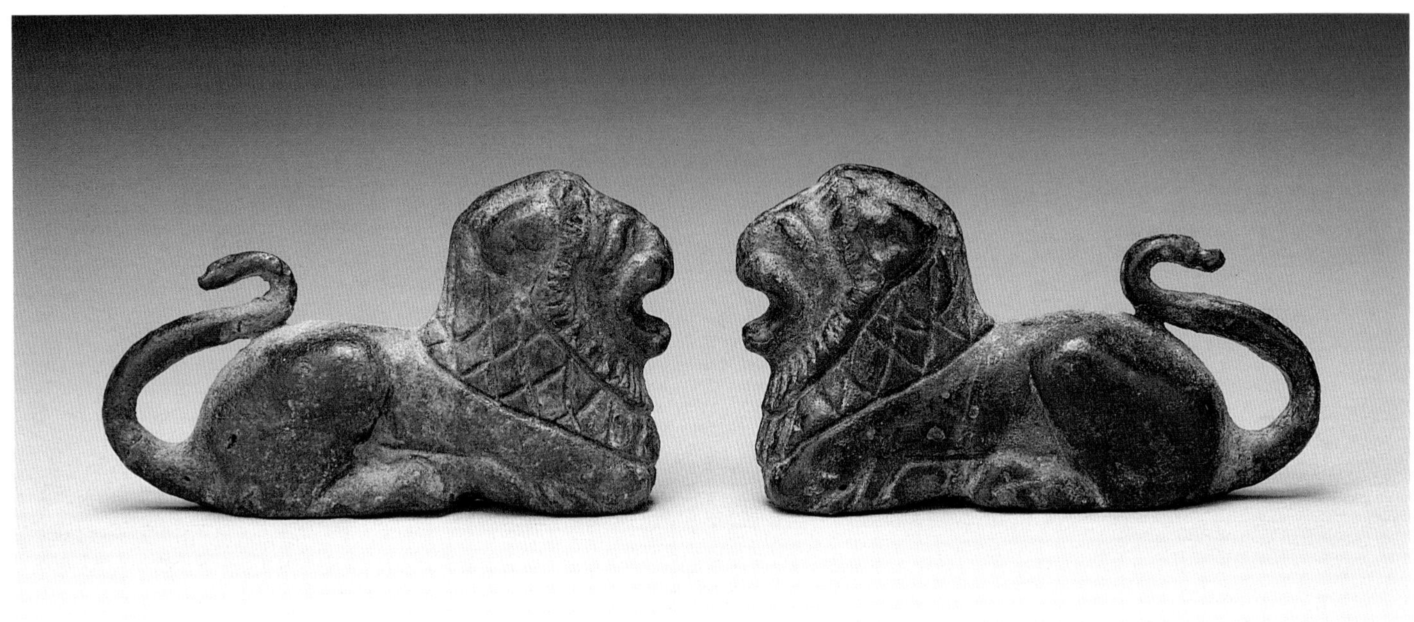

LIONS WERE A FAVORITE subject in Etruscan, Greek, and Near Eastern art. The Etruscans often used bronze representations of the lion to decorate armor, furniture, and carriages, and especially as fittings on bronze vessels. These ornamental attachments generally appeared in groups, so this pair of lions probably decorated the same vessel or other object. They may have been positioned back to back or confronted in a heraldic arrangement, serving in a dual capacity as decorative and guardian entities. Their small scale and the fact that their forepaws were excluded from the form (they appear to be hidden beneath the creatures) indicate that their original setting was purely decorative and probably subsidiary.

In their crouching pose, the lions are depicted snarling with their ears pinned back. Their eyes are narrow ridges, their whiskers and ruffs are hatched, and their manes are rendered in a stylized triangle pattern. Their hind legs extend from the haunches in low relief along their bodies. The tails do not cling to the bodies except for the slight attachment for stability at the base of the small curve; this is typical of Etruscan lions and distinguishes them from Greek ones.

PUBLICATIONS: Hoffmann 1970, 195, no. 91.

REFERENCES: Brown 1960, 115; Muscarella 1974, nos. 83–85; Hall 1987, 210, no. 118; Haynes 1985, no. 13. For a pair of cast couchant lions attached to the rim of an Etruscan bronze vase see Jucker 1991, 26, no. 7.

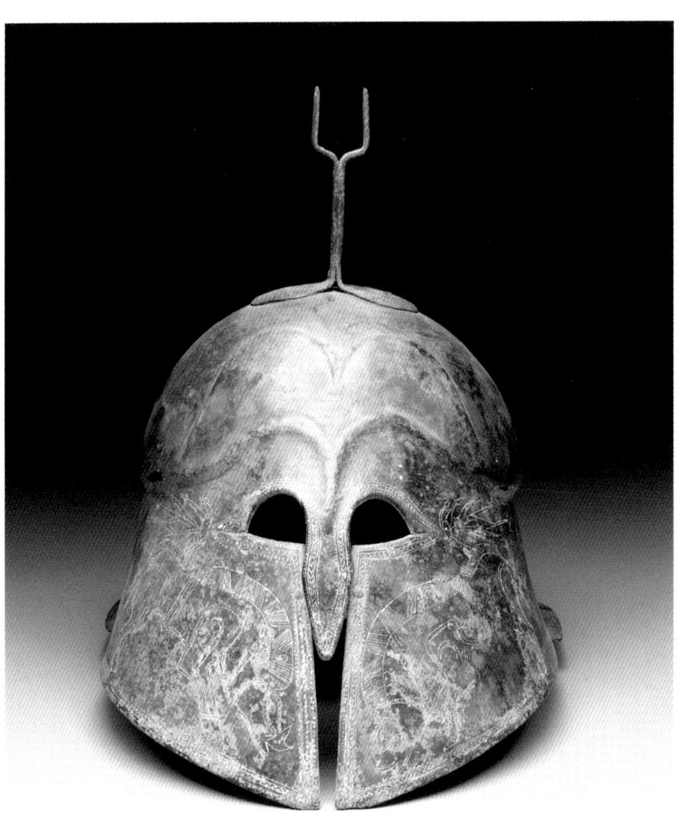

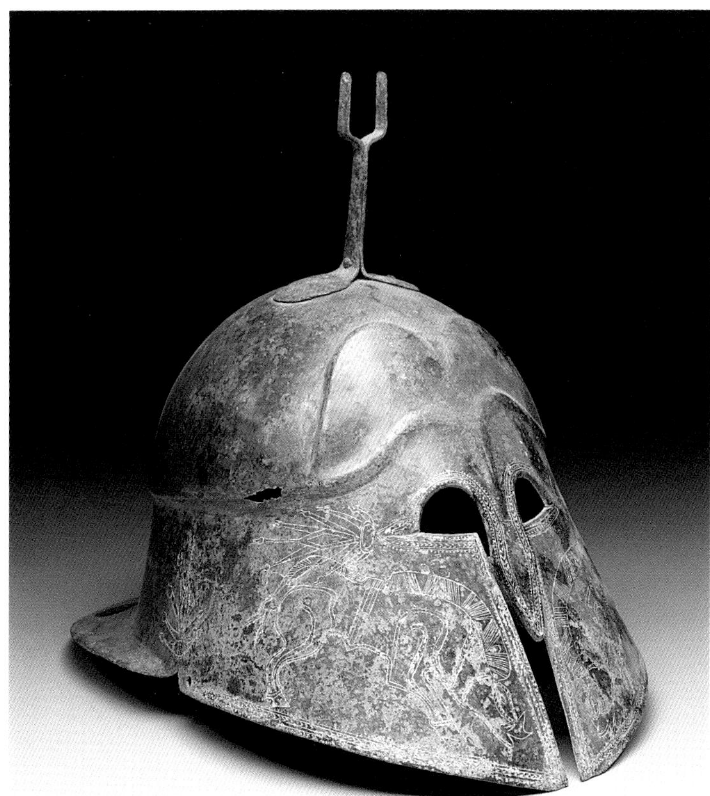

34.
Helmet

Apulian-Corinthian, early fifth century B.C.
Bronze
H. 27.1 cm, L. 30.5 cm, D. 22.1 cm
Dallas Art Association purchase, Edwin J. Kiest Memorial Fund, 1966.8

A SOUTH ITALIAN adaptation of the Corinthian type of Greek helmet produced a smaller version in Etrusco-Apulian style. On this example, the double-pronged crest-mount is supported by two flat, oval-shaped extensions, which are fastened to the crown of the helmet by two rivets. The skullpiece is offset from the face and sides by a pronounced ridge, which drops diagonally from the forehead and runs beneath the large, embossed eyebrows and toward the rear of the helmet. The small, closely set eyeholes are outlined with an incised herringbone pattern between lines and a dot band, which continues around the narrow nose guard and along the edge of the cheekpieces. A pair of wild boars at bay confront each other on the cheekpieces. Their stiff bristles and stylized body markings are indicated with incising. A palmettolike flower motif is incised on the outer edges of the eyeholes and on the sides of the helmet. A helmet liner was once anchored to the rivets in the

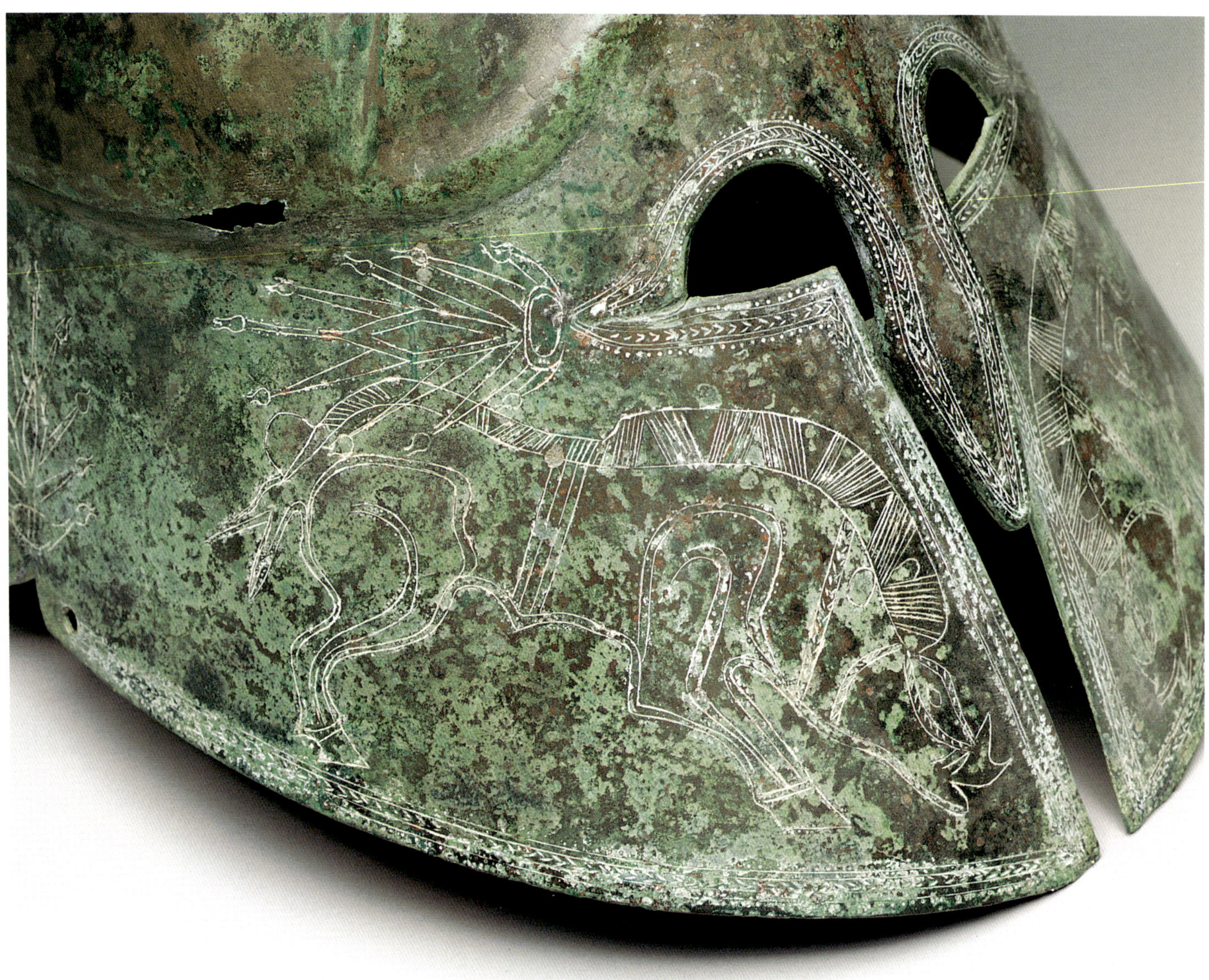

crown and to a hole on either side of the helmet.

This helmet with its small holes was not worn over the face but pushed back on the head, exposing the face and allowing the otherwise horizontally flared neck guard to rest diagonally at a nearly parallel angle to the neck. The small notches on the sides of the helmet are reminiscent of larger ones on later Corinthian helmets; such notches prevented the lower neck or shoulders from being scraped when these helmets were worn over the entire head. Wild boars decorated some of the Corinthian helmet prototypes but occur more frequently on extant Apulian-Corinthian helmets. With its high crest, incised animal and floral motifs, and patternized subsidiary decoration, this helmet belongs to a large group of ceremonial armor of the type that was frequently placed in warriors' tombs. Its preservation is excellent and superior to most of the Apulian-Corinthian helmets that have survived.

PUBLICATIONS: Hoffmann 1970, 162, no. 77; Bromberg 1979, 65, no. 74; Hase 1982, 103 with illustration; Bottini 1988, 134, no. A17.

REFERENCES: For a nearly identical Apulian-Corinthian helmet with confronted boars see Jucker 1991, 92, no. 110. For a helmet with perforations surrounding the eyeholes and cheekpieces for attaching the helmet liner to bronze pins see Comstock and Vermeule 1971, 404, no. 582. For ancient Italian helmets see Stary 1986, 25 ff. For the Apulian-Corinthian type specifically see Bottini 1988, 107–36, and 418–29, nos. 38–43.

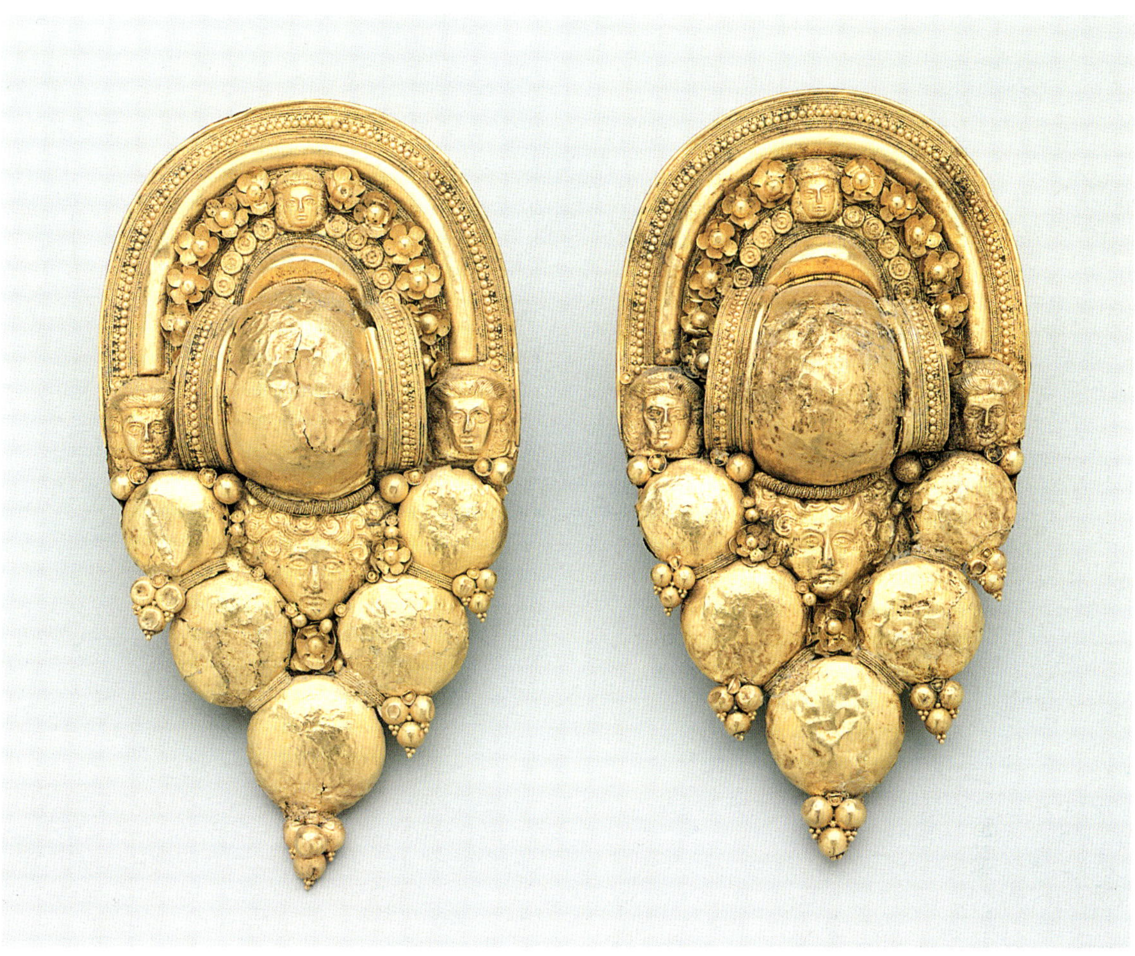

35.

Pair of earrings

Etruscan, fourth–third century B.C.
Gold
H. 11.7 cm, W. 6.5 cm, D. 3.5 cm and
H. 11.4 cm, W. 6.5 cm, D. 3.5 cm
Gift of Mr. and Mrs. Cecil H. Green, 1966.25.a–b

THESE LARGE AND ELABORATE earrings are a common late Etruscan type; two similar pairs in the DMA's gold collection were acquired in 1991. They are sometimes called *a grappolo* earrings because the triangular bottom part looks like a bunch of grapes. This is an exceptionally rich example, with fine maskettes and very intricate filigree and granulation. The upper part consists of a horseshoe-shaped band decorated with filigreed wire patterns and a row of granulation. At the base of the horseshoe is a semicircular section of a bent tube flanked by parallel rows of filigree and granulation. Above this "leech"-shaped ornament is a semicircle of stamped rosettes and stamped disk ornaments surmounted by a maskette. There are also maskettes on either side of the central ornament. Below this upper area is an inverted triangle of five flattened capsules, each with small clusters of granulated globules hanging from it. There are rosettes in the interstices and a central mask with dramatic waving hair. The earrings were formed by repoussé and have undergone considerable repair on the lower halves. Such earrings are worn by female figures in Etruscan funerary sculpture.

PUBLICATIONS: Hoffmann 1970, 466, no. 215; Bromberg 1979, 65, no. 75; Bromberg 1983, 103, no. 100.

REFERENCES: Higgins 1980, 151, and pl. 42D; Cygielman 1990, 35, pl. 71, and 36, pl. 72; Cristofani and Martelli 1983, 223, no. 239; Marshall 1911, 255, no. 2252, and 256, nos. 2258 and 2259; Richter 1940, 54, and fig. 172.

36.

Mirror: double pipe player and winged Lasa

Etruscan, early third century B.C.
Bronze
H. 26.7 cm, W. 14.4 cm, D. 0.7 cm
Dallas Art Association purchase, Edwin J. Kiest Memorial Fund, 1966.7

THE TWO FIGURES ENGRAVED on the back of this hand mirror are juxtaposed so as to balance the composition within the circular frame. A male youth clad in a long chiton with a cloak over his left arm plays the double pipes. His cheeks are inflated, his lips puckered, and his fingers positioned on the instrument. A headband holds his hair in place. At right is a winged Lasa, one of the charmingly attractive Etruscan fantasies in the circle of Turan, who represents the Etruscan equivalent of Aphrodite. She is nude except for a simple necklace, bracelets, and sandals. The straps crisscrossing her torso may represent an unnecessary apparatus to fasten the wings to her body, a feature not generally found on the many images of Lasas on Etruscan mirrors, since the wings would be part of the spirit's form. Perhaps the wing straps on the Lasa are a conflation of visual accounts of images of the mortal Icarus, who required identical supports for his wings as seen in Etruscan art. The emphatic gesturing of the Lasa's hands, the twisting of her head to one side, and the movement expressed through her right leg indicate that she is dancing to the music performed by the attendant youth. Behind her is an open chest, which perhaps alludes to toilet items associated with the boudoir, and a woven satchel suspended above. Surrounding the figural scene is a wreath, its pattern perhaps reflective of floral designs found on South Italian red-figure vases. A frontal-faced female head with leaves, perhaps a wreath, in her hair is beneath the two figures in the transitional space between the disk and handle. The bronze tang beneath this image would have been inserted into a handle of a different material, probably wood, bone, or ivory.

Although the Egyptians, Greeks, and Romans used mirrors in daily life, the Etruscans produced hand mirrors in greater numbers; over three thousand examples the animal style that dominates the vases are known today. Mythological characters and winged figures such as Erotes, Boreads, Sirens, Thanatos, and Hypnos are used as decorations. Prominent among the mythological scenes shown on mirrors are love stories, either with happy endings, such as that of Odysseus and Penelope, or with a tragic element, such as those of Helen and Paris, Aphrodite and Adonis, and Atlanta and Meleager. The winged Lasa was a favorite image on Etruscan mirrors (cf. Mitten and Doeringer 1967, no. 215); and a Lasa in a pose similar to that on the DMA mirror takes the form of a *patera* (offering pan) support and appropriately gazes into a mirror (Kozloff and Mitten 1988, no. 50). Mirrors were originally utilitarian in the hands of Etruscan women, who appreciated the romantic sagas, scenes of domestic life, and other matters of feminine concern depicted on them. Although mirrors were used by both women and men in other Mediterranean cultures, they were the property of women in ancient Etruria, where a profound symbolic significance was attached to them. Here the mirror was considered a receptacle for the soul of the person whose image was reflected on its surface. The Etruscan word *hinthial* means both "soul" and "reflected image." This dual concept is similar to that in ancient Egypt where the word *ankh* means "life" but also denotes a mirror. Many Etruscan mirrors have been retrieved from the graves of women, indicating not only their desire to take earthly possessions of value into the next world, but that the owners did not want to leave behind the device that had contained their souls in life.

PUBLICATIONS: Grummond 1982, 199, no. 35.

REFERENCES: For the decoration, dating, and uses of Etruscan mirrors see Grummond 1981, 54–58; Roberts 1982, 31–54. For an image of a winged Lasa on a mirror see Mitten and Doeringer 1967, 211, no. 215. For a winged Lasa holding a mirror see Kozloff and Mitten 1988, no. 50. For the various interpretations of Lasas see Grummond 1982, 114–15.

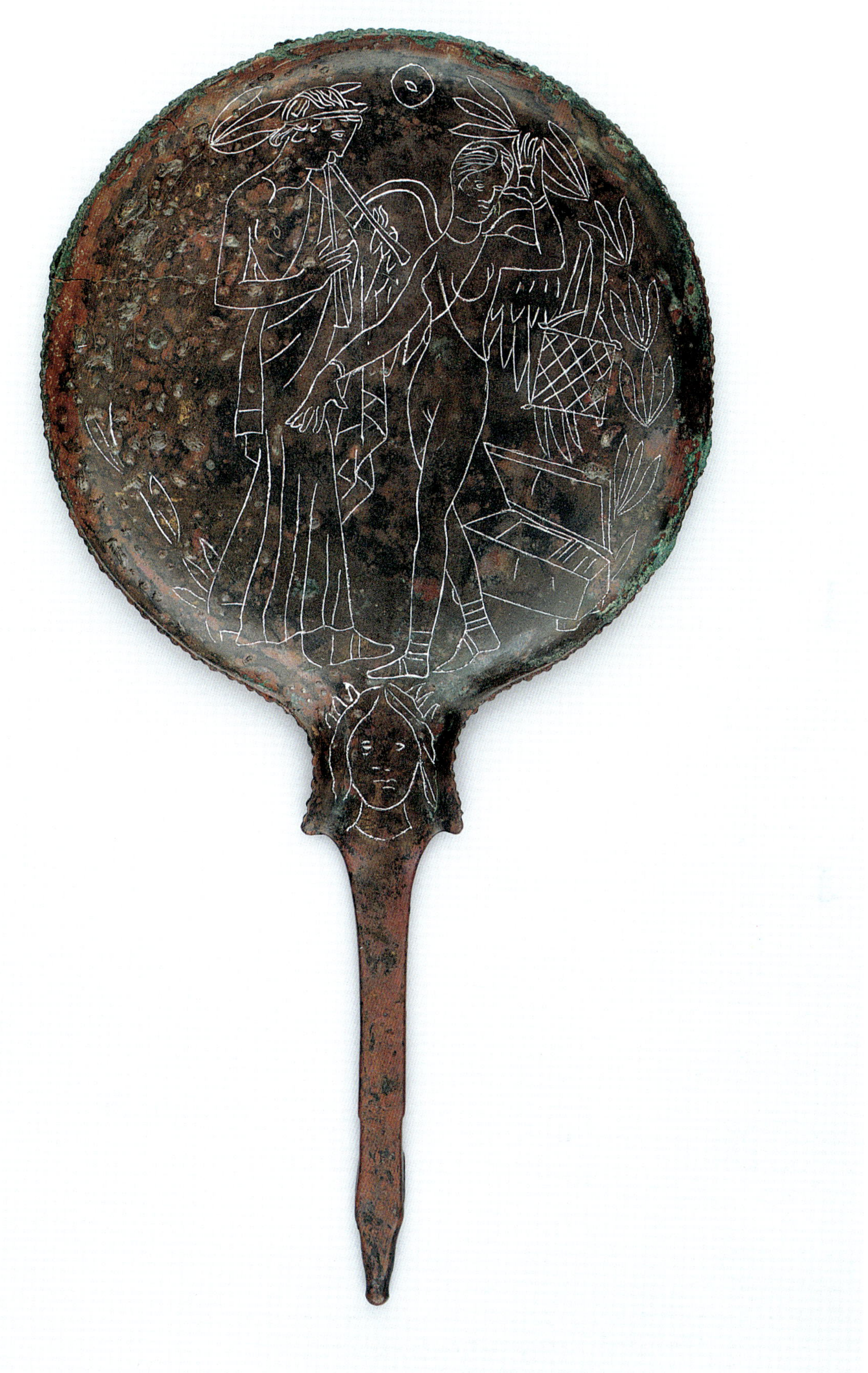

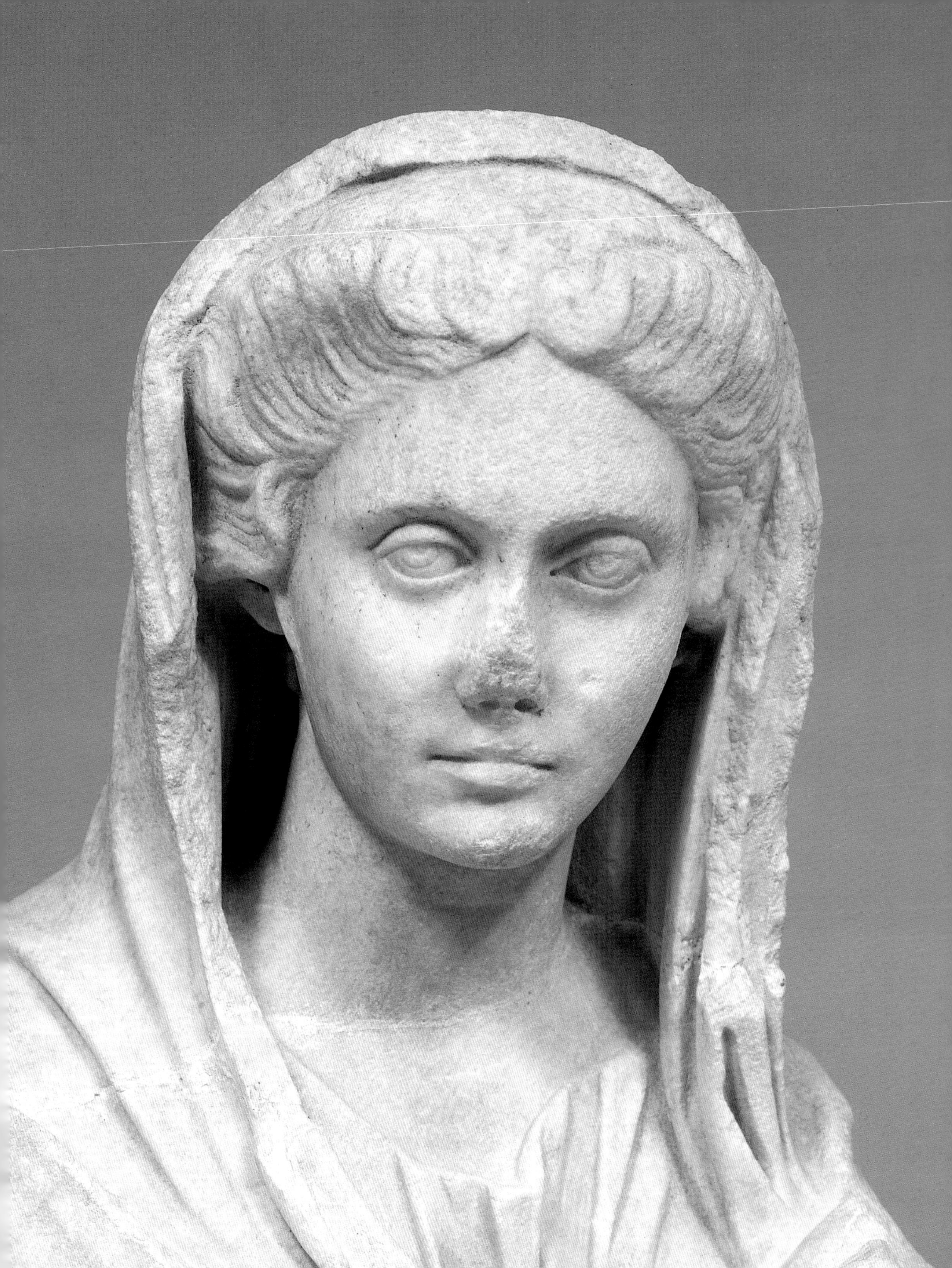

Chapter 6

Rome: Art in an Imperial Society

But conditions were different in the atria of our ancestors where it was portraits that were looked at, and not statues by foreign artists, either in bronze or marble. Wax impressions of the face were set out on separate chests, so that they might serve as the portraits which were carried in family funeral processions, and thus, when anyone died, the entire role of his ancestors, all who ever existed, was present.

—Pliny, *Natural History*

Let others more skillfully mold breathing images of bronze. . . . You, Oh Romans, must rule with might over the nations of the world.

—Virgil, *Aeneid*

Republican Rome scorned art. The founders of the Roman Republic in the sixth and fifth centuries B.C. believed in austere virtue, warlike strength, loyalty, self-sacrifice, and puritanical self-denial. The historian Livy's *History of Rome,* Book I, paints a picture of early Rome as a community of heroes, dedicated to the common good of the Roman state. Whether this ideological view of expanding Roman society is correct or not, by the late third century B.C. Rome had absorbed both the Etruscan city-states to the north and the Greek cities in Magna Graecia to the south. Rome was now poised for the conquest of the entire Mediterranean, a conquest that would bring native Italic cults, arts, and values face to face with the sophisticated civilization of the Hellenistic Greek world. In the next two centuries, Rome became the heir to these Hellenistic kingdoms in the East, and Roman art became the last, and in some ways the greatest, synthesis of Greek style and local taste.

At first, the Roman conquerors of Magna Graecia and the mainland Greek states, in the manner of conquerors anywhere, removed a mass of sculptures and decorative arts to Rome as triumphal loot. They also, in an eclectic manner, adapted their own portrait sculpture and architecture to Greek styles and employed Greek artists. The earlier influence of Etruscan art, with its own rich adaptation of Greek art, meant that Roman Italy was no tabula rasa, and that the values of early Roman culture also influenced the way in which Greek art was adopted. This is exemplified by the well-known sculpture of a prominent Roman from Delos, now in the National Museum in Athens, which places a realistic Roman head on a heroic Greek nude body. In a very significant way, the complex Roman confrontation with Greek art was a paradigm for all the later "classical revivals" and "renaissances," in which the enduring images of Greek cult religion were simultaneously embraced and subtly changed by later peoples. The Laocoön, a work apparently made for Roman patrons by Greek sculptors (Agesander, Athanadoros, and Polydoros of Rhodes) in the first century B.C. or A.D., is significantly different in its veristic violence from dramatic, but still idealized, sculptures of divine combat such as the reliefs on the Hellenistic Great Altar of Zeus from Pergamon.

The Roman Empire succeeded the Hellenistic Greek kingdoms in the East and dominated the entire Mediterranean Basin from the Straits of Gibraltar to the highlands of Anatolia, the Levant, and Egypt. The empire also extended the trade networks of the Greek East; not only did the Syrian Orontes River flow into the Tiber, as the satirist Juvenal acidly said, but Roman ships and military roads expedited trade everywhere. If Greek art and philosophy were the major gifts of ancient civilization to a future Europe, Roman law, technology, and political organization were an equally important future legacy. It was the image of a majestic, all-powerful state, *Roma Aeterna,* that was to pass on the concept of civilization, via the Roman Catholic Church and the Holy Roman Empire, to Dark Age Europe.

Art played an important role in the crucial symbolic formulations of the early empire under the shrewd politician Octavius Caesar, later to become the first Roman emperor, Augustus. Augustus was fully aware of the publicity value of images. Like Seti I and his son Ramses II in Egypt, Augustus consciously deployed traditional art forms in a new imperial way. The great Prima Porta statue of Augustus of the early first century A.D., in the Musei Vaticani, in Rome, recasts a Greek athlete-hero as a Roman general. Augustus, barefoot and noble in appearance, wears a resplendently decorated suit of realistic armor, although he was neither athlete nor soldier. This is the godlike king visible in the DMA bust of Seti I: wise, powerful, beneficent, and beautiful.

The value of realistic portraiture in Rome had its roots in early Roman religion. The images of ancestors were carefully preserved in the tombs of patrician families. The first *imagines*, or death masks, were probably modeled in wax from the actual features of the dead person, but by at least the first century B.C. these images appeared in the form of portrait sculptures. A fusion of this Roman concern with images of the dead and the interest in portraiture found in Hellenistic art led to the remarkable gallery of brilliant portrait sculptures —one of the finest artistic achievements of the Roman Empire. The faces of Rome are unforgettable, from the pudgy portrait of the crazed Emperor Nero to the grand nobility of Marcus Aurelius, the philosopher-emperor, whose equestrian statue was visible in Rome throughout the Middle Ages and, until recently, graced Michelangelo's Piazza Campidoglio on the Capitoline.

Portraits of people associated with the imperial family were the most important creations of Roman sculptors; the prototypes were created in imperial workshops at Rome and then duplicated for distribution across the empire. Such statues served as visual icons for the Roman administration, and were especially important because many emperors received divine honors in the provinces. However, portraits were valued throughout Roman society. Those who could afford a funerary monument immortalized their life in portrait form. Often this goal was achieved before death by purchasing a ready-made figure to which a portrait head could be attached in life or added by the family after death. Egypt, Greece, and Rome shared the custom of memorializing the dead person in portrait sculpture, which served as a testimonial to the value of his or her life. Whatever an individual's view of the afterlife, it was a Roman family's duty to preserve images of the dead for posterity. Portraits also reaffirmed the identity, personality, and ideal value of living people, as they were to do in Renaissance and post-Renaissance sculpture derived from Roman portraiture. Jean-Antoine Houdon's plaster bust of George Washington in the Museum collections is a good example of later attempts to achieve immortality through idealizing portraits.

The DMA has two fine marble busts of this type. An Antonine head (cat. no. 38), formerly a part of the Norbert Schimmel collection, is close to the type of the young Marcus Aurelius in the Museo Capitolino in Rome. A rich example of early Antonine baroque style, the boy has the innocent pathos of youth; his delicate features and wide eyes are almost overpowered by the great mass of elaborately drilled curls.

The DMA's other head (cat. no. 37), also formerly from the Schimmel collection, is a stylistic and psychological contrast to the portrait bust discussed above. The treatment of the young man's features is crisp and austere; the effect is both more complex and more ambiguous. The youth glances sideways, almost evasively, and his pursed lips create a troubled expression. There could hardly be a better example of the range of possibilities opened up by the unique combination of plastic power and psychological penetration in Roman sculpture. Roman imperial sculptors raised portraiture to the ideal level of Greek art through their brilliant treatment of hair, flesh, and facial forms, while at the same time dramatizing the actual appearance of a real person through idiosyncratic features and an expressive glance. The head of this young man is superbly modeled and textured, with a subtle glow in the marble suggestive of the energy of youth, but the spirit speaking through those side-cast eyes is as elusive as life itself.

The second-century-A.D. statue of a woman (cat. no. 39), like the Antonine head of a youth, represents some of the main values of Roman society. The statue is a monument to a well-to-do *mater familias*, an honored wife and mother. As in the Prima Porta Augustus, the woman's symbolic role is emphasized by the use of a much earlier Greek sculptural type. The woman's body type probably goes back to Greek sculpture of the fourth century B.C. This Small Herculaneum figure type, named after a statue found at Herculaneum, appears frequently in Roman sculpture. The heavy drapery and concealing mantle indicated, for a Roman audience, purity, modesty, and virtue. Although these may be thought to have become archaic values by the second century A.D., the original Roman idea of a marriage based on chastity and loyalty retained its religious sanctity throughout Roman history. In Roman eyes, the virtue of marriage paralleled the virtue of the Roman state and was one of its supports. Consequently, distinguished Roman men and women were often shown clasping one another's hands, in the formal bond of marriage, on their sarcophagi.

The head of the statue would have been a contemporary addition to the stock body type. Gentle, distinguished, and sad, the sculpture speaks of the best traditions of Roman society. It is quite unlike some of the harder and more theatrical personifications of Roman imperial women. The lady does, however, embody the fundamental Roman belief in family, marriage, and ancestral traditions, which, like Roman law, were to become an integral part of Roman Christianity.

The funerary significance of a traditional Roman marriage is described in the Augustan poet Propertius's elegy to a great lady related to the emperor's family:

> When the maid's robe of purple was laid aside before the torch of marriage, and a new wreath caught up and bound my hair, I was wedded to your couch, my Paullus, doomed, alas! to leave it thus. Behold the legend on this stone: To one and one alone was she espoused.
>
> My life was changeless; through all its days it knew no slander: between the torch of marriage and the torch of death ours was a life of high renown. (Propertius, *The Elegies* 4.33–36, 45–46)

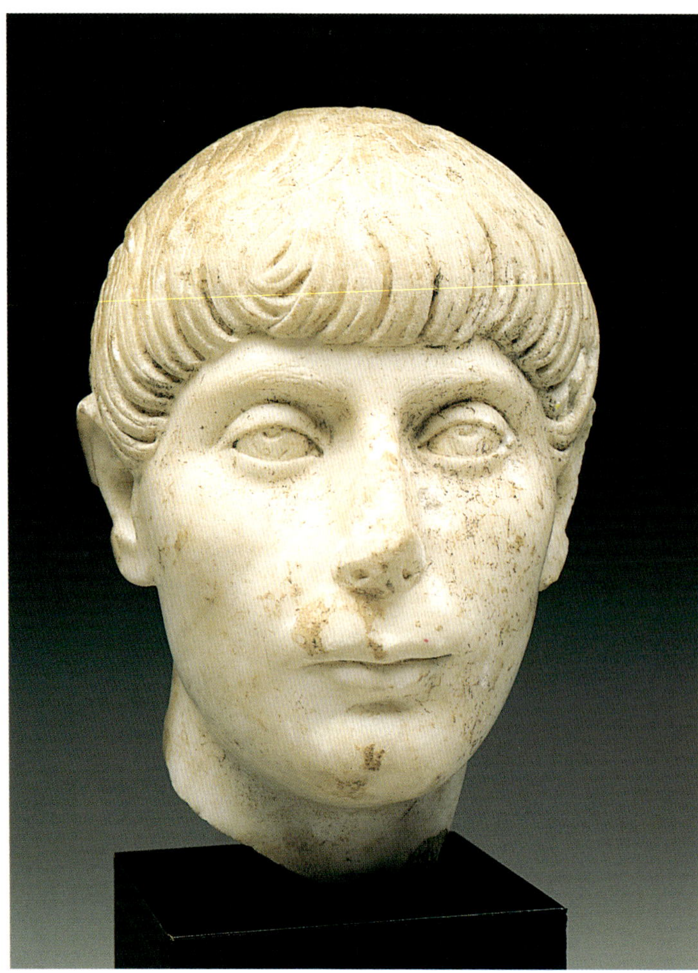

37.

Head of a young man

Roman, second century A.D.
Marble
H. 22.5 cm, W. 16.5 cm
Anonymous gift in memory of Edward Marcus, 1981.169

THIS FINELY MODELED HEAD of a young man is depicted with compact hair, muted eyebrows, heavy-lidded eyes that appear to gaze off to his upper right, and a soft, non-committal expression of the lips. The high cheekbones and angular nose contribute to a sense of dignity and individuality marked by a subdued and aloof mood created by the sleepy expression of the eyes and the reserved mouth. The ears, although partially broken, hug the sides of the head and do not detract from the oval form of the hair and face. The smooth, glossy surface of the face produces an interesting contrast with the formalized pattern in the locks of hair. The delicate modeling of the face balances the strong sense of skeletal structure beneath the finely stretched skin. Ultimately the sculptor has created an image of refined nobility, reserved and somewhat withdrawn, bearing an expression of smugness, and endowed with an air of formalism promoted by the hairstyle, but having a strong sense of individuality.

The back side of the head was attached by a square dowel. The pattern of the hair would presumably have continued on the posterior portion of the head, which is now lost. The smooth surface of the marble around the edge of the "slice" and the rough area in the center along with traces of sintering on the surface indicate that the cut is ancient.

The linear treatment of the thick hair with the frontal locks coming nearly straight down over the brow, and the side locks arranged forward and sweeping over the ear, are clear reflections of Trajanic hairstyles. This hairstyle remained in vogue during the subsequent Hadrianic period. A very close example to the hairstyle on the DMA head is worn by a youth whose statue, now in The Nelson-Atkins Museum of Art, Kansas City, Missouri, derives from Emperor Hadrian's villa near Tivoli. The faint and delicate eyebrows of the DMA head, as well as the short crescents in the pupils of the eyes, are also similar to Hadrianic portraiture.

PUBLICATIONS: Muscarella 1974, no. 97; Bromberg 1983, 104, no. 101.

REFERENCES: For portraits of Trajan see esp. Fittschen and Zanker 1985, Beilage (Supplement) 18. For the statue of a youth in The Nelson-Atkins Museum of Art see Vermeule 1981, 318, no. 273.

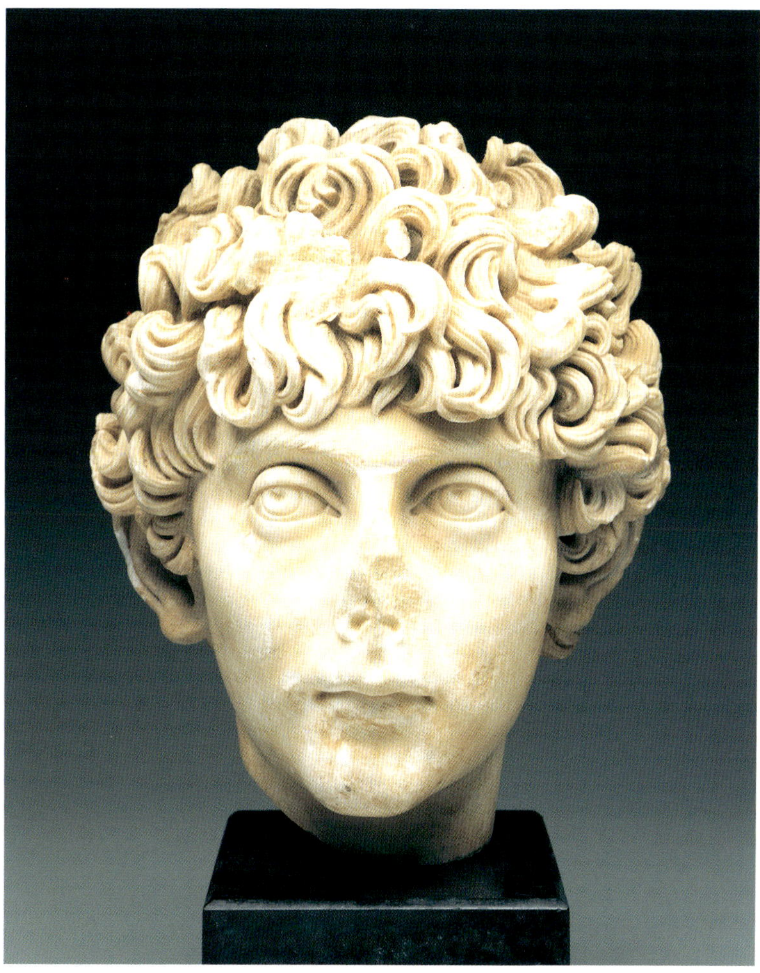

38.

Head of a youth

Roman, Antonine, c. A.D. 140–170
Marble
H. 27.9 cm, W. 21.6 cm
Gift of Norbert Schimmel, in memory of Betty Marcus, 1984.163

THIS MASTERFULLY CARVED head of a Roman youth beautifully illustrates the refined style that portraiture could attain in the immediate wake of the Hadrianic period. The deeply cut, massive curls transform the hair into a highly textured crown, animated by the sharp contrasts of light and shadow; this in turn differs markedly from the soft, smooth surfaces of the face. The head is pulled slightly to the right by the twist of the neck and the sidelong glance of the deeply set eyes. Combined with the boyish impression imparted by the narrow jaw and small mouth with nearly quivering lips, disheveled locks of hair, and relatively large, protruding ears are clear traits of sensitivity and intelligence expressed in the high cheekbones, narrow shank of the nose, and large, dreamy eyes beneath distinctive eyebrows.

The plastic rendering of the eyes consists of a carved semicircle designating each iris, and modified, crescent-shaped drill holes for the pupils. The deeply cut tear ducts terminating the thick upper lids, which close over the top of the pupils, contribute to the sleepy appearance of the gaze, a typical stylistic trait of portraiture in this period.

The refined styling of the face, combined with the mass of lavish curls, is remarkably similar to portraits of Marcus Aurelius in his youth, and it may be presumed that the style of such official portraits had a direct impact on fashion for court followers and others close to the emperor. The idealized expression of the nobility of youth exemplified in this portrait also finds a close parallel in official portraits of the family members of Antoninus Pius.

PUBLICATIONS: Muscarella 1974, no. 96.

REFERENCES: For Antonine portraiture see Wegner 1939; Harrison 1953, 38, no. 28; Vermeule 1965, 394–95, fig. 52; Clairmont 1966; Kraus 1967, 258–59, and pls. 310 and 311; Kleiner 1992, 268–77.

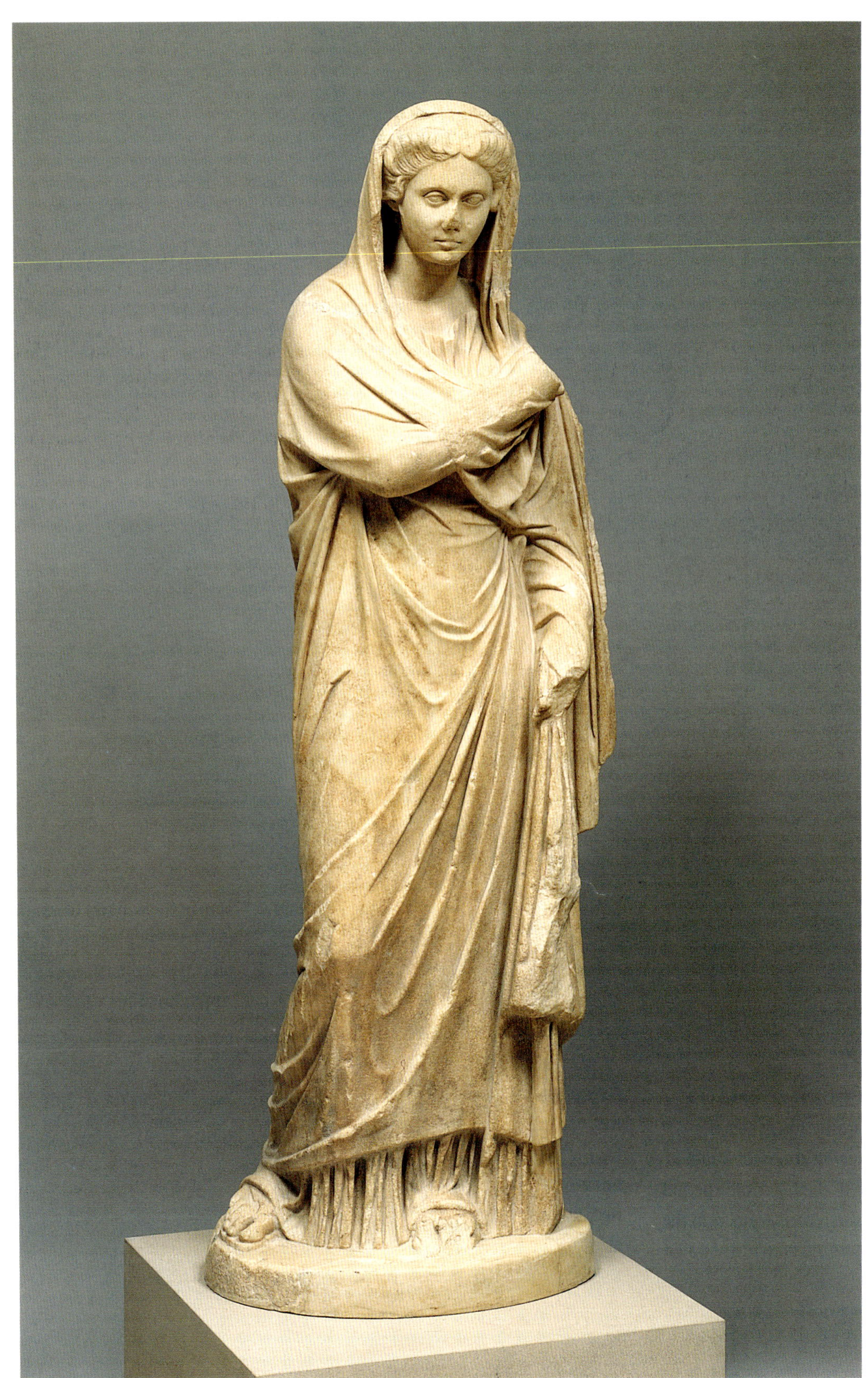

39. Figure of a woman

Roman, second century A.D.
Marble
H. 175.9 cm, W. 71.8 cm, D. 44.8 cm
Gift of Mr. and Mrs. Cecil H. Green, 1973.11

THIS LIFE-SIZE FIGURE of a woman served as a commemorative or funerary statue. The majestic image of feminine Roman nobility seen here is derived from fourth-century-B.C. models created by followers of Praxiteles or sculptors in the circle of Lysippus. The positioning of the arms, feet, and drapery folds clearly characterizes this statue as one of a number of similar marble figures found in the ancient theater at Herculaneum and known as the Small Herculaneum type. An example of this type, as well as the Large Herculaneum type, is now in Dresden.

The DMA statue wears a long chiton, or tunic, which can be seen below her neck and over her sandaled feet. Her himation, or mantle, is worn over the chiton, embracing the figure in a series of magnificent folds, and has been pulled up over her head to create a veil. Through the drapery folds, the form of the female figure is realized and the body animated. The angle of the bent elbow, the diagonal of the extended hand, the gentle convex planes of the stomach, and the protruding impression of the right knee are all created and yet muted by the drapery. The woman moves forward, her left foot trailing behind, while she secures the placement of her veil with her left hand. In place of significant action, here the figure is subdued and pensive, indicating the reflective state of mind associated with a commemorative or funerary image, as well as conveying the desirable attitude associated with Roman women of noble rank.

In the creation of portrait images, Roman sculptors followed the tradition of representing Demeter and Persephone, mother and daughter, by the Large and Small Herculaneum types, respectively. The Large Herculaneum type was generally used for portraits of older women while the Small type was the form for younger ones. In classical mythology, Persephone was the bride of Pluto (Greek Hades), and Demeter was often depicted mourning her loss to the underworld. Therefore either of these mythical subjects offered an ideal context for funerary sculpture.

The DMA statue follows the formula for the Small Herculaneum type except that the figure wears a veil, which is often associated with a bride and is more commonly an attribute of the Large Herculaneum type. According to Margaret Bieber, the blending of the two Herculaneum types, specifically the depiction of the Small Herculaneum type with a veil, began in the late second century A.D. and continued into the early third century. On the DMA figure, the mouth is small; the head is slightly bowed; and the eyes, carved to reveal the irises and pupils, are somewhat downcast. The hairstyle is distinctive, combed up from the face and bearing a pronounced central divide. The face resembles portraits of Faustina the Younger, daughter of the emperor Antoninus Pius, and his wife, Faustina the Elder. Faustina the Younger became the wife of the emperor Marcus Aurelius. Aspects of the hair and face, however, deviate from accepted portraits of Faustina the Younger, leaving the DMA statue without clear identification.

PUBLICATIONS: Bromberg 1979, 67, no. 78; Vermeule 1981, 326, no. 280, and color pl. 25; Bromberg 1983, 105, no. 102.

REFERENCES: For the Large and Small Herculaneum statues in Dresden see Richter 1951, 184–91, figs. 24 and 28. For the Small Herculaneum type with a veil see Bieber 1962, 129. For marriage in Roman funerary art see Walker 1985, 48–49. For female portraiture under the Antonines see Kleiner 1992, 277–80.

40.
Head of a priest

Roman, Palmyrene, c. A.D. 150–250
Limestone
H. 54.6 cm, W. 22.9 cm, D. 26.7 cm
Gift of the David T. Owsley Discretionary Fund and the Alvin and Lucy Owsley Foundation, 1994.51

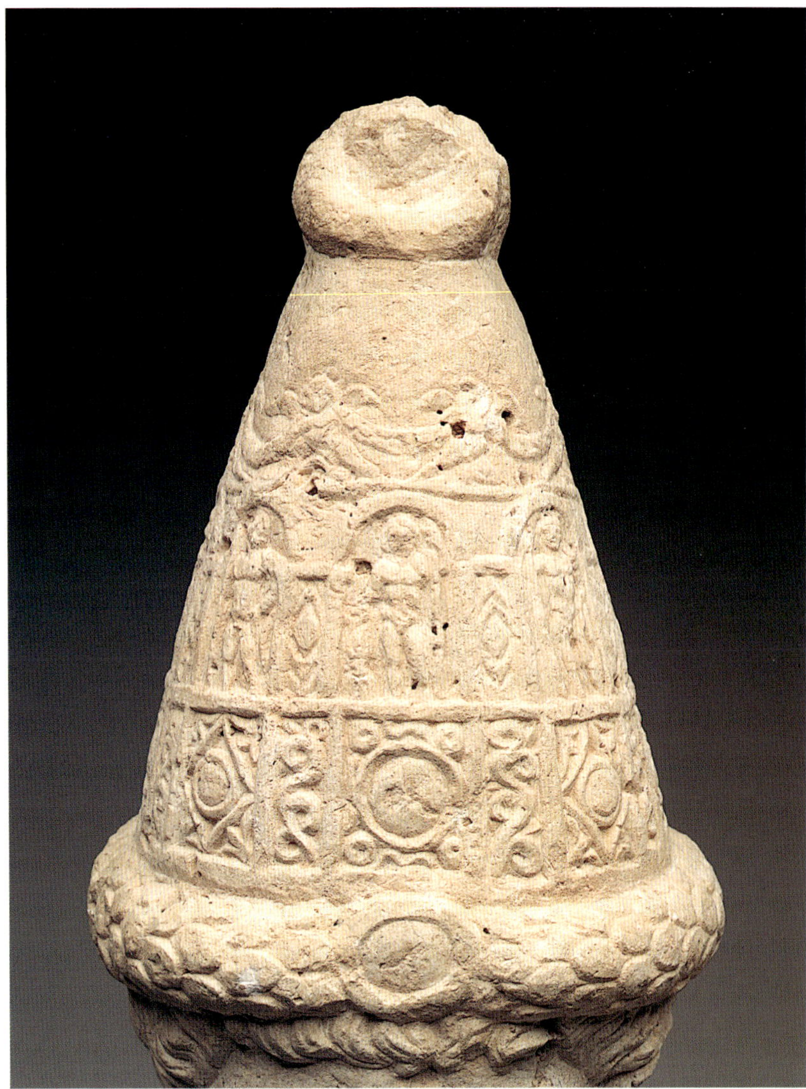

THIS ROMAN IMPERIAL portrait head, which is in excellent condition, adds to two areas of the Museum's ancient art collection: Roman portraiture and Near Eastern art. Roman portraits from the late second to the early fourth century A.D. are frequently masterpieces of subtle modeling and expressive psychology. The native Roman taste for realism in portraiture was broadened to include suggestions of personality and even religious temperament during this period. The face and hair of this portrait head are carved with the rich, sensuous realism of portrait sculpture in this cosmopolitan era of the Roman Empire. However, the priestly role represented by the man's conical headdress is specific to the Asian parts of the Roman Empire.

Similar elaborate representations of priests are found in Asia Minor and in the arts of Palmyra, as well as in Syria proper, where this head originated. Many examples of Palmyrene portrait sculpture may be found in museums in both the United States and Europe. In a Palmyrene funerary group in the National Museum, Damascus, depicting a husband and wife, the man wears a headdress that fully covers his hair and is decorated with a wreath and priest's bust, indicating his profession. The relief of Aphlad, also in the National Museum, Damascus, depicts a priest in a cap similar to the one on the DMA head, but with his hair showing under its rim. Other analogies to this head may be seen in Anatolian sculptures of priests, such as a fine funerary portrait in the Adana Museum, Turkey, in which the headdress indicates the man's role as a priest in his lifetime.

The conical headdress goes back centuries in Near Eastern religious art. Originally the mark of a divinity, by the time of the Roman Empire it was the regalia of priests of various Syrian and Anatolian deities. A priest of the Anatolian mother-goddess Cybele in the museum in Ostia, Italy, wears such a headdress. The well-known frescoes from a synagogue in Dura-Europus, Syria, now in the Damascus museum, also show priests wearing such headdresses. However, the idealized nude Greek figures ornamenting the headdress on the DMA head represent a complete fusion of Near Eastern beliefs and Greco-Roman style. The incised eyes, which give the figure a hypnotic intensity, are typical of such late Roman portraits and are often emphasized to suggest the spiritual state of the person represented. The syncretic character of religion and culture in the eastern parts of the Roman Empire are well represented by this handsome head. It carries on the tradition of Roman portraiture represented by the DMA's two great second-century portraits of young men (cat. nos. 37 and 38).

REFERENCES: Inan and Rosenbaum 1966, 204, no. 282, and pl. 157; Bianchi Bandinelli 1971; Klengel 1972. For the Palmyrene sculpture of a woman and a priest see Weiss 1985, 397 ff., and for the Aphlad relief see 409 ff. For Roman portraiture in the eastern empire see Vermeule 1968.

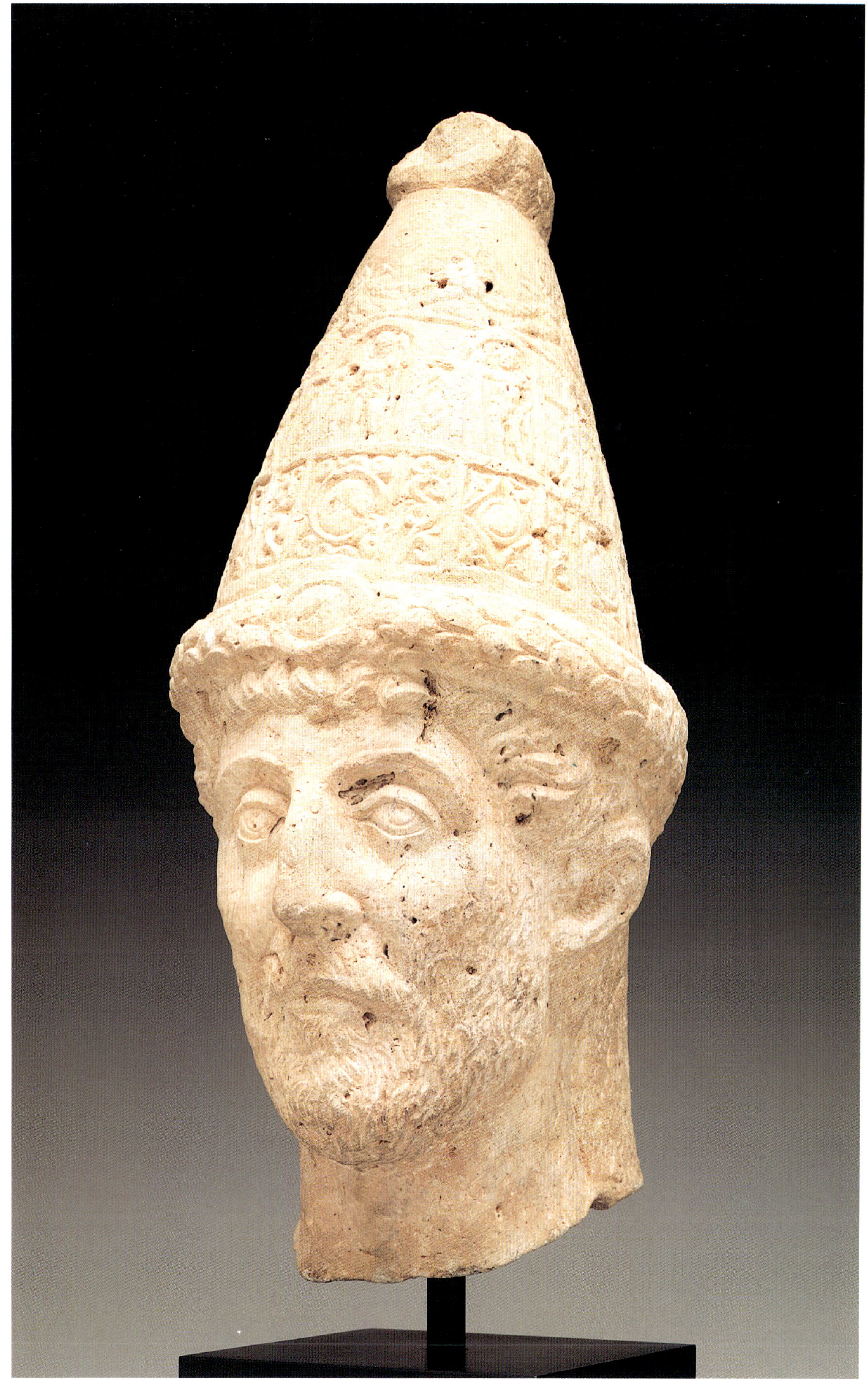

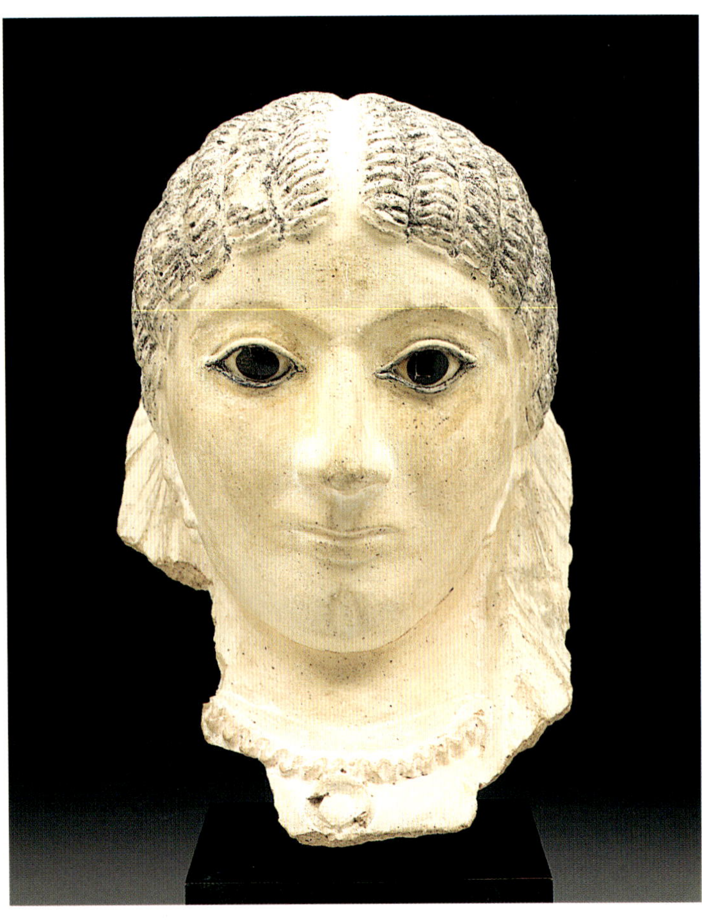

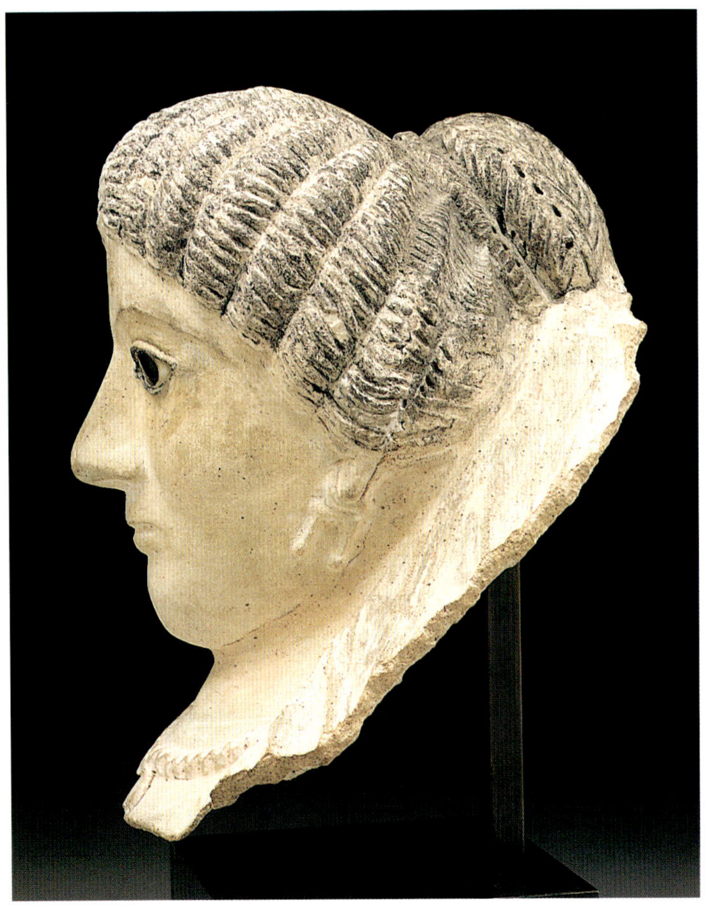

41.

Mummy portrait

Egyptian, Roman Period, late second century A.D.
Cartonnage, paint, bronze, glass
H. 24.8 cm, W. 17.8 cm
Green Estate Acquisition Fund, 1995.82

THE PRACTICE OF MAKING plaster mummy masks to place over the embalmed body of a dead person had a long tradition in Egypt, ultimately going back to the reserve heads of the Old Kingdom. When the Greeks of the Hellenistic age and later the Romans of the Empire ruled Egypt, they adopted this custom. The well-to-do Greco-Roman elite ordered such plaster or cartonnage masks to suit their own artistic taste. This Roman portrait mask is an interesting counterpoint to the Museum's marble figure of a standing woman (cat. no. 39). The mask blends the idealism of Greek art with realistic Roman style, creating a head that is both beautiful and psychologically forceful. The woman wears recognizable types of late second-century A.D. earrings and necklace, similar examples of which are in the DMA's ancient jewelry collection. The inlaid eyes and the remains of paint on the cartonnage give the portrait a remarkably lifelike appearance. While the style of the head is Roman, the funerary symbolism of the portrait head, which implies eternal life, is Egyptian. This syncretism of belief and style is also seen in the contemporary portrait paintings in encaustic paint over wood from the Fayum area of Egypt. Like the Museum's Syro-Roman head of a priest (cat. no. 40), this head illustrates the spread of Roman ideas of portraiture in the eastern Empire.

REFERENCES: Parlasca 1966; Grimm 1974; Spanel 1988, 132–33; D'Auria, Lacovara, and Roehrig 1988, 202.

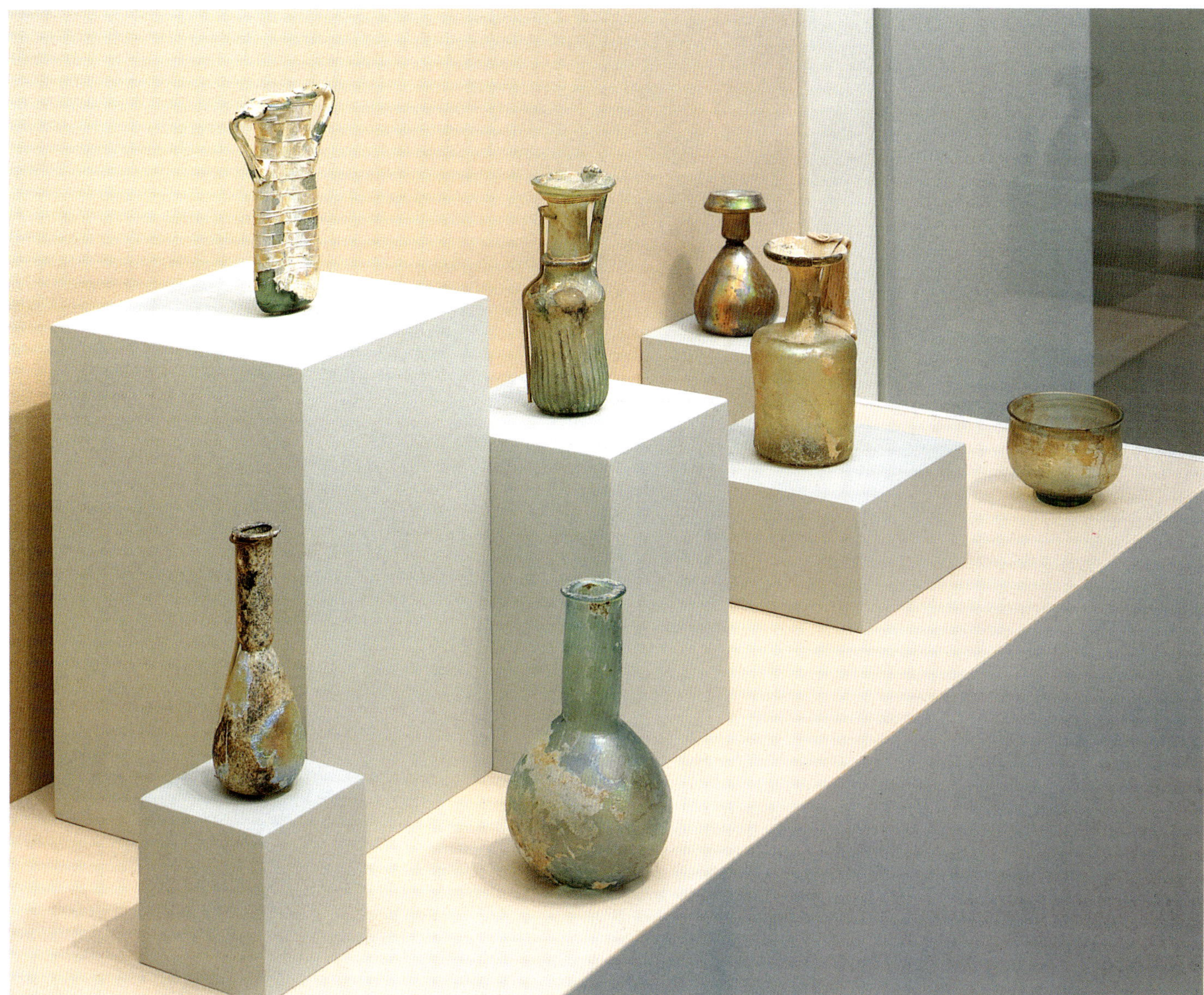

42.
Vessels

Roman, second–third century A.D.
Glass, painted ceramic
Dimensions vary
Gift of Helen L. Williams, 1967.12.14, 1967.12.15, and 1967.12.15; Gift of Margaret J. and George V. Charlton, R.1971.1; Roberta Coke Camp Estate, 1975.29, 1975.30, and 1975.31; gift of Blanche Erlanger, 1988.64 and 1988.65

GLASS HAS BEEN USED as a form of artistic expression for approximately 3,500 years. First appearing in the form of small beads in Mesopotamia, glass was soon shaped around preformed cores of earth to make hollow vases. During the middle of the first century B.C., a process for blowing glass into a variety of shapes was invented, probably along the Levantine coast. This process revolutionized the glass industry and created the basis for the mass production of glass vessels during the Roman era. With the blowing technique established, glass became a desirable and inexpensive commodity, available in diverse colors and decorative enhancements, and glass had the unique quality of allowing the contents of a vessel to be seen through its walls.

A small sampling of glass in the DMA collections illustrates only a portion of the variety of shapes and decorative possibilities found in Roman glass vases. The first example is a large bottle (overleaf, left) that was free blown and shaped while the glass was hot by turning the vase against pincers to create the neck and lip, and to form a flat surface for the base. The vessel may have been used for the storage of perfume and

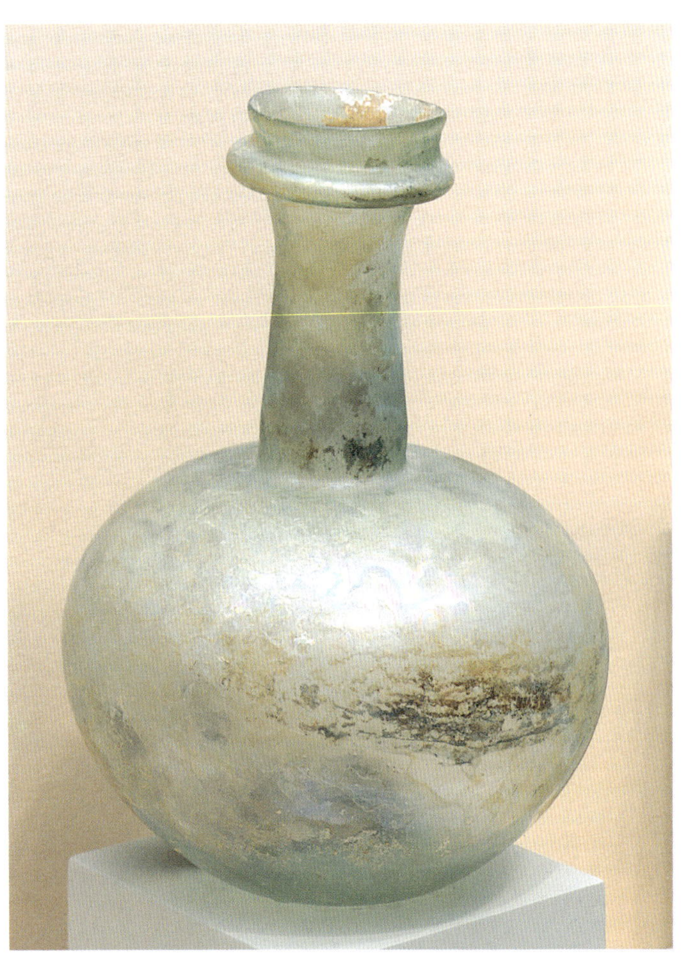

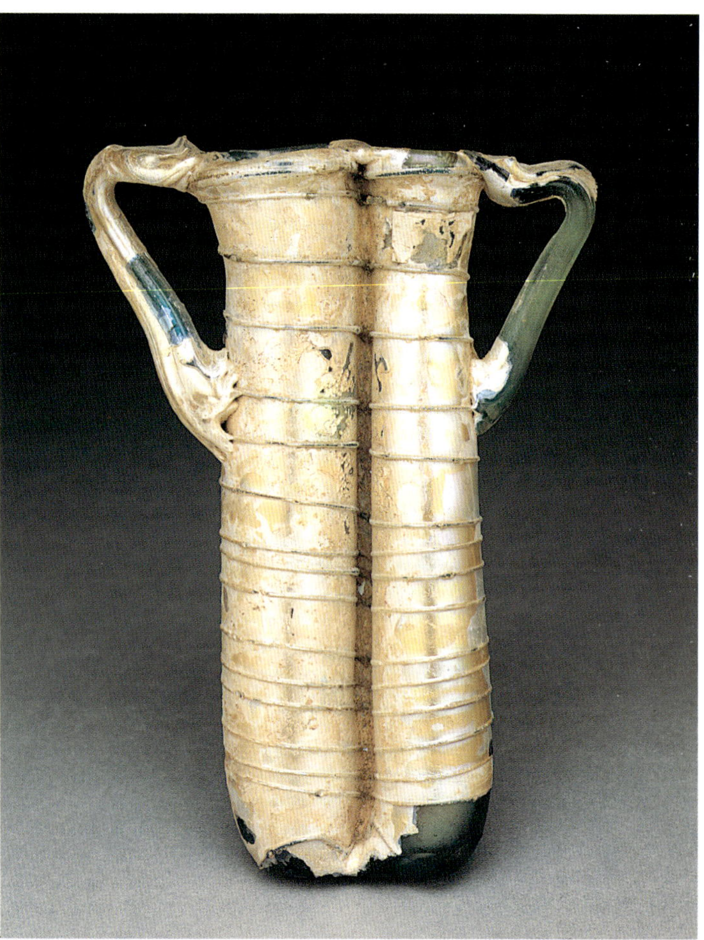

would have had a stopper, perhaps of glass. Although the vase is translucent, the frosted or pitted opaque effect has an iridescent quality. The second vase, a double unguentarium (above, right), was very popular in the east Mediterranean, especially in the glass centers of Syro-Palestine. The delicate double form is crafted by folding a glass tube in half, bonding the two equal parts, and attaching a pair of angular handles from the lips. A veneer of glass was applied over the green glass shape, and snake-thread decoration spirals around each half of the vase. The third glass vase is a very fine, small bowl with an outwardly turned rim and a ring foot for stability (overleaf, far right). The pale green glass is translucent, showing off its thin walls, and has no need of additional ornament to enhance its beauty.

Roman glass centers are known to have existed in nearly every quarter of the Mediterranean and beyond, from Syria to France and Germany and from Egypt to Greece, Yugoslavia, and Italy. A few glassworkers signed their works, and a number must have moved from one center to another, meeting the demand for fragile objects of art that did not travel well.

REFERENCES: For Roman glass see Forbes 1966; Harden 1956; Harden 1969; Price 1976, 110–26.

43.

Votive plaque with seated figure of Pluto

Roman, second–third century A.D.
Silver over copper
H. 18.7 cm, W. 8 cm, D. 0.3 cm
Gift of Norbert Schimmel, 1982.18

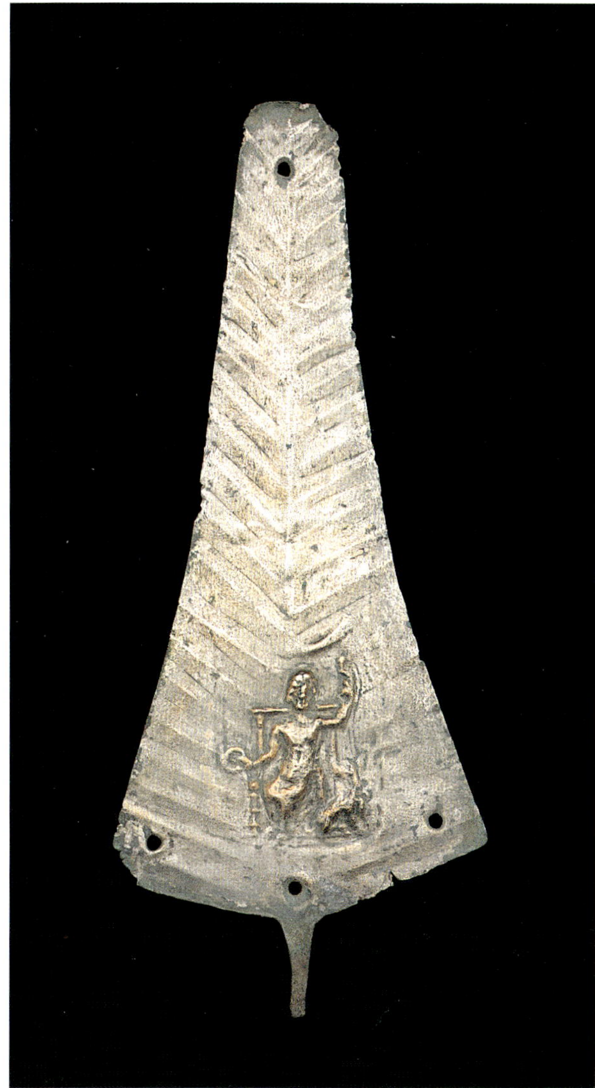

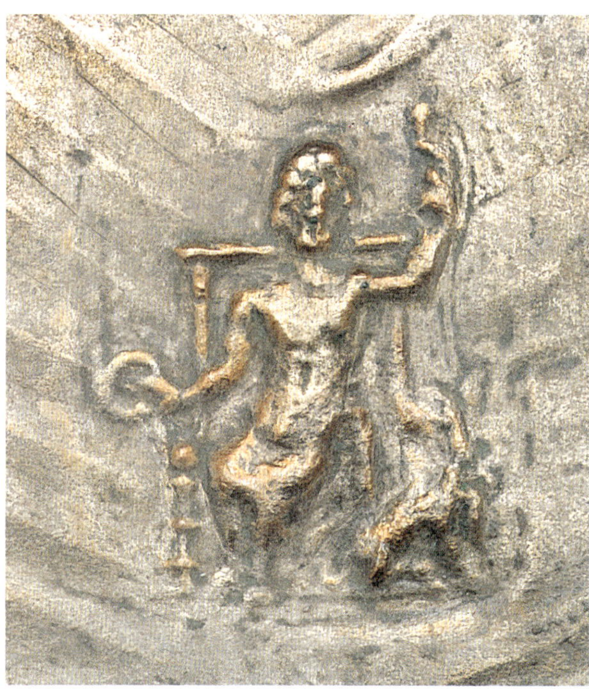

THE SILVER AND COPPER EX-VOTO in the form of a leaf or feather is one of three similar pieces found together in Tunisia. The group once belonged to Norbert Schimmel, and one piece is now in the Metropolitan Museum of Art, New York. The thin hammered silver sheet accented by raised diagonal ribs is ornamented by an enthroned male figure wearing a himation and holding a scepter in his raised left hand. Possibly he is extending a *phiale* (offering cup) in his right hand. The beard and pose of the figure suggest a powerful deity like Jupiter (Greek Zeus), Serapis, or Pluto (Greek Hades). The figure at his left seems to be a dog, which would indicate that the figure is Pluto, the brother of Jupiter and lord of the underworld, accompanied by his dog, Cerberus. The figure is worked in repoussé. These funerary plaques seem to have been nailed to votive offerings to commemorate a departed relative. There are four holes for attaching the piece, one at the top and three across the bottom.

REFERENCES: For the companion Schimmel piece see The Metropolitan Museum of Art 1992, 60, no. 57.

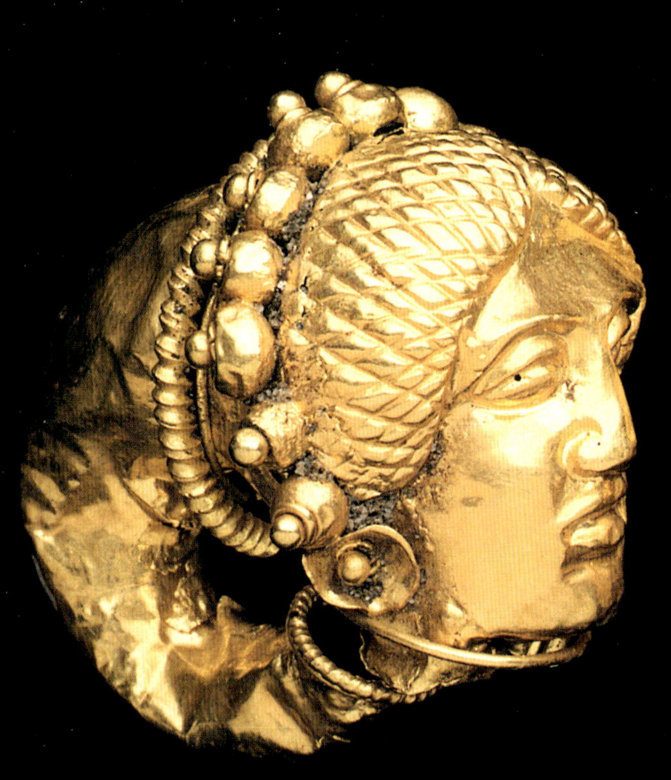
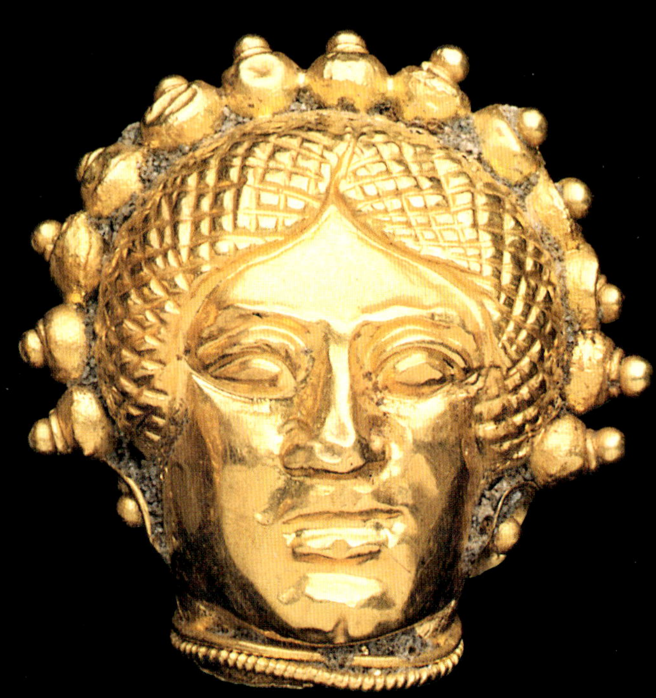

Chapter 7

Ancient Gold: The Spread of Imagery

Gold is Zeus' child, nothing erodes or consumes it. It conquers the mind of man and is the most powerful of possessions.

—Pindar, *Olympian Odes I*

GOLD, THE UNDYING METAL, came close to being a metaphor for the undying gods in the ancient world. As a rare and valuable material, whose readiest sources were mostly on the fringes of the Mediterranean world in Thrace, Anatolia, the Caucasus, India, and East Africa, gold was treasured like gemstones, ivory, precious resins, rare woods, and amber. These valuable raw materials were devoted to the most expensive artworks and to objects with religious significance, such as cult statues. Gold, however, which was easily worked and essentially indestructible, remained throughout antiquity a medium for royal equipment and for the kind of luxurious ornaments that would be buried with their owners in tombs. The jewelry and gilded furnishings of King Tutankhamun's tomb in Egypt and the spectacular, often Greek-made gold ornaments buried with Scythian chieftains in the tomb mounds of southern Russia are striking examples of precious gold workmanship consigned to darkness in order to accompany the spirit of the dead person in the afterworld.

Because gold ornaments were buried with the dead so often, it is possible to follow in great detail the development of ancient jewelry styles. And because these pieces were made as much for religious, magical, or symbolic reasons as for ornamental ones, gold jewelry embodies the mythology of antiquity. Earrings reflect the magic compulsion of desire in Aphrodite and Eros. Bracelets and rings call upon the sacred snakes of the underworld deities. Lions, emblems of royal power and fertility in nature, are frequent figures in bracelets, rings, and earrings. God figures like Dionysus and Athena were often represented, whether as protective amulets or as charms for their worshipers.

The DMA now owns an important group of gold ornaments from the collection of Dr. Athos Moretti, a European collector who has also given ceramics and jewelry to museums in Basel and Berlin. This collection is rich in major types of Greek and Etruscan jewelry from the seventh to the first century B.C. There are a few Roman imperial works. These ornaments reflect in exquisite miniature the stylistic history of more monumental art. They are sculptures on a small scale. To look at the fifth-century-B.C. Etruscan earrings with female heads (cat. no. 47) in the Severe style of Early Classical art, or the Hellenistic Greek medallion with the frontal head of Dionysus crowned by vine leaves (cat. no. 49), is to see how major sculptural types could be adapted for personal use with no loss of majesty.

The most refined techniques of gold working, such as granulation, filigree, repoussé, and the use of enamel and glass with gold, passed from Egypt, Minoan Crete, and the Near East to the Mycenaean Greeks in the second millennium B.C. The later Greeks and the Etruscans in central Italy also added Near Eastern ideas and techniques to their remarkably brilliant craftsmanship in gold during the Orientalizing and Archaic periods. Though metalworking, especially in copper, bronze, and iron, was highly developed in all early societies north of the Mediterranean, fine jewelry work was often influenced by imported luxury goods, including decorative work on furnishings, as well as by jewelry itself. The Mycenaean Greek kings patronized Minoan Cretan craftsmen, some of whose masterworks from the royal graves at Mycenae still survive in the National Museum in Athens. Greek adaptations of Cretan style also appear. The same rich mixture of styles, influences, and elaborate techniques occurs in Greek and Etruscan gold work in Italy from the eighth to the seventh century B.C. The earliest Etruscan jewelry, as seen in the Regolini-Galassi tomb at Cerveteri, already demonstrates a bravura, highly ornamental style using some imagery from the Near East.

During the sixth, fifth, and fourth centuries B.C., Greece and Etruria created a splendid array of gold jewelry, intricate in workmanship and classically refined in form. Whatever the meaning of these luxury ornaments in life, their burial with the dead conveyed a funerary message. The wreaths and diadems, for instance, of which the DMA has a number of fine examples, would have been worn in life at banquets, as victors' prizes in war or athletic competitions, and on religious or civic occasions, but their burial defined a different kind of triumph.

Many of the Greek pieces in the DMA collections come from Magna Graecia, the Greek city-states in southern Italy and Sicily. These communities were generally richer than the older cities of mainland Greece and Ionia; our word "sybaritic" comes from Sybaris, one of these luxury-loving towns in Magna Graecia. The South Italian cities were also devoted to mystic cults, like those of the philosopher-magician Pythagoras or the Orphic rituals, which claimed to carry out the beliefs of the legendary musician Orpheus. All these cults professed a more positive view of existence after death than was common in the classical age. Unlike the stark classical Greek view of death and human fate, these cults shared with the Eleusinian cult of Demeter and the northern cult of Dionysus a hope for some kind of personal immortality.

In considering the effect of such beliefs on jewelry, it is hard to draw the line between the DMA's pair of earrings with Nike (victory) figures, which were probably simply left with the dead woman as prized personal possessions, and the medallion with the head of Dionysus (cat. no. 49), which may have referred to religious beliefs. Certainly sphinxes, which appear on a fine Etruscan clasp and also on diadems in the Museum collections, had a funerary meaning in the ancient world since they guard graves. One late ring bezel shows Oedipus answering the Sphinx's riddle concerning the meaning of existence. Images of gods like Athena, Aphrodite, and Dionysus imply a belief in the gods' power during life and intimations of their power after death.

The Etruscans, whose elaborate painted and sculptured tombs testify to their vivid interest in the afterworld, were expert goldsmiths. The granulated detail on the best of the Museum's Etruscan fibulae, or brooches, is so minute it demands magnification. Yet these miracles of small-scale ornament were manufactured with simple means. The equipment of ancient gold workers, described graphically in Egyptian tomb paintings and Pompeian frescoes, was no more complicated than those used by African villagers today. Gold dust or small ingots were melted and refined in clay or stone vessels over charcoal fires, with oxygen supplied by leather bellows or blowpipes. Cold metal was worked by copper hammers, chisels, and cutting tools. Hammering gold into thin sheets was a basic technique, as was repoussé modeling, in which the sheet was raised from behind by a leather-covered punch. The lost-wax casting method used for bronze weapons, vessels, and statues was rarely used in gold work because working sheet gold made a rare material go as far as possible. Simple gold jewelry shapes could be enriched by granulation (fixing a pattern of gold globules to a resin base that would disappear when heated) or filigree (making patterns with gold wire). Glass could also be combined with repoussé gold ornament, as in the very rare blue glass bracelet with lion-head finials (cat. no. 46), the unusual ornament in the form of an aegis, or the more common Hellenistic and Roman necklaces with glass beads *(pasta vitrea)*.

Sources for gold in the Archaic and Classical periods were fairly limited. Riverine gold deposits in Anatolia (the foundation for the myths of King Midas, whose touch turned things to gold, and the fabulously wealthy King Croesus) were important, as were deposits on the Aegean Islands of Siphnos and Thasos and north of Greece in Macedonia, Thrace, and Scythia, where local rulers often employed Greek craftsmen. After Alexander the Great's conquests of Egypt and the Near East in the late fourth century B.C., raw gold became more readily available in the Mediterranean. It came from as far away as the Caucasus, India, and the highlands of East Africa. These rich resources in both gold and gemstones are apparent in the polychrome jewelry of Hellenistic Greece and its successors in the Roman Empire.

One spectacular Greek or Early Roman ornament in the collections is a snake armlet (cat. no. 52). Snake bracelets, which were worn in pairs on the upper arms, date back to Early Classical times in both Greece and Italy. Snakes were symbols of the underworld and a part of apotropaic images like the snake-haired Medusa, or Gorgon. Hermes Psychopompos, leader of spirits into the underworld, had a snake-headed herald's wand, or *kerykeion* (caduceus), like the DMA's fine bronze example (cat. no. 21). Underneath the shining splendor of the entire gold collection—works originally meant to be worn by men and women as a sign of wealth and power in life—lies a more fundamental meaning. Gold was imbued with a mysterious power and was one of the ways people could communicate with the gods who rule human life. The nature of much of the gold imagery in the collection is as ambiguous as the character of ancient religious cults themselves. The pieces of jewelry represent love, fertility, and power as well as war, violence, and death, as evidenced by their incarnation as the monstrous Gorgon, which can be a protective charm; the flowers of springtime; the grapes of Dionysus; and Athena's warlike helmet and shield.

One view of gold in the ancient world was prosaic: gold was wealth.

> And in this way a distribution was made of the Persian concubines, the gold, the silver, the beasts of burden and all the other valuables. (Herodotus [trans. Rawlinson] 9.81)

Another view shows gold's affinities with the divine world, as expressed in the *Homeric Hymn* to the love goddess Aphrodite:

> She was clothed in a robe more brilliant than gleaming fire and wore spiral bracelets and shining earrings, while round her tender neck there were beautiful necklaces, lovely, golden, and of intricate design. (*Homeric Hymn to Aphrodite* [trans. Athanassakis] 86–90)

44.
Fibula of the *sanguisuga* type

Etruscan, c. 630 B.C.
Gold
L. 12.9 cm
Museum League Purchase Funds, The Eugene and Margaret McDermott Art Fund, Inc., and Cecil H. and Ida M. Green in honor of Virginia Lucas Nick, 1991.75.5

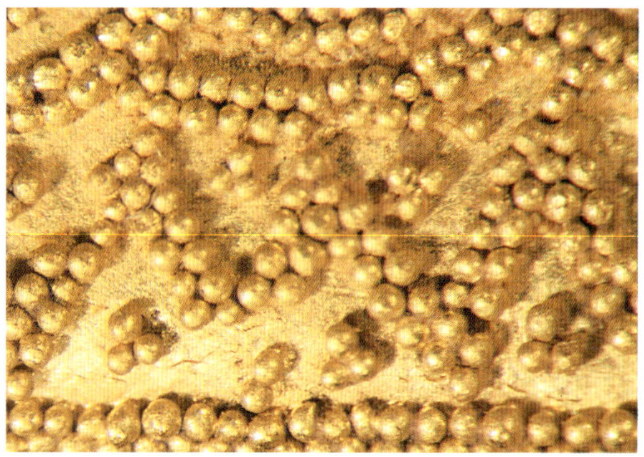

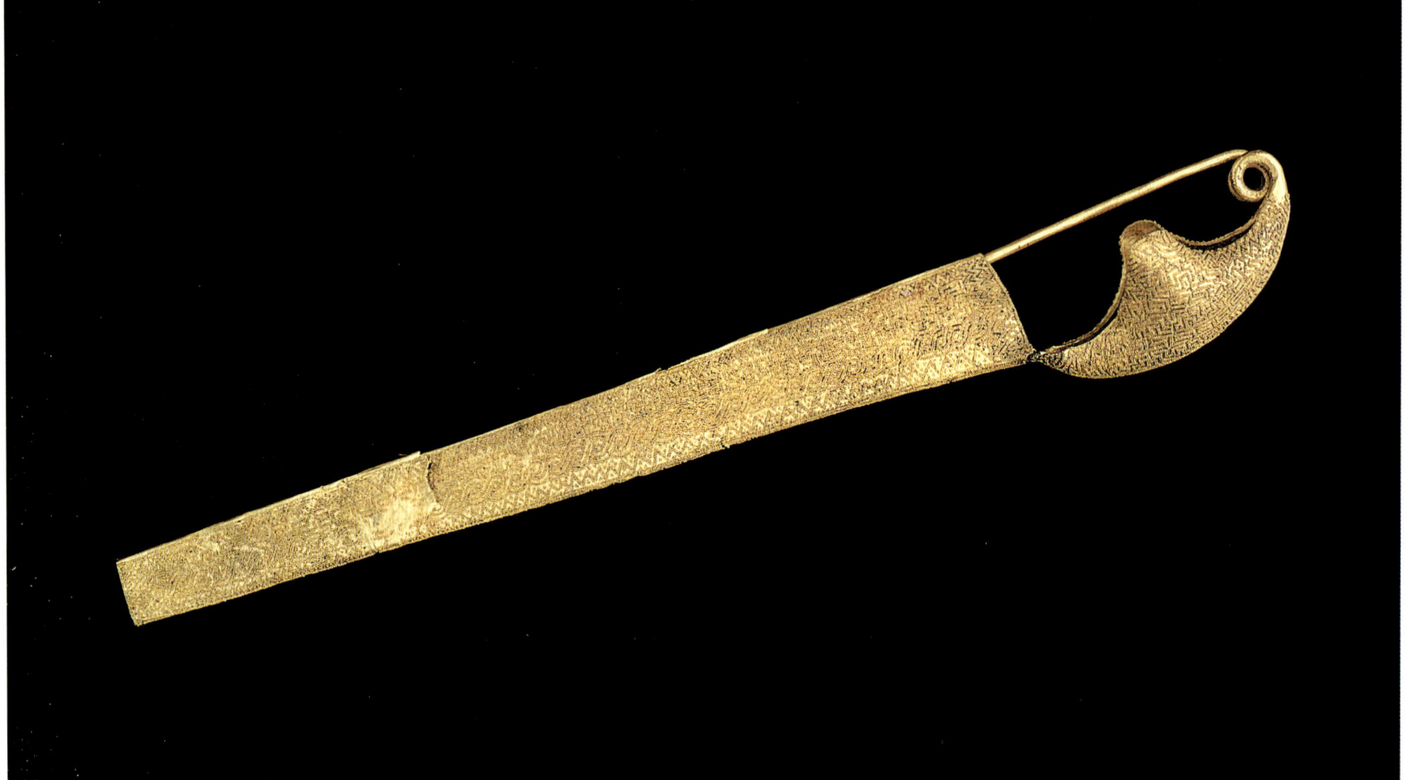

BROOCH SAFETY PINS in the shape of leeches (Italian *sanguisuga*) or boats were very common in Etruria during the seventh century B.C. They generally have a bow-shaped head and straight foot. Historically, this kind of ornamental clothes fastener derived from Villanovan bow-shaped brooches. This example is one of the finest in the DMA collections, with extremely minute and delicate granulated ornament. In the granulation technique, minute globules of gold were dropped upon a resin base on the object to be decorated. Once the piece was heated, the resin base evaporated, leaving the granulation pattern fused with the base. This piece is decorated with a guilloche (rope) pattern surrounded by an overall field of granulation. Inscribed in Etruscan lettering on the inside of the rim is *"mi mulu arathia lethana chailus prasnaia."*

REFERENCES: Cristofani and Martelli 1983, 139, no. 99, and 143, no. 106; Marshall 1911, 131, no. 1381; Carducci 1963, 9, pl. 9b; Cygielman 1990, 59, pl. 197.

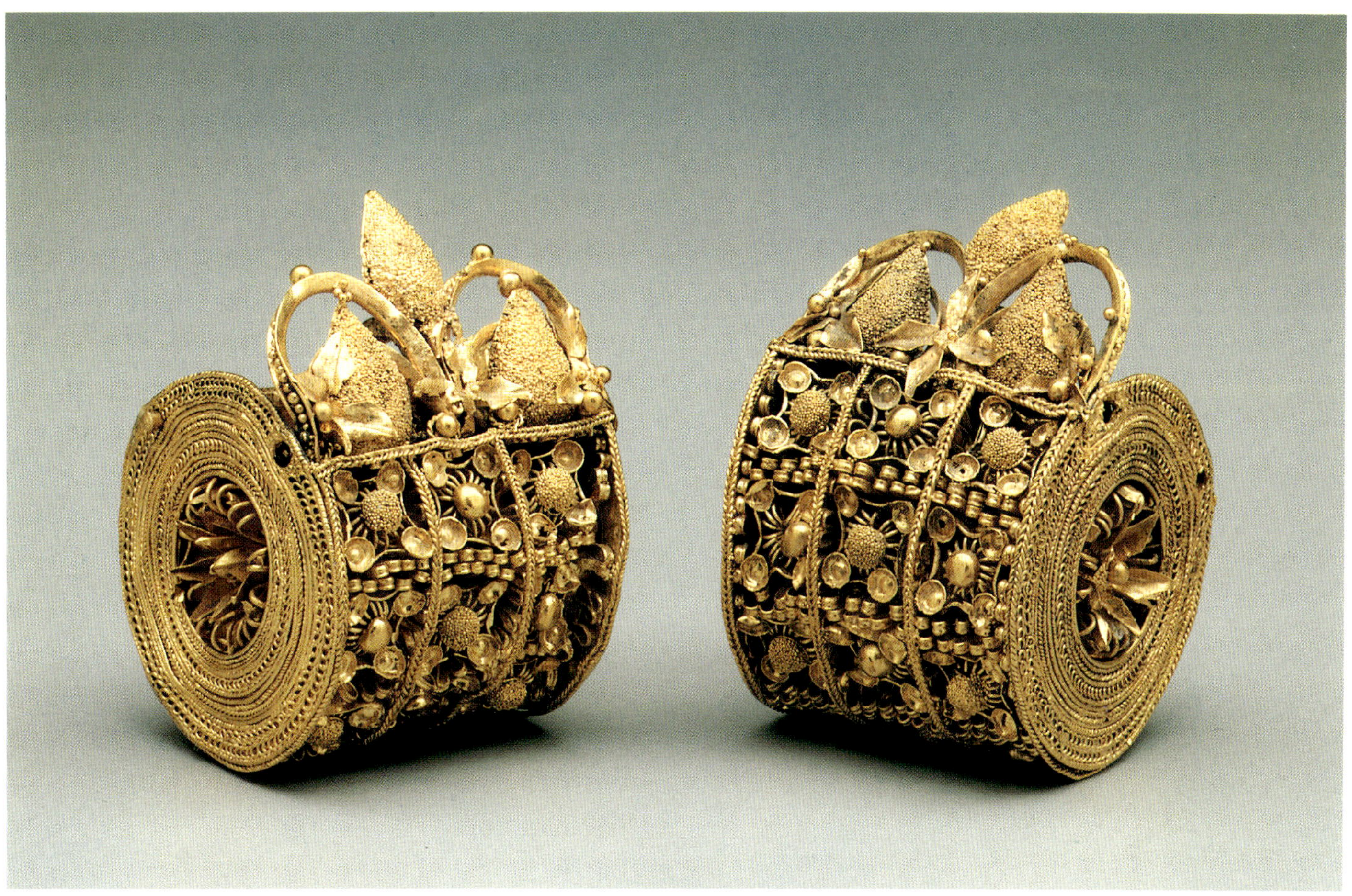

45.

Pair of *a bauletto* earrings

Etruscan, late sixth–early fifth century B.C.
Gold
H. 3.2 cm, W. 2.2 cm, D. 2.5 cm and
H. 3.5 cm, W. 2.2 cm, D. 2.5 cm
Gift of Mr. and Mrs. James H. Clark, 1968.13.a–b

ETRUSCAN ARCHAIC JEWELRY exhibits a masterful combination of luxuriant richness and formal restraint. These basket-shaped earrings are of a type named *a baule* or *a bauletto,* from the Italian word for valise. Such earrings were constructed by bending sheet gold into a cylindrical shape and then ornamenting it with filigree wire. This pair is essentially intact except for the silver hoops by which the earrings were suspended over the wearer's ears and the hinged pin to which the hoops were attached. Holes for the pin are still visible. The outside of the cylinders is decorated with three rows of square compartments composed of wire plaits, each compartment holding rosettes formed of filigree. The central cup of alternating rosettes is covered with granulation. The same fine powdered granulation, called "dust granulation," covers the bud-shaped forms on the projecting piece, which conceals the earring's attachment to the ear. Each end of the cylinder is ornamented with rows of beaded filigree wire; one end has a rosette with petals in the center, while the other end is open. This extraordinarily complex type of ornamentation appears to be an Etruscan invention.

PUBLICATIONS: DMFA 1968; Hoffmann 1970, 464, no. 214; Bromberg 1983, 103, no. 100.

REFERENCES: Oliver 1966, 280, fig. 22; Higgins 1980, 138; Marshall 1911, 114, nos. 1286 and 1287–88, and 117, nos. 1303–5; Greifenhagen 1970, pl. 72.4.

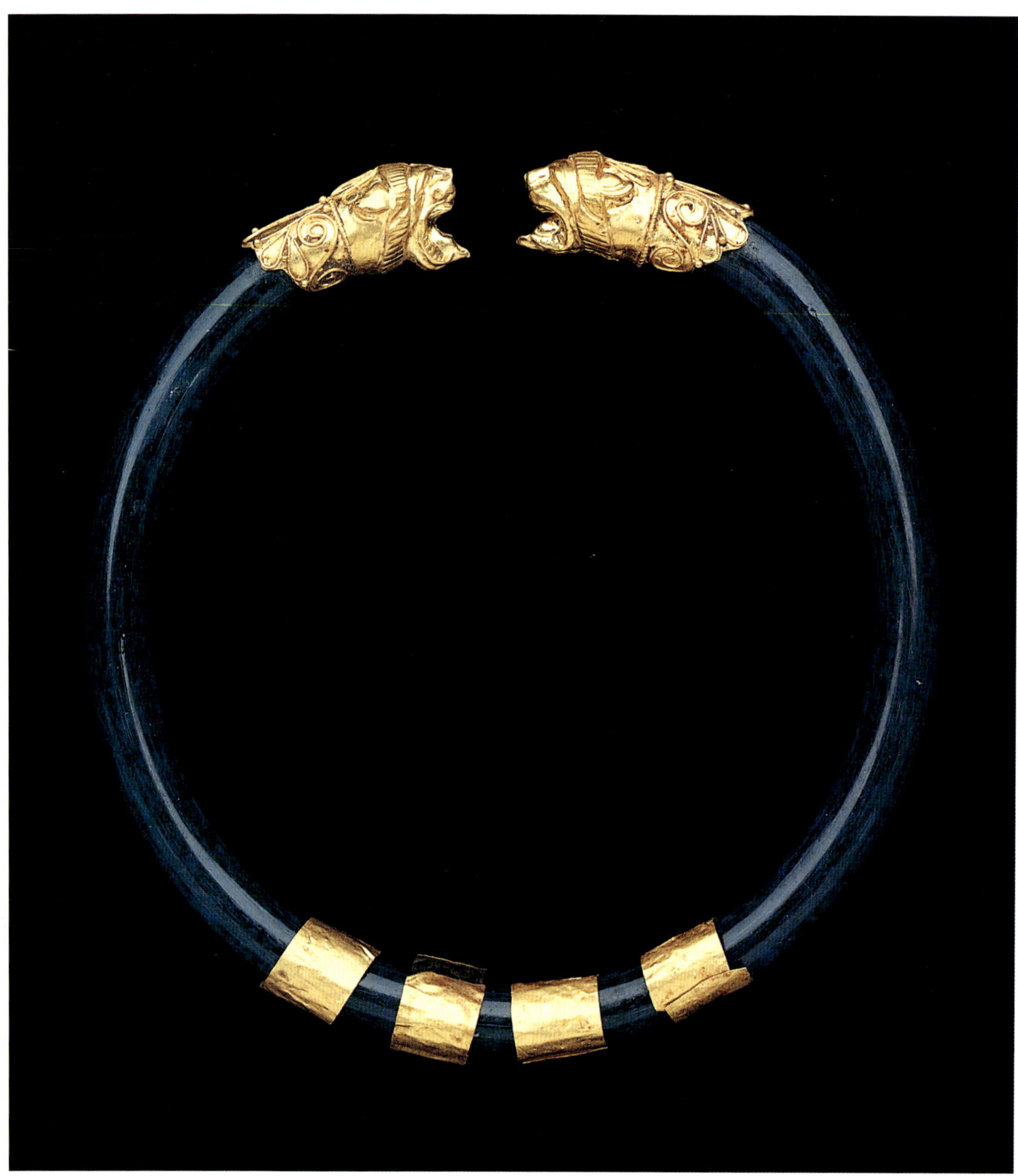

46.

Lion-head bracelet

Etruscan, late sixth century B.C.
Gold, blue glass
DIAM. 8 cm
Museum League Purchase Funds, The Eugene and Margaret McDermott Art Fund, Inc., and Cecil H. and Ida M. Green in honor of Virginia Lucas Nick, 1991.75.21

THE BLUE GLASS HOOP of the bracelet terminates at each end with a lion head made of sheet gold. Behind the base of each lion head is a collar decorated with two spirals and a palmette in filigree. The four loosely fitted gold bands on the hoop slide back and forth. This is a very rare piece; one other complete example that has survived is a bracelet found in a tomb in Monte Autò, now in the Museo di Villa Giulia in Rome. Fragments of glass hoops have been found in Italy, indicating Etruscan workmanship, though the style of these lion heads appears to be Greek. The Benaki Museum in Athens has a pair of animal finials in the form of rams from a necklace of the same type, but the hoop is missing. Depictions of lions were common in art all over the ancient world, from Egypt and the Near East westward. They had a range of meanings: royal power, fertility, guardian spirits, warlike prowess and triumph, and in some cases perhaps triumph over death.

REFERENCES: Cristofani and Martelli 1983, no. 174; Bromberg 1990, 40, pl. 15.

47.
Pair of earrings with female heads

Etruscan, second quarter of fifth century B.C.
Gold
H. 2.5 cm
Museum League Purchase Funds, The Eugene and Margaret McDermott Art Fund, Inc., and Cecil H. and Ida M. Green in honor of Virginia Lucas Nick, 1991.75.29.a–b

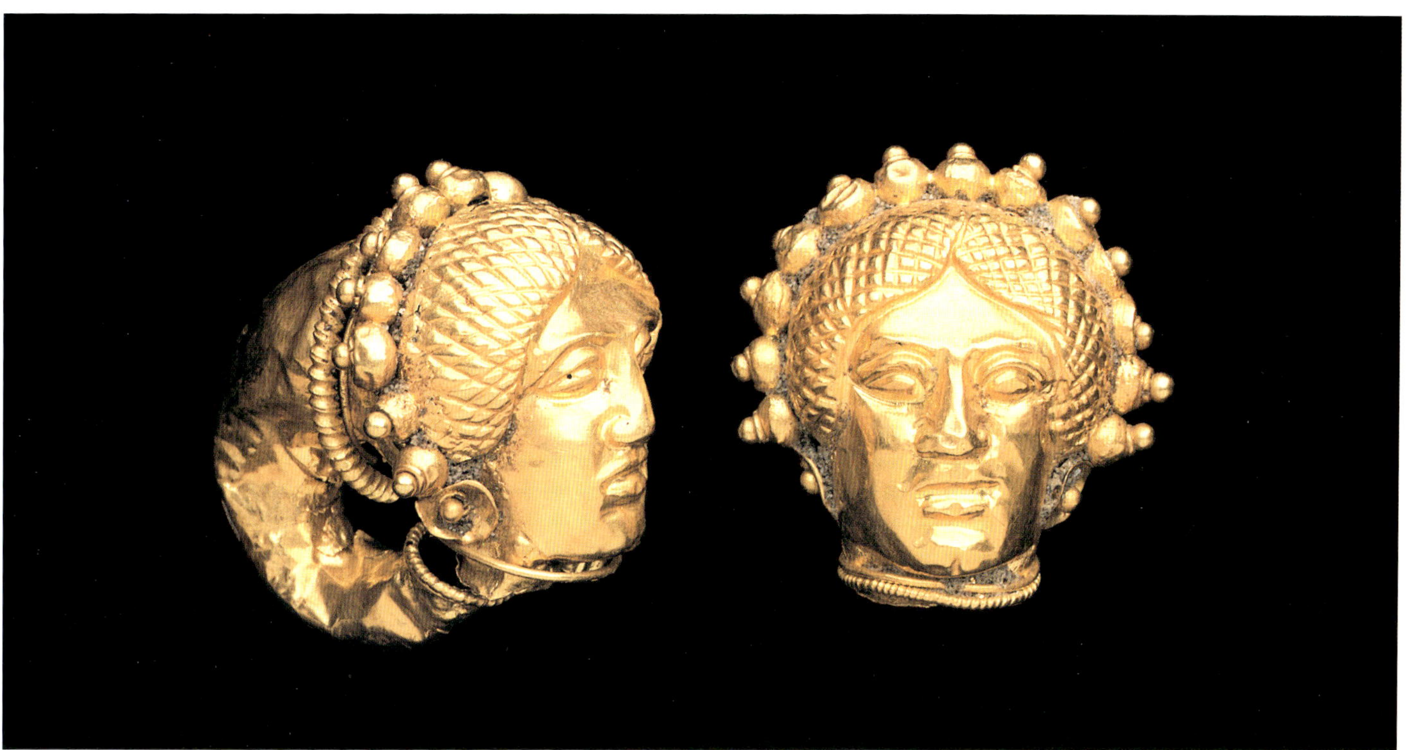

THE PURE EARLY CLASSICAL features of the female heads on these earrings recall the Severe style sculptures at Olympia. Some of the richness of Archaic ornamentation is still evident in the masses of heavy hair indicated by cross-hatching, in the diadem of hollow globules, and in the minute necklace and rosette earrings worn by the figures. The hollow, curved tube that forms each earring has a beaded ring at the end. Whether the women are maenads or deities, they have the remote calm of classical art. Like some of the late *korai* sculptures in the Acropolis Museum, the figures represent the artistic moment when the more decorative style of Archaic art was giving way to the grand idealizations of the Classical age.

REFERENCES: Marshall 1911, nos. 2196 and 2197.

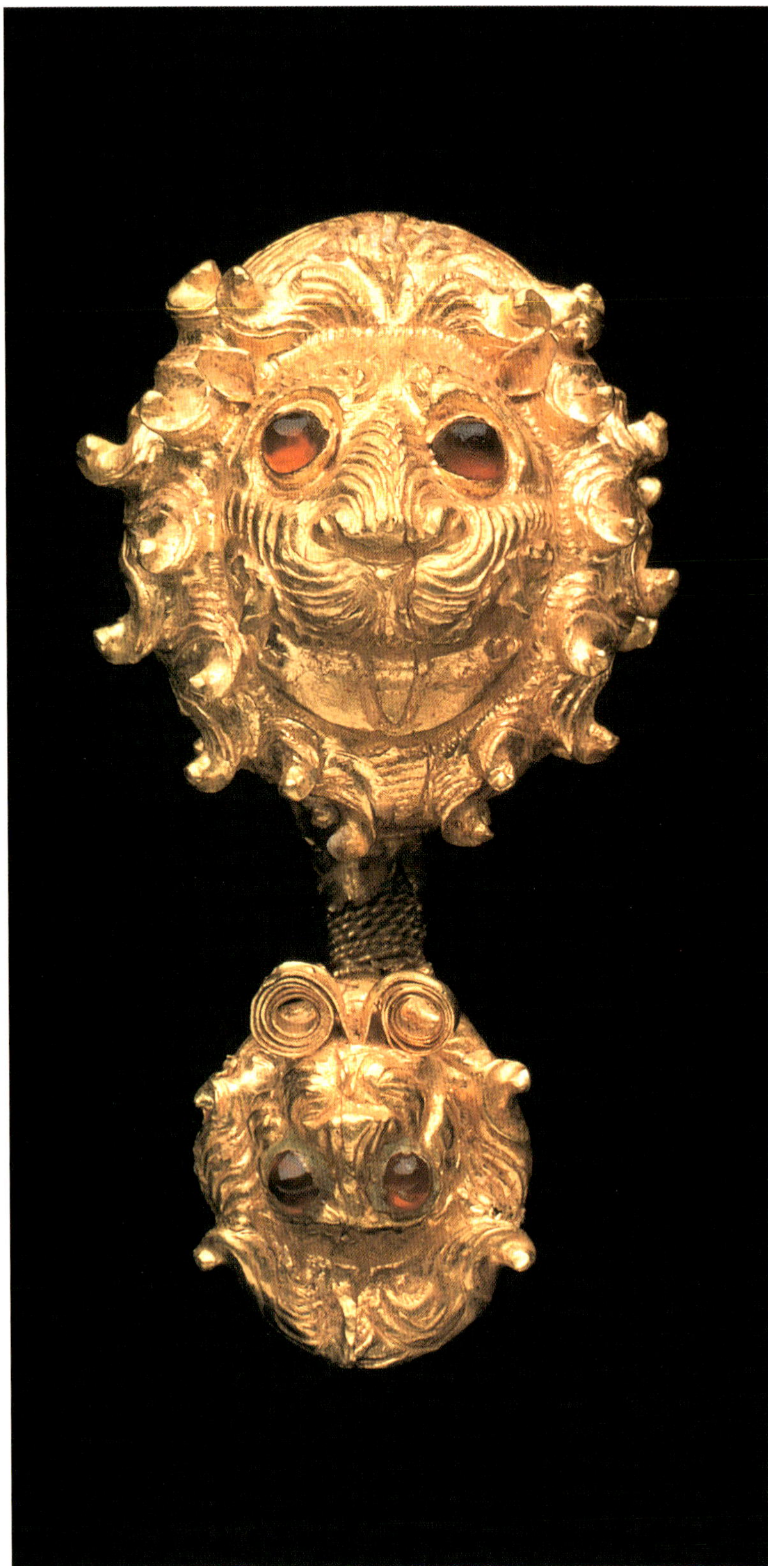

48.

Lion-head earring

Greek, third century B.C.
Enameled gold, garnet
H. 3.9 cm
Museum League Purchase Funds, The Eugene and Margaret McDermott Art Fund, Inc., and Cecil H. and Ida M. Green in honor of Virginia Lucas Nick, 1991.75.64

THIS IS A SUPERB EXAMPLE of the flamboyant baroque style found in the Greek settlements in Italy. After the conquests of Alexander the Great, the Hellenistic world had readier access to gold and gemstones than ever before. Coloristic works like this became common. The hollow hoop was made in two sections. The upper end is surmounted by a large lion head decorated with filigree and perhaps some traces of enamel. The lion's mane is particularly well defined by chasing. The lower end has a smaller lion head, which can be removed. Both heads have garnet eyes.

REFERENCES: Deppert-Lippitz 1985, 225, no. 160 (similar work in Berlin); Juliis 1984, 181, no. 107, and 181–86, nos. 108–17.

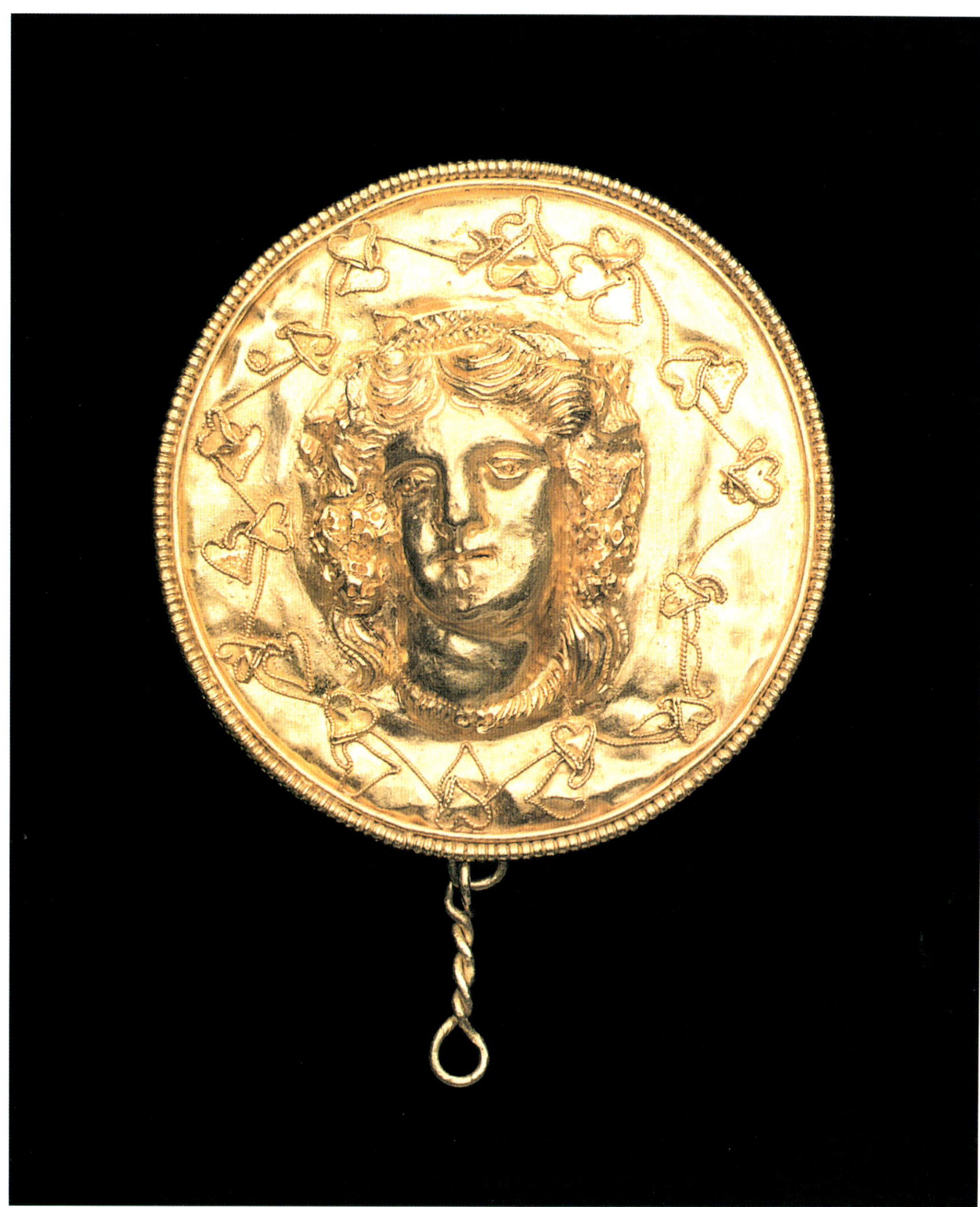

49.

Medallion with the head of Dionysus

Greek, Hellenistic, third–second century B.C.
Gold
DIAM. 4 cm
Museum League Purchase Funds, The Eugene and Margaret McDermott Art Fund, Inc., and Cecil H. and Ida M. Green in honor of Virginia Lucas Nick, 1991.75.71

THE MEDALLION CONSISTS of a flat disk decorated with a relief head of Dionysus in the center and edged with plain and beaded wire. Dionysus wears ivy and grape leaves in his hair and bunches of grapes over his ears. He is also adorned with a wreath composed of sheaves of wheat and a heavy necklace or collar formed from twisted wire. A continuous vine of ivy leaves in fine filigree is in the background. On the back are clamps for attaching the medallion to a diadem, strap necklace, or breast bands. A twisted wire and loop at the bottom of the medallion could also be used to attach it to another object. The figure of Dionysus is slightly crushed and the mouth area has been repaired.

PUBLICATION: Hoffmann and Davidson 1965, 234ff., fig. 95a.

REFERENCES: Axmann 1986, 267, no. 64.

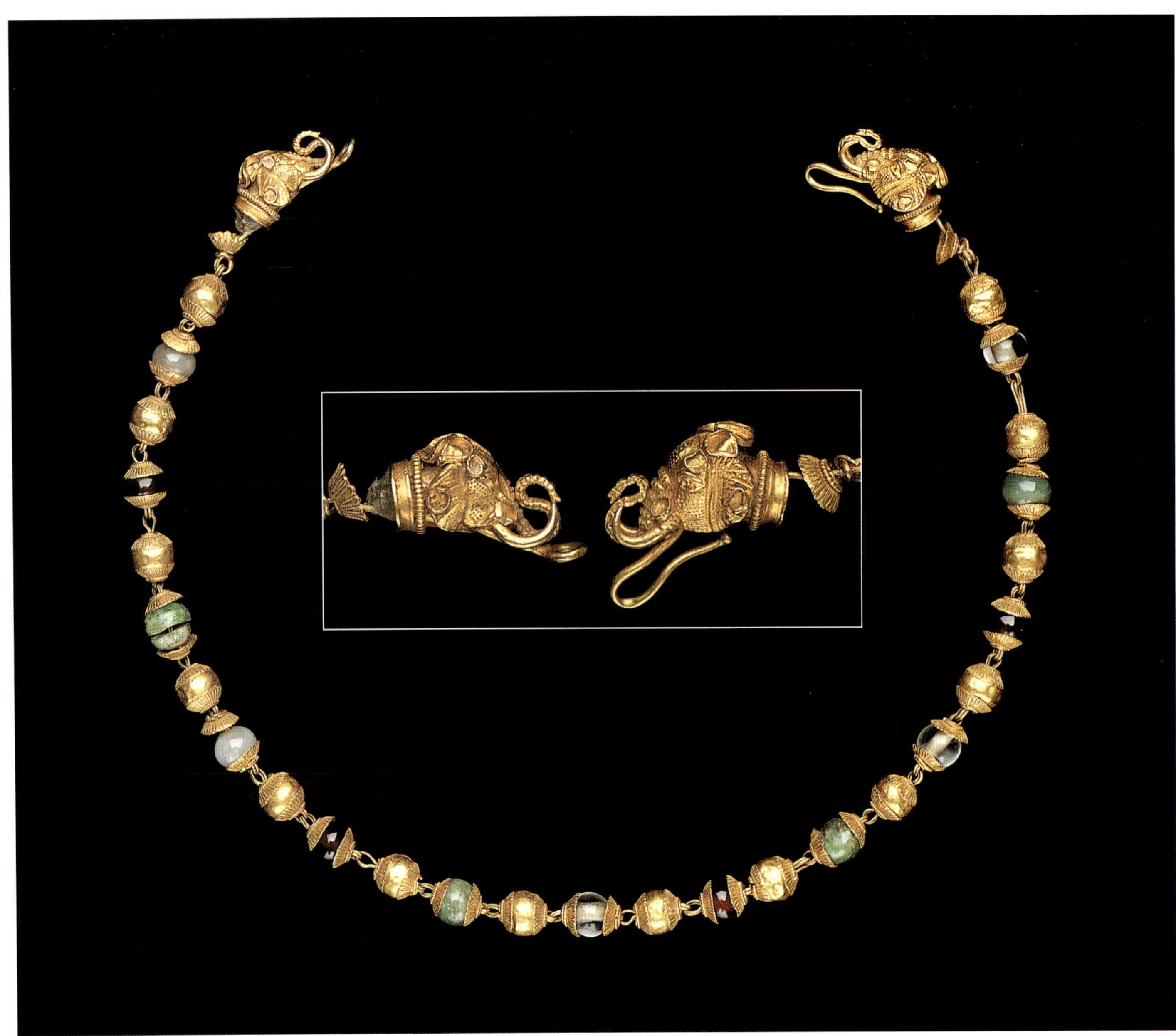

50.

Elephant-head necklace

Greek, Hellenistic, second century B.C.
Inlaid gold, gemstones, rock crystal
L. 37.5 cm
Museum League Purchase Funds, The Eugene and Margaret McDermott Art Fund, Inc., and Cecil H. and Ida M. Green in honor of Virginia Lucas Nick, 1991.75.79

THIS RICH NECKLACE IS composed of twenty-seven beads made of sheet gold, emerald, rock crystal, and garnet and held in place by pairs of rosette cups. Each bead is threaded on a double-wire loop, linked at each end to the neighboring loop. The elephant-head finials are bejeweled and finely chased. Each elephant trunk is made of a flat gold piece that has been notched and bent. At the base of each head is a collar with beaded wire. One head has a wire hook under it, the other a loop. As lavish as the finials still appear, they once had wreaths and ear ornaments of small gemstones, the settings of which remain. This unique work may refer to Dionysus's triumphal procession from India accompanied by Oriental animals.

REFERENCES: There is no exact parallel. For animal finial necklaces see Hoffmann and Davidson 1965, 132 ff., figs. 46a and 46b (also in the DMA collection); Juliis 1984, 222, no. 155, and 223, no. 156.

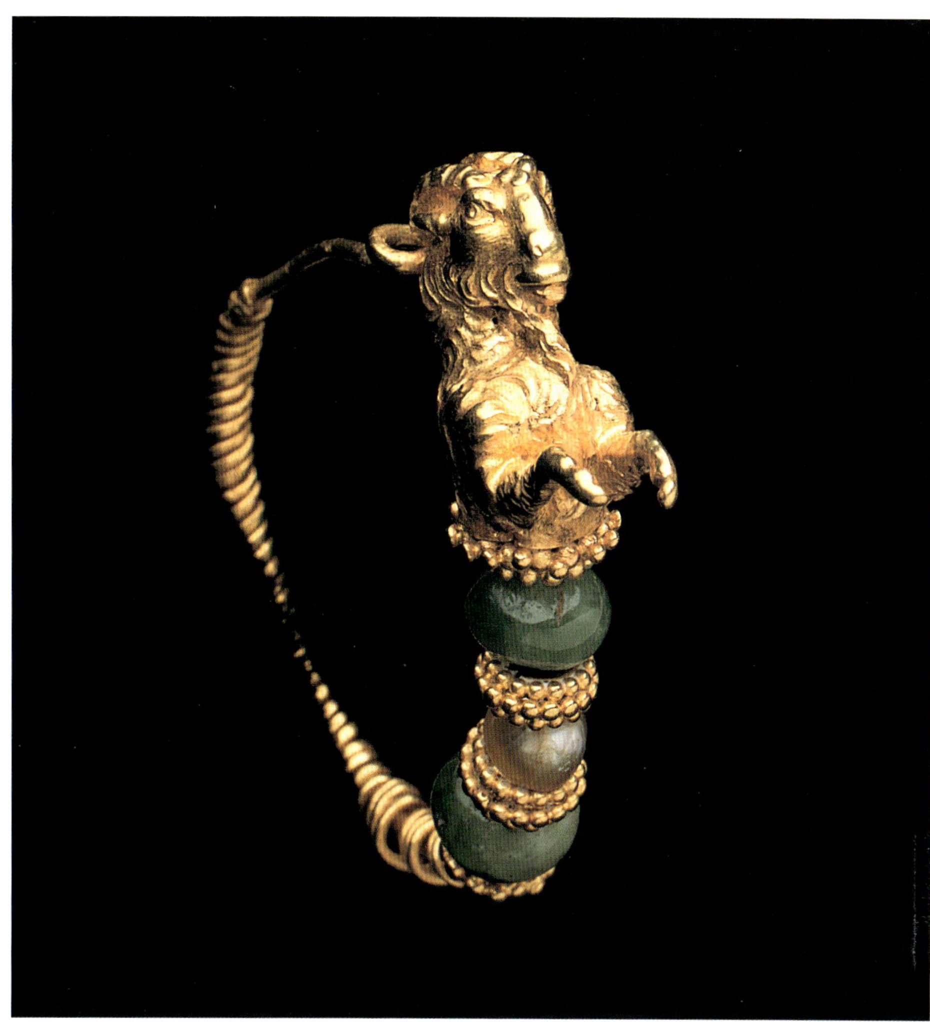

51.
Goat protome earring

Greek, Hellenistic, second–first century B.C.
Enameled gold and pearl
H. 3.5 cm
Museum League Purchase Funds, The Eugene and Margaret McDermott Art Fund, Inc., and Cecil H. and Ida M. Green in honor of Virginia Lucas Nick, 1991.75.81

THE SPIRAL-WOUND HOOP is separated from the goat protome by a pearl set between two large emerald beads. The pearl is separated from the emeralds by two rings, each consisting of three rows of coarse granulation. Similar granulated rings form the transition to the goat on one end and the spiral hoop of the earring on the other. The head and shoulders of the goat, including the beard and ears, were made in two halves, which were joined mechanically. Textural chasing suggests the goat's hair. The projecting forelegs were made separately from the body and attached. This is a very sculptural work: the goat springs forward with powerful energy.

PUBLICATIONS: Hoffmann and Davidson 1965, 108, no. 29.

REFERENCES: Amandry 1953, nos. 304 and 305.

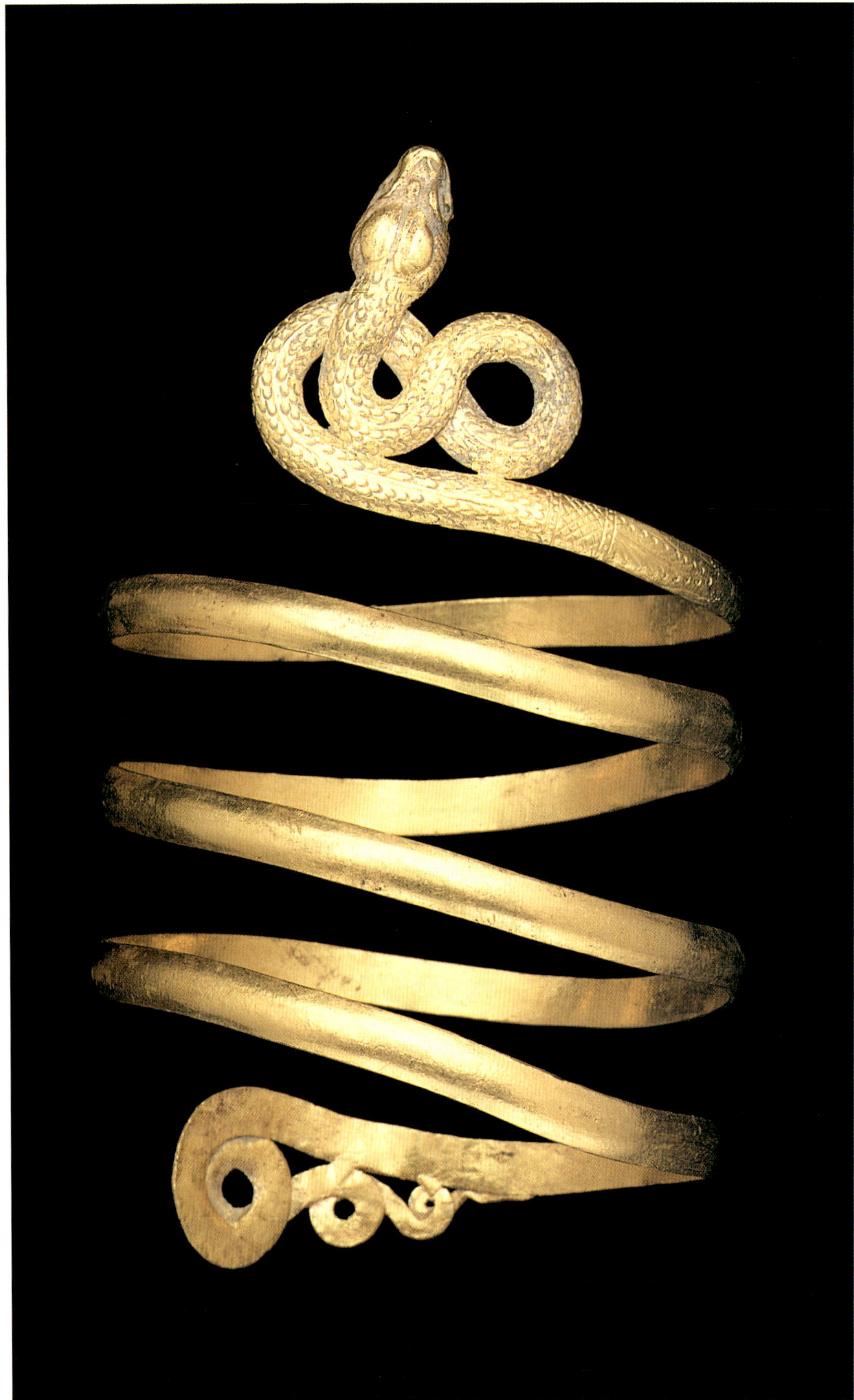

52.

Snake armlet

Greek or Roman, probably first century B.C.
Gold
DIAM. 8 cm
Museum League Purchase Funds, The Eugene and Margaret McDermott Art Fund, Inc., and Cecil H. and Ida M. Green in honor of Virginia Lucas Nick, 1991.75.92.1

SNAKE ARM BRACELETS date back to the Classical period in Greece. They were worn in pairs on the upper arms. This example consists of a plain, flat, coiled gold band, with the head and curled body of the snake forming one end and the curled tail the other. The modeling of the snake's head is quite realistic, as are the carefully chased details of the snake's scales.

REFERENCES: Deppert-Lippitz 1985, 269, no. 201; Higgins 1980, pl. 51, fig. C; Juliis 1984, 247, no. 172, and 248, no. 173; Bromberg, 1990, 57, pl. 40.

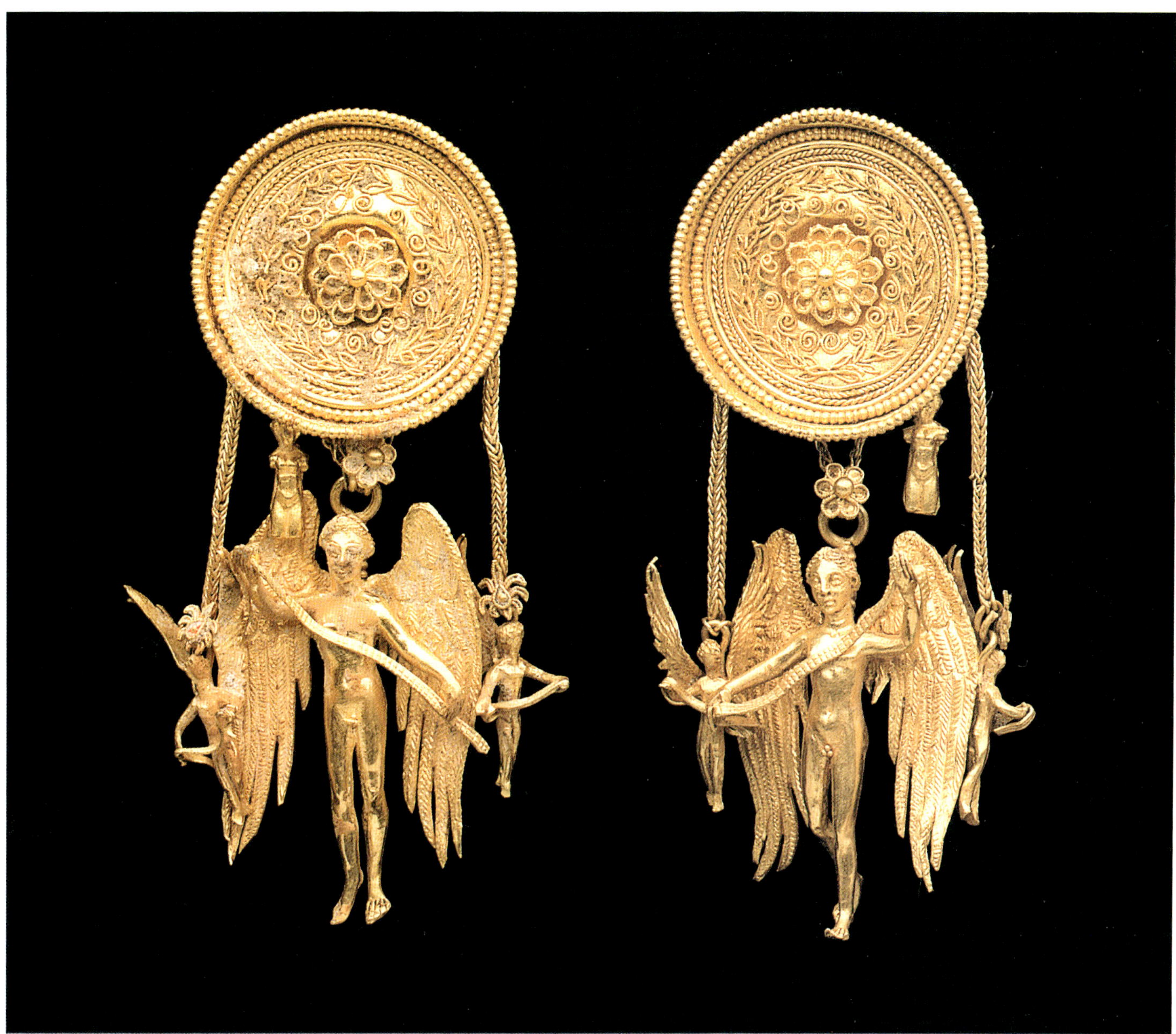

53.
Pair of earrings with Erotes

Greek, late fourth century B.C.
Gold
H. 5.4 cm, DIAM. (of disk) 2.2 cm
Green Estate Acquisitions Fund, 1995.25.a–b

THIS FINE PAIR OF EARRINGS with dangling Eros figures is a recent addition to the collection. Each earring is a miracle of refined miniature work, combining decorative filigree work with small-scale sculptural modeling. The details on the main figures are very fine, with the feathers of the wings clearly indicated. Eros, the god of love, was an especially popular subject in women's earrings, bringing sexual grace and seductiveness to the wearer. The fillets held out by the Eros figures crown the wearer with the prize of love and beauty. The small nude torsos attached to each disk are an unusual feature of these earrings. Reynold Higgins interpreted such torsos as amulets.

REFERENCES: Higgins 1980, pl. 48d; Williams and Ogden 1994, 96–97, no. 49; Deppert-Lippitz 1985, 192, pl. 20.

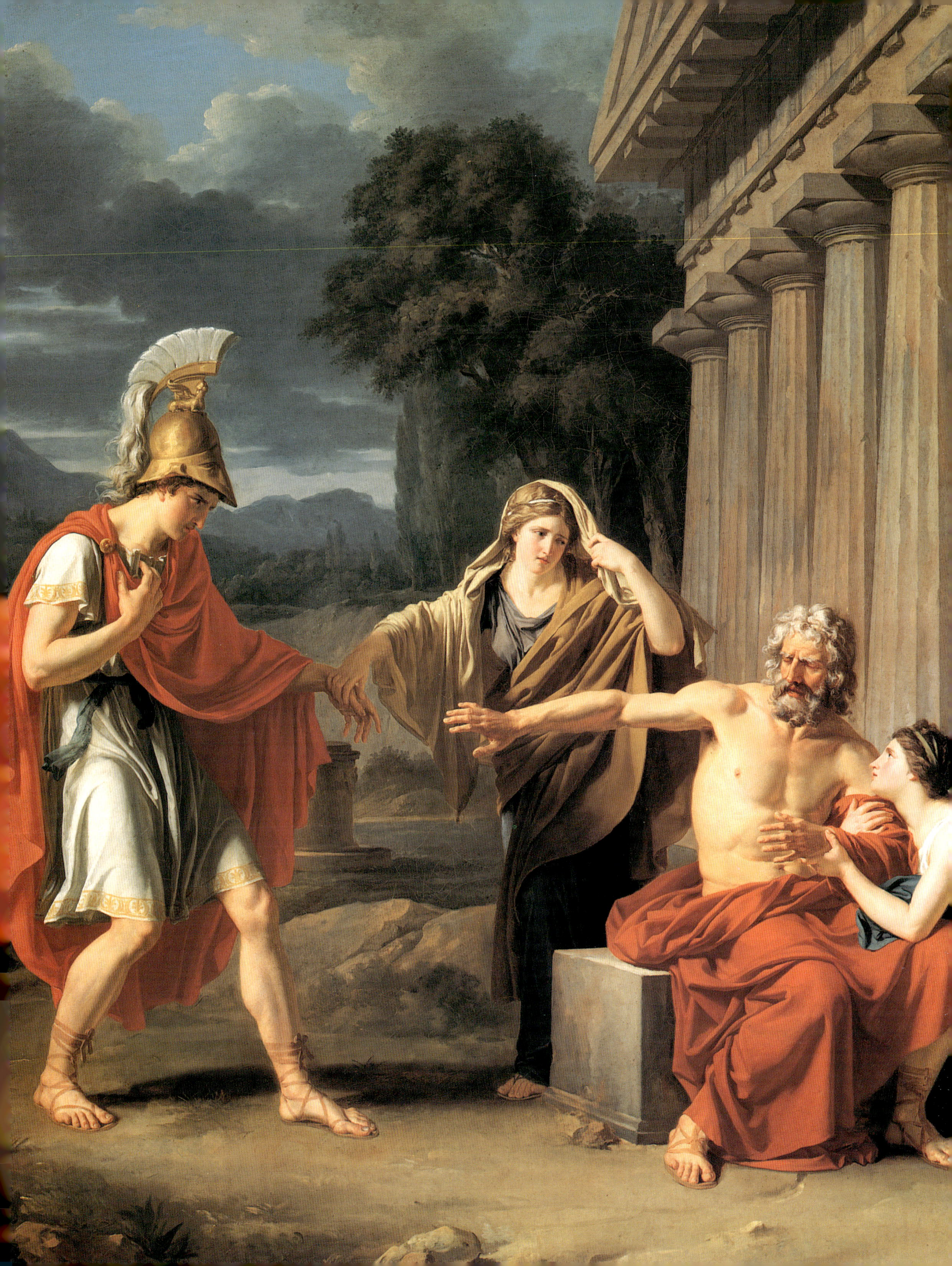

Chapter 8

The Classical Legacy: Myth in Later European Art

But more than all did the most gracious Raffaello da Urbino, who, studying the labors of the old masters and those of the modern, took the best from them, and, having gathered it together, enriched the art of painting with that complete perfection which was shown in ancient times by the figures of Apelles and Zeuxis.

—Giorgio Vasari, *Lives of the Most Eminent Painters, Sculptors and Architects*

While the imagery of the classical world did not totally disappear with the coming of Christianity, its appearance in art underwent a transformation. Sometimes purely antique forms were used for Christian subjects, as with the heroic nude figure of Jonah on a relief in the Museo Pio Cristiano in the Vatican. Other times late Greco-Roman narrative style was used to tell biblical stories, as in early Byzantine manuscript illustrations. An actual antique work was sometimes incorporated into a medieval treasure, like the Roman cameo in a Carolingian crown in the cathedral treasury at Aachen. Roman sarcophagi were sometimes reused by medieval Christians; numerous examples exist in the Campo Santo at Pisa. Late antique art passed north of the Alps via Byzantine Ravenna and Carolingian monastic workshops to become part of a new Christian visual world. It is thus too simple to speak of ancient art based on Greco-Roman cult religion as disappearing for a millennium, only to be reborn in the Italian Renaissance of the fifteenth century. What actually happened is both more complex and more interesting.

The fourth century A.D. witnessed two major imperial decrees that effectively brought ancient civilization to an end. In 313, Constantine I issued the Edict of Milan, which legalized the practice of Christianity within the Roman Empire, and in 391 Theodosius I officially closed the pagan shrines, making Christianity the state religion. While the means through which Greco-Roman civilization had thrived were now irreparably gone, over a thousand years of classical culture had made an indelible impression on the society that now struggled to become Christian, so its survival in Western civilization was virtually guaranteed. The forms through which classical culture permeated the Late Antique/Early Christian era were various, some lingering in altered states into the Middle Ages, others reemerging with tremendous impact toward the end of that period and in the Renaissance.

An immense array of classical literature recounting the sagas of mythological characters who filled the works of poets from Homer (eighth century B.C.) to Apuleius (second century A.D.) survived into the Middle Ages. The perpetuation of these mythological tales in Medieval art and literature, however, was drastically reduced because Christian themes and iconography superseded those of the pagan world. Perhaps due to the Greek origins of Constantinople, survival was stronger in the Byzantine East than in the Latin West. Mythological gods and heroes in classical attire illustrate a number of Byzantine ivory carvings and illuminated manuscripts. Photius, a patriarch of Constantinople during the ninth century A.D., collected passages from nearly three hundred Greek texts in his *Myriobiblion*, which was illustrated with images probably based in part on those from Apollodoros's *Bibliotheca* (second century A.D.) and works of Conon, a Roman mythographer of the first century A.D.

Unable to deny the classical tradition completely, Christian leaders often adapted classical myths to Christian philosophy, clothing them, as it were, in Christian dogma. It was simple to alter the meaning of a mythical subject, making it acceptable to Christian doctrine by assigning biblical names to classical images. Furthermore, traditional imagery was often perpetuated by artists who reverted to accepted formulae when confronted with the task of illustrating episodes from a new religion that lacked an established iconography. Other Christian writers attempted to divert belief in the pagan gods as divine beings by use of euhemerism, a rationalizing process that interpreted mythical characters as ordinary people of heroic stature or extraordinary accomplishment. This concept was named after its founder, Euhemerus of Messene (c. 300 B.C.).

While church fathers in the Latin West attempted to eradicate the deep-rooted remnants of the pagan world, the burgeoning scientific community in the late Middle Ages and early Renaissance adopted Arab astrological charts illustrated with classical gods and heroes derived from Hellenistic forerunners. One of the greatest of these was the computations of the Greek astrologer and geographer Ptolemy of Alexandria (second century A.D.) whose calculations were followed by scholars until the sixteenth century, when they were superseded by the work of Copernicus. The presence of these mythological characters on astrological charts, often accompanied by Greek, Latin, or Arabic texts enumerating their names, spheres of influence, and even attributes, was tolerated by the Christian community since Christian scholars accepted the notion of stellar influence and maintained that the classical divinities had been reduced to demonic forces that, albeit subject to God Almighty, still moved the heavenly bodies.

In the late Middle Ages, a growing interest in mythological tales from classical antiquity led artists and poets to turn to works such as Guido delle Colonne's *Historia destructionis Troiae* (1287) in their efforts to satisfy court officials who desired to be linked with the great "lords and ladies" of Troy. The heirs of Trojan heroes, so Virgil tells us in the *Aeneid,* were the founders of regal and aristocratic lines in Italy, and members of European nobility envisioned themselves as their ultimate descendants. The choice of Trojan versus Greek nobility underscored the rift within the Christian Church at that time, represented by Greek Orthodoxy in the East and Roman Catholicism in the West.

Other important works focusing on classical mythology were soon to follow. Among them were *Ovid moralisé* (early fourteenth century) and Giovanni Boccaccio's *De genealogia deorum gentilium* (Genealogies of the Pagan Gods, c. 1351–1360), which was translated into Italian, French, and Spanish. Here, as in other related writings, the mythological tales were used for the purposes of allegory and moralizing. Furthermore, although the renewed interest in mythological subjects brought them into wider circulation, they were clad in medieval attire and set within a medieval atmosphere. Poets not painters were the first to reach out to their literary antecedents to become the intellectuals who set the standards for reviving the classical gods and heroes. This means of representing ancient divinities in contemporary guise continued into the sixteenth century. Despite their respective attributes of a peacock and the caduceus, when Juno and Iris appear on a maiolica charger of the mid-sixteenth century (fig. 1) they are clad in contemporary dress and placed beside Renaissance architecture, all subordinated to a magnificent pastoral setting.

By the fifteenth century, humanists in Italy like Leon Battista Alberti were not so much rediscovering antiquity for the first time, as more consciously using ancient literary sources for their own sake. It was no longer necessary to "moralize" classical sources in a Christian manner. At the same time, artists felt free to adapt surviving examples of ancient sculpture and architecture in a new way, rethinking Greco-Roman deities for court patrons who accepted classical culture as a set of values parallel to Christianity, or complementing it. Alberti himself said: "I shall define beauty to be a harmony of all the parts, in whatsoever subject it appears" (*De re aedificatoria* [trans. Leoni] 6.2). Plato would have applauded this point of view. The philosophic basis of humanist thought in fifteenth-century Italy was Neoplatonism, as adopted by thinkers like Alberti and Pico della Mirandola and later by Giambattista Vico. In their minds, antique myth and classical imagery were not incompatible with Christian dogma and could be used to illustrate the most profound Christian truths. It was this great synthesis of classical values with Christianity that made possible works like Raphael's Stanza della Segnatura (1510–1511) in the Vatican or Michelangelo's paintings in the Sistine Chapel (1508–1512). Thanks to the importance of humanists in education, the forms of ancient civilization became a dominant cultural force in European society.

Allegorical imagery for writers and artists alike was given a major stimulus with the printing of Andrea Alciati's *Emblemata,* first with 104 images in 1531 and soon after with more than two hundred examples. Other widely circulated texts, destined to be inspirational to artists, perpetuated the notion of allegorical imagery. Yet Renaissance artists required a closer scrutiny of tangible remains from the classical past before they altered their manner of depicting the characters and their stories in what was by now viewed as the grand glorification of the classical heritage. Foremost in this pursuit was Poggio Bracciolini, who was one of the earliest scholars to begin developing an archaeological approach to the study of antiquity. In his quest for knowledge about antiquity, he combined a desire to collect ancient literary texts with a passion for collecting classical portrait busts. His contemporary Flavio Biondo applied his many talents to the study of the visible antiquities of Rome. With the fresh approach of an enthusiast, he sought an understanding of ancient buildings as they once existed. His illustrated studies of the monuments of ancient

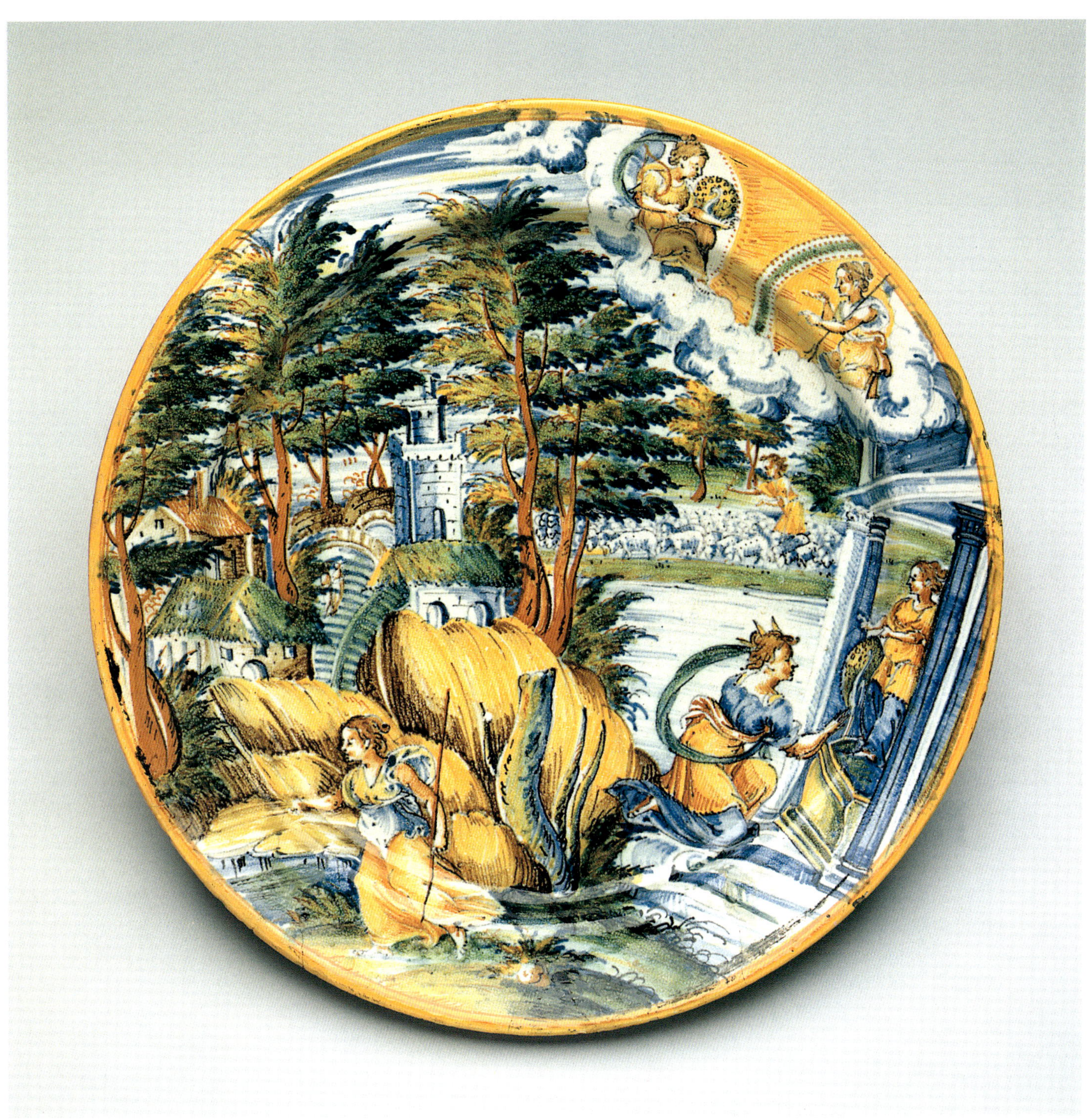

Fig. 1. Charger, Faenza, Italy, c. 1555. Tin-glazed earthenware, diam. 43.2 cm. Dallas Museum of Art, gift of Sarah Dorsey Hudson, 1990.169.

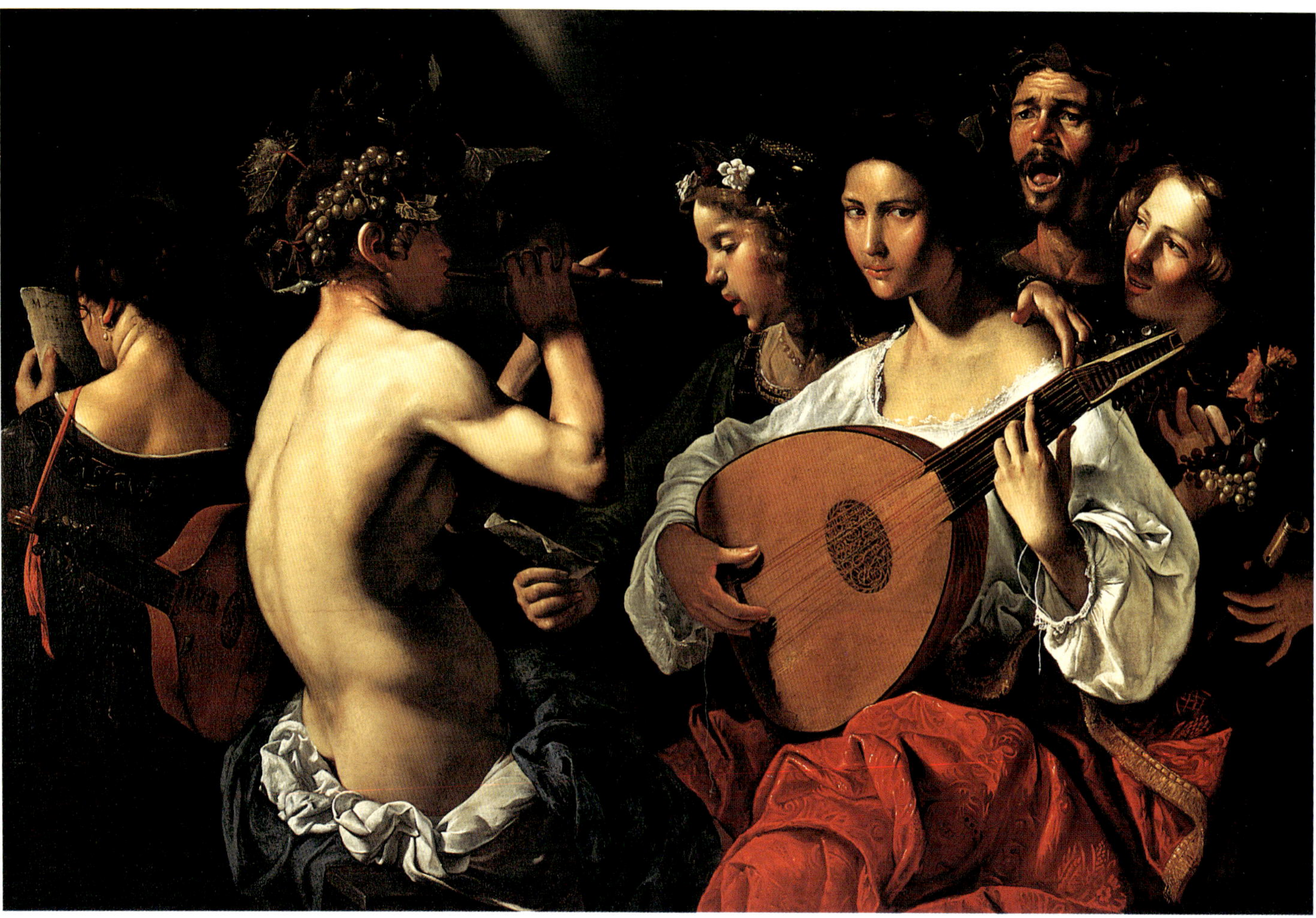

Fig. 2. Pietro Paolini, *Bacchic Concert*, 1625–1630. Oil on canvas, 117.5 × 174.6 cm. Dallas Museum of Art, The Karl and Esther Hoblitzelle Collection, gift of the Hoblitzelle Foundation, 1987.17.

Rome (*De Roma instaurata*, 1446) and of Italy (*Italia illustrata*, 1474) typify the changing attitude toward classical forms in the early Renaissance. Biondo's work became a source of inspiration for artists as well as a point of departure for others like himself, such as Andrea Fulvio, who published his *Antiquitates urbis* in 1527 at the urging of Pope Leo X.

The rapid discoveries of classical art both in and outside of Italy brought about a greater interest in their forms than there had been during the preceding millennium. Such magnificent works as the Apollo Belvedere, found by the mid-fifteenth century, and the Laocoön and the Sleeping Ariadne, unearthed at the beginning of the sixteenth century, drew immediate attention in the artistic community. Collections of antiquities grew at an enormous rate in the hands of the papacy, the nobility, and to a lesser extent, the artists themselves. Furthermore, the presence of antiquities in public and private collections allowed them to be copied in sketchbooks and reproduced in plaster casts, and enabled their images to be disseminated through the growing medium of prints, all to the benefit of artists seeking to depict their subjects in a natural form.

The humanist movement in the Renaissance also released an overt interest in the erotic and sensuous aspects of the human form, which were more easily depicted through mythological themes than by images of saints. Fully established in the Renaissance, this focus was readily carried into the Baroque period. The DMA's *Bacchic Concert* (fig. 2) by Pietro Paolini is an early seventeenth-century work that reflects a complex adaptation of ancient art to a modern setting. Influenced by Caravaggio's work, especially *The Lute Player* (c. 1594, Hermitage Museum, St. Petersburg), Paolini also used an antique model, probably the Ludovisi Mars in the Museo Nazionale delle Terme, for the mostly nude figure of the pipe player. This is a darkly resonant vision of the wine god, whose gleaming flesh is contrasted with the figures in contemporary Renaissance costume. Their sly, ambiguous appearance is an interesting approximation to the rustic half-animal followers of the god in ancient times. The sumptuous figure of Bacchus, set off by drapery around his hips and wearing an extraordinarily rich and glowing grape leaf and ivy crown, is a vivid embodiment of the ecstatic power of music and wine. Only one figure in the composition looks directly out of the painting; all the others are elliptical in glance and enigmatic in expression. The dark, demonic side of Dionysiac cult is a subtext of this very sophisticated painting. The glowing seminude form of the Bacchic flutist dramatically accents the scene of revelry and harvest celebration so characteristic of the ancient Dionysiac cult. In addition to the subtle display of sensuous flesh, other Dionysiac images include the suggestive pose of the young girl's fingers holding the phallic-shaped flute and pinching the intoxicating bunch of grapes, the mysterious and alluring back view of the woman scrutinizing a sheet of music, the open charm of the two vocalists, and the seductive glance of the female lute player as she entices the viewer to partake of the scene.

The importance of classical myth in art passed from Italy to seventeenth-century France, where it became the foundation of French academic art. Painters like Nicolas Poussin, who had studied in Rome, considered antique models to be a necessary source for a style of ideal grandeur suitable for the French monarchy and court. Nicolas Mignard, who spent much of his professional life in Avignon but ultimately worked for the court, is represented at the Museum by a grand classical subject, *The Shepherd Faustulus Bringing Romulus and Remus to His Wife* (fig. 3), the foundation myth of Rome. The she-wolf lurking in the background to the right is partly a real wolf, partly a recollection of the lean and shaggy nurse-mother of Rome in the Museo Capitolino in Rome. The central figures resemble Neo-Attic marble reliefs, an impression heightened by the clear, crisp primary colors. Although the ambience of the poor shepherd's hut is

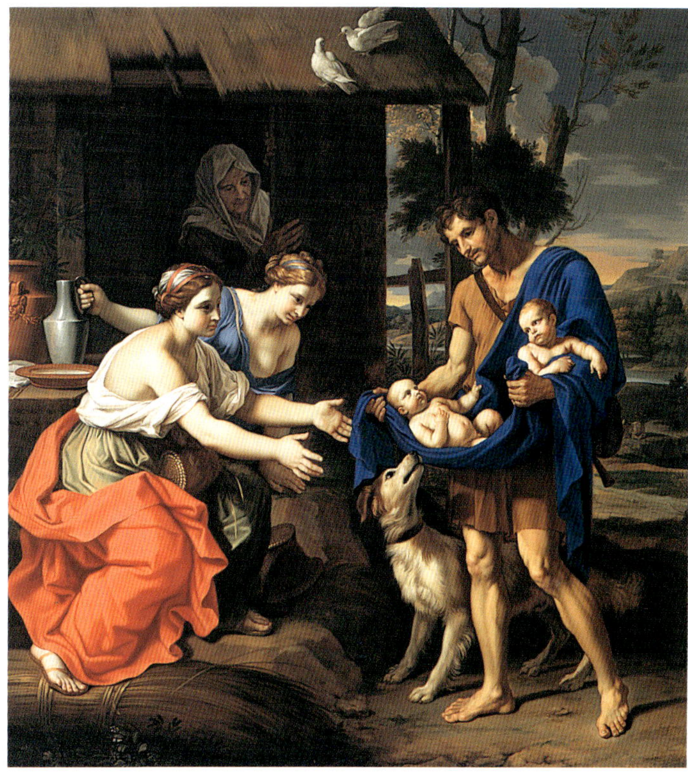

Fig. 3. Nicolas Mignard, *The Shepherd Faustulus Bringing Romulus and Remus to His Wife*, 1654. Oil on canvas, 148.6 × 145.1 cm. Dallas Museum of Art, gift of Mr. and Mrs. Algur H. Meadows and the Meadows Foundation, Incorporated, 1970.25.

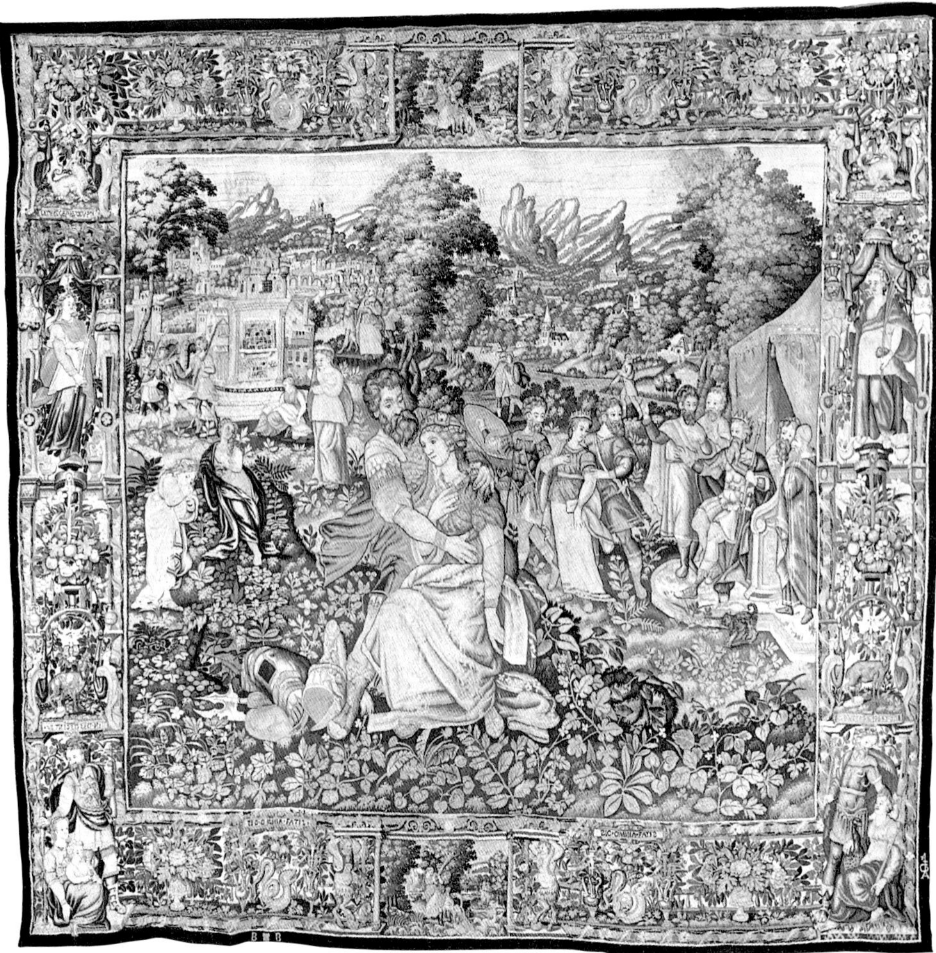

Fig. 4. Jacob Geubels I, Brussels, Belgium, *The Rape of Rhea Silvia, Mother of Romulus and Remus, by Mars,* from the series *The History of Romulus and Remus,* c. 1575–1605. Wool, 315 × 322.6 cm. Dallas Museum of Art, anonymous gift, 1981.93.FA.

Arcadian, the sculptural treatment dignifies and ennobles the humble setting. An interesting comparison in the treatment of Roman mythology is the DMA's baroque tapestry (fig. 4) depicting the story of Rhea Silvia, the Vestal Virgin who bore Romulus and Remus to the war god Mars. Erotic tones present in the tapestry are also evident in the Mignard painting. The lush display of drapery contrasted with the bare flesh of Acca, wife of the shepherd Faustulus, and the exposed breast of her maid (ostensibly to indicate her continued nurturing of the infants Romulus and Remus, who were suckled by the she-wolf) are combined with symbols of married love in the pair of doves on the roof.

The seventeenth century also experienced a particular sentimentality for antiquity, which reaches its apogee of expression in landscape painting. The pastoral settings characterized in the poetry of Theocritus (third century B.C.) and Virgil (first century B.C.) were represented in pictorial form by such masters as Claude Lorrain and Nicolas Poussin, among others, who often added the haunting presence of crumbling ruins to their scenes. In so doing, they generally minimized the importance of the mythological characters in their paintings—subordinating them to the architectural elements or the overwhelming presence of nature—and thereby infusing the scene with a penetrating sense of nostalgia, as well as a subtle reference to a lost Golden Age.

The works of Antoine Coypel, a royal painter like Nicolas Mignard's brother Pierre, represent the moment toward the end of Louis XIV's reign when the grand style was giving way to more sensuous, coloristic painting. His *Alliance of Bacchus and Cupid* (fig. 5) has a grace and casual air that is lacking in the high seriousness of Mignard's work. The putto playing with Bacchus's masks and leopard (which the child treats like a tame cat) are charming vignettes, while the adolescent Venus presiding from a pillow-soft cloud is distinctly enticing. The succulent Cupid tempts an equally youthful Bacchus with a wine cup. Altogether the painting looks like a *jour de fête* in some golden fairy-tale country, full of air and shadows; it is quite different from the mythic clarity of the Mignard scene.

Coypel's anticipation of the rococo style is fully realized in Jean-Baptiste-Marie Pierre's wonderfully romantic *The Abduction of Europa* (fig. 6). Pierre, too, was a court painter. His grand scene sums up the way eighteenth-century sensuality could be idealized in myth. Elements representing male sexuality and the forces of nature surround Europa: the startlingly suggestive sea monster; the equally lascivious nude Triton reclining above it; Zeus in full figure as a

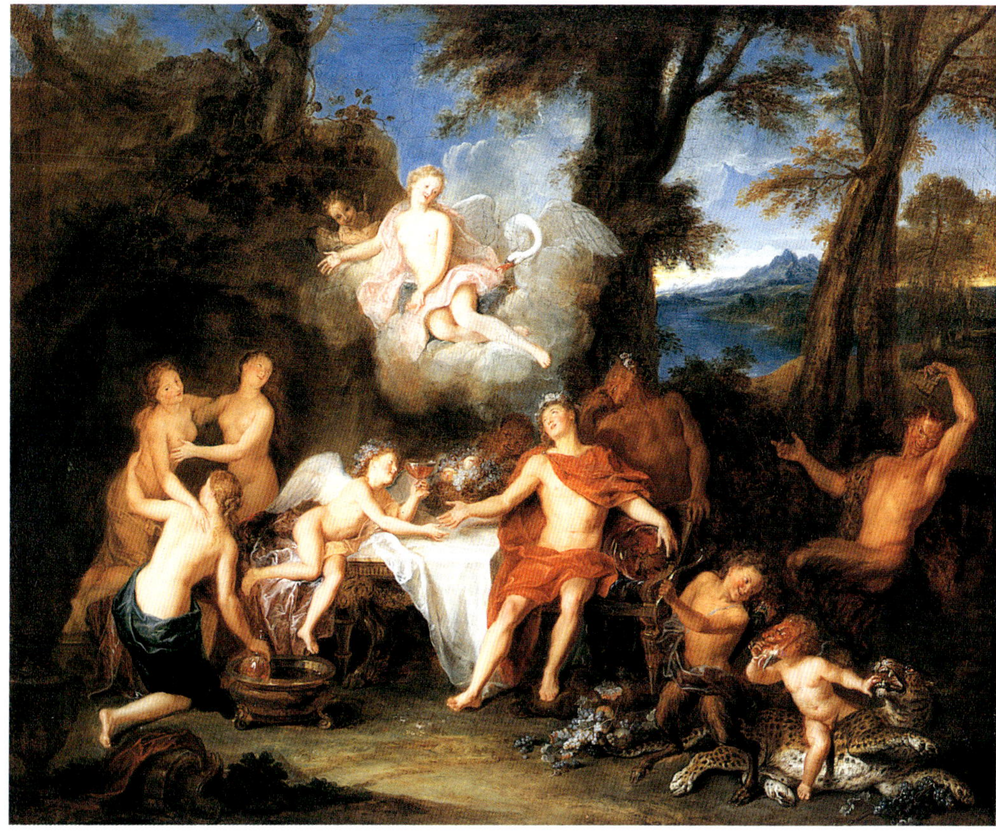

Fig. 5. Antoine Coypel, *The Alliance of Bacchus and Cupid*, c. 1702. Oil on canvas, 75.6 × 94 cm. Dallas Museum of Art, Foundation for the Arts Collection, Mrs. John B. O'Hara Fund, 1990.144.FA.

garlanded bull; and Zeus's alter ego, the eagle, screaming overhead. These potent forces form the groundswell of seduction upon which the girl is carried away. Europa herself is a sunlit central figure of froth and foam, heralded by flying cupids with garlands of flowers. If the scene is a rape, the only evidence of regret is in the girl's mild backward glance at the safe shore of home. Primarily Europa is the radiant center of a symphonic celebration of love, caught up peacefully by the great organ swell of impassioned nature. She says farewell to her past, only to be crowned by the airy cohort of fertility and power. Ovid's elegant romances in the *Metamorphoses* find an eighteenth-century equivalent in this work.

The eighteenth century witnessed the magnificent discoveries from the excavations in buried towns and villas on the slopes of Mount Vesuvius on the Bay of Naples. Beginning officially in 1748, the excavations at Pompeii produced an enormous wealth of artifacts, many of which were distributed across Europe. Herculaneum, too, had numerous artworks taken from its deep soil; they were studied and published starting in 1757 in a multivolume series entitled *Antichità di Ercolano*. These publications, filled with mythological subjects, eventually gained great attention and brought many travelers, including Johann Joachim Winckelmann, on the "grand tour" to Herculaneum and Pompeii. Winckelmann's *Geschichte der Kunst des Altertums*, published in 1764, would have profound effects on neoclassicism.

A Wedgwood cameo (fig. 7) in the DMA collections admirably illustrates the way in which decorative artists adapted classical motifs in the late eighteenth century. Josiah Wedgwood first called the relief *Night*, and indicated that the figures on the cameo were modeled after an antique *Venus and Cupid*. In the 1779 catalogue of his works, he changed the title of the cameo to *Ceres and Triptolemus*. Wedgwood's model has been attributed to an antique gem of Venus and Cupid illustrated in Lionardo Agostini's *Gemmae et sculpturae antique* (1685). An image virtually identical to the Wedgwood cameo appears in Bernard de Montfaucon's *L'Antiquité expliquée par Montfaucon*, published in 1722. The figure is entitled *Venus and Cupid* and is based on a gem in the Maffei collection. Wedgwood owned a copy of Montfaucon's compendium and was presumably familiar with this illustration. It is not clear why Wedgwood ultimately thought of the figures as the corn goddess Ceres and her protégé, Triptolemus, despite the winged figure of the boy, which is closer to Cupid.

Whatever the source of the image, the figures are extraordinarily graceful and rhythmic, with the dignified and maternal goddess

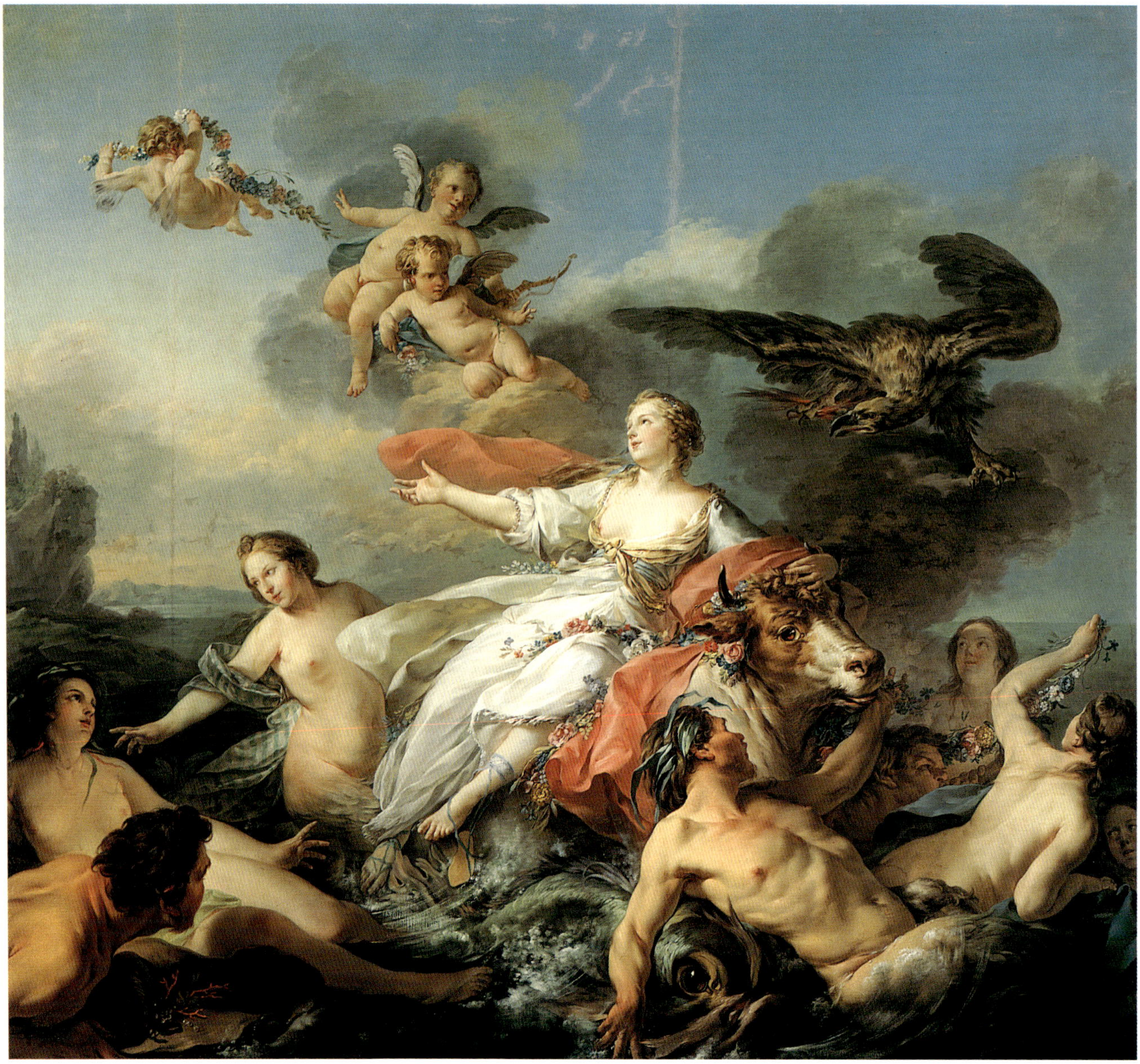

Fig. 6. Jean-Baptiste-Marie Pierre, *The Abduction of Europa,* 1750. Oil on canvas, 243.8 × 275.6 cm. Dallas Museum of Art, Foundation for the Arts Collection, Mrs. John B. O'Hara Fund, 1989.133.FA.

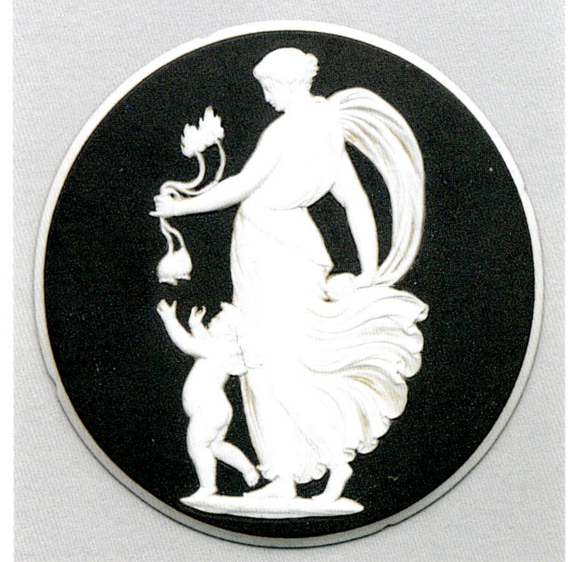

Fig. 7. *Venus and Cupid,* Josiah Wedgwood Factory, Staffordshire, England, c. 1790–1800. Jasper, diam. 6 cm. Dallas Museum of Art, anonymous gift, 1991.412.87.

holding out a lushly detailed sheaf of poppies to her winged child. Both figures suggest a dancing movement well fitted to the circular frame. For Wedgwood, the mythological meaning of the original image was probably less important than its decorative quality. That the artist worked from a book illustration rather than an original art object indicates how very widespread the repertory of classical imagery had become by this period.

Another interesting example of the Wedgwood factory's use of ancient styles and motifs appears in the DMA's crocodile teapot (fig. 8), manufactured around 1810. Wedgwood's *rosso antico* ("antique red") ceramics, with figures in raised relief, refer back to both the contrast of red and black on Greek vases and the raised relief designs on Roman red-colored Arretine wares. The piece is a fine example of Egyptianizing styles popular during the early nineteenth century.

While Wedgwood was not trying to produce authentic hieroglyphics on their ceramics, as some European designers did, the array of symbols found on the teapot include very common Egyptian motifs of religious or magical significance to the Egyptians themselves. Moving in a circle from the area below the teapot handle, these include: a winged sun disk, the Anubis jackal, an ankh or sistrum, a *ba* bird, an altar for offerings, another sun disk, a ram-headed god (probably Khnum), a sphinx, the Maat feather, a sun disk, a goose, a Canopic jar, the goddess Hathor as a crowned cow, a sun disk, and a pair of crocodiles. The Wedgwood emblems are visually correct in relation to their Egyptian prototypes. The source for these motifs was probably illustrations in books showing Egyptian images. By the nineteenth century, figures that were used in Egypt as part of hieroglyphic scripts, as amulets or as the subject matter of art, had become raw material for decorative design.

Just as myth in art was used by the ancient Romans and the medieval church to foster allegorical notions and moralizing dictums, so was classical myth used, in antiquity and later, for political propaganda. One of the most intense periods of its use in this manner was during the French Revolution. Neoclassical French art of the late eighteenth century returned to the relieflike structure of the Mignard painting (fig. 3), but with an ideological, as well as a formal, intent. Jacques-Louis David's neoclassical works created before the French Revolution pictured a stern Roman moral for an Enlightenment audience. The work of his colleague Jean-Antoine-Théodore Giroust, whose 1788 Prix de Rome painting has fortunately survived intact, also underlines the moral meaning of ancient myth. *Oedipus at*

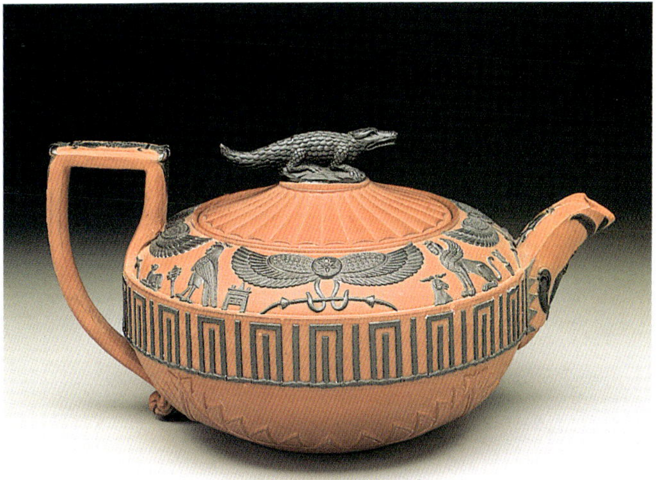

Fig. 8. Teapot, Josiah Wedgwood Factory, Staffordshire, England, c. 1810. *Rosso antico*, basalt, 20.3 × 11.4 cm. Dallas Museum of Art, The Barbara and Hensleigh Wedgwood Collection, gift of the Dallas Antiques and Fine Arts Society, acquired 1996.

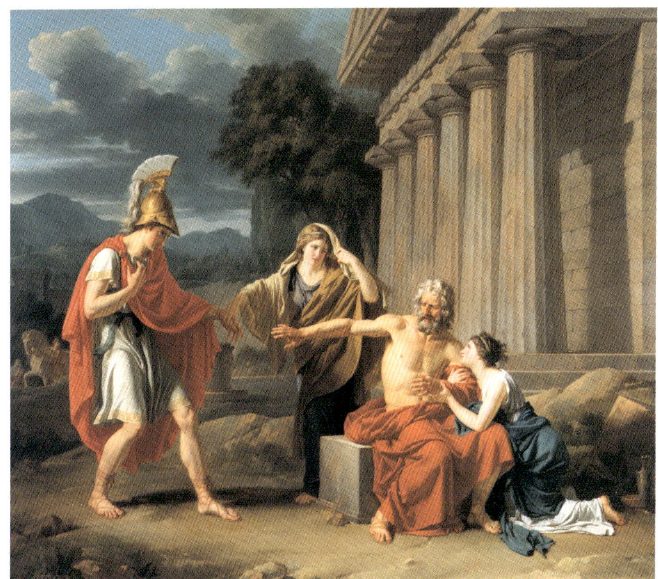

Fig. 9. Jean-Antoine-Théodore Giroust, *Oedipus at Colonus*, 1788. Oil on canvas, 164 × 194 cm. Dallas Museum of Art, Foundation for the Arts Collection, Mrs. John B. O'Hara Fund, 1992.22.FA.

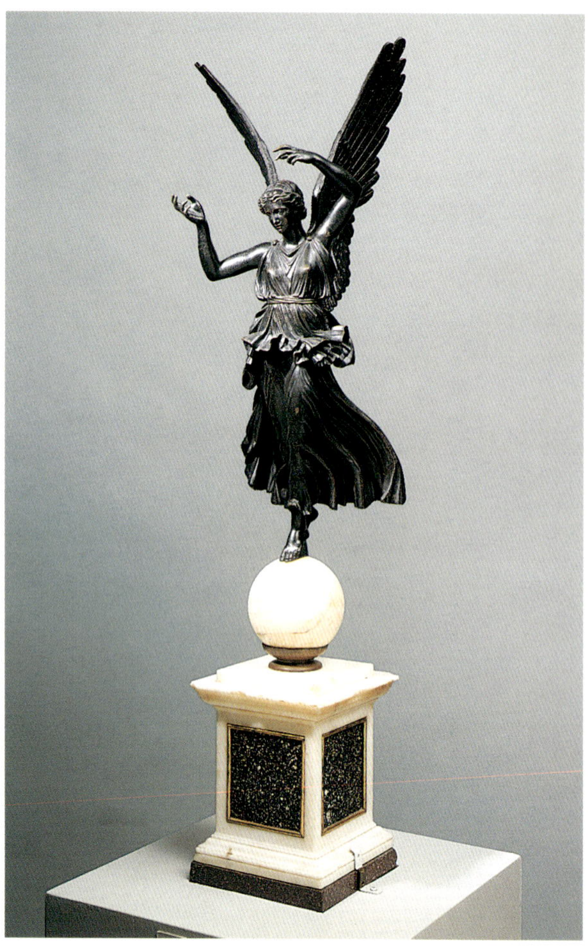

Fig. 10. Antonio Canova, *Victory*, c. 1813. Bronze, alabaster, 85.7 × 17.8 × 20.6 cm. Dallas Museum of Art, Foundation for the Arts Collection, Mrs. John B. O'Hara Fund, 1979.40.FA.

Colonus (fig. 9), based on Sophocles' last play, presents the dramatic moment when the aged and blind Oedipus cursed his son Polynices for engaging in warfare at Thebes against his brother, Eteocles. The solemn curse uttered by the splendidly painted old man occurs against a temple setting meant to suggest a sacred Greek shrine. Sophocles' play is a mighty meditation on the meaning of the gods' curse on Oedipus, his future fate, and the relationship of gods and men. Giroust dramatizes this great theme with classical economy. Against the Doric temple facade, the still noble and fiery Oedipus, speaking with patriarchal wisdom and agonized experience, rejects the pleas of his daughters and casts out his feckless son.

The columns of the Doric temple have been faithfully copied from the monolithic examples at ancient Corinth. Ruined blocks of stone and archaeologically authentic Greek vases fill the right-hand corner of the scene, while the equestrian group at the far left does double service as the local statue at Colonus noted by Sophocles in his play and as the groom with mount that Polynices has left on the periphery of the sanctuary while he addresses his father. Giroust has based the distinguished head of Oedipus on a Roman copy of a famous Hellenistic portrait of Homer, good examples of which are in Boston and London, and which had previously appeared on canvas in Rembrandt's famous painting *Aristotle with the Bust of Homer* (1653, Metropolitan Museum of Art, New York). While Sophocles wrote of the blind Theban king being given refuge in the territory of democratic Athens, Giroust depicted Oedipus in the guise of the blind but highly respected poet of antiquity in order to inspire patriotism and champion democracy among his French audience. This painting was produced only a year after David's *The Death of Socrates* (1787, Metropolitan Museum of Art, New York), which, in reference to the trappings of another noble antique theme, emphasized that people should be prepared to surrender their lives for their ideals. In both paintings, the artists have endowed their respective heroes on the verge of death with aged, noble heads surmounting classically athletic bodies, bestowing on them an element of the divine. The portrait of Homer copied by Giroust for his Oedipus is reminiscent in its ring of thick curls of the magnificent marble bust of *Zeus Otricoli*, now in the Vatican, which was discovered between 1776 and 1784. This combined sense of Homeric nobility and Olympic divinity in Giroust's champion from the distant past gave greater emphasis to the importance of his political theme. The imagery of Oedipus with his daughter Ismene pleading across his knees would be utilized in 1811 by another defender of the Revolution, Jean-Auguste-Dominique Ingres, when he painted his captivating scene of *Jupiter and Thetis* (Musée Granet, Aix-en-Provence, France), with the god's head also inspired by the Otricoli bust.

Giroust's painting makes a serious effort to grapple with the meanings implicit in ancient art in a way that would not happen again until the twentieth century. Despite the extent to which nineteenth-century artists, especially academic artists, worshiped antique models, the actual use of such models tended to be theatrical, decorative, or conventional. Eugène Delacroix's daring use of the head of the Venus de Medici for the head of Liberty in his *Liberty Leading the People* (1830, Musée du Louvre, Paris) had few followers. Antonio Canova's *Victory* (fig. 10) figure was originally designed as part of a heroic sculpture of Napoleon in the guise of a Roman emperor, which is now in Apsley House in London. Smaller versions of the Nike figure Napoleon is holding in his right hand were also made. Canova's classically correct representation of Nike alighting on an alabaster globe supported by a pedestal recalls with uncanny clarity the windswept form of Paeonius's marble statue atop a tall pillar

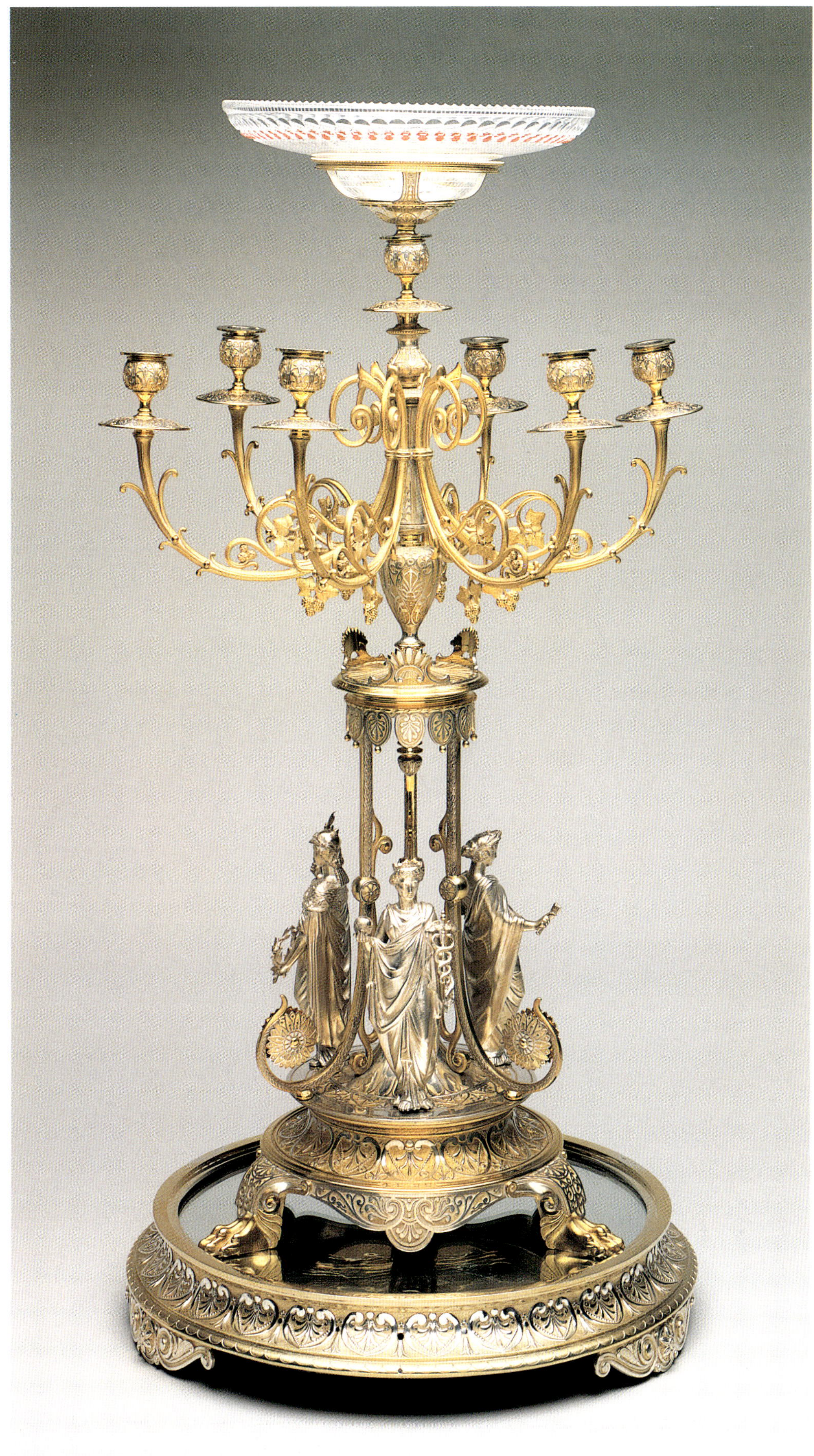

Fig. 11. Candelabrum for dessert service, Frederick Elkington & Co., Birmingham, England, 1876–1877. Silver, 78.7 cm. Dallas Museum of Art, gift of the Meadows Foundation, Incorporated, 1988.44.a.

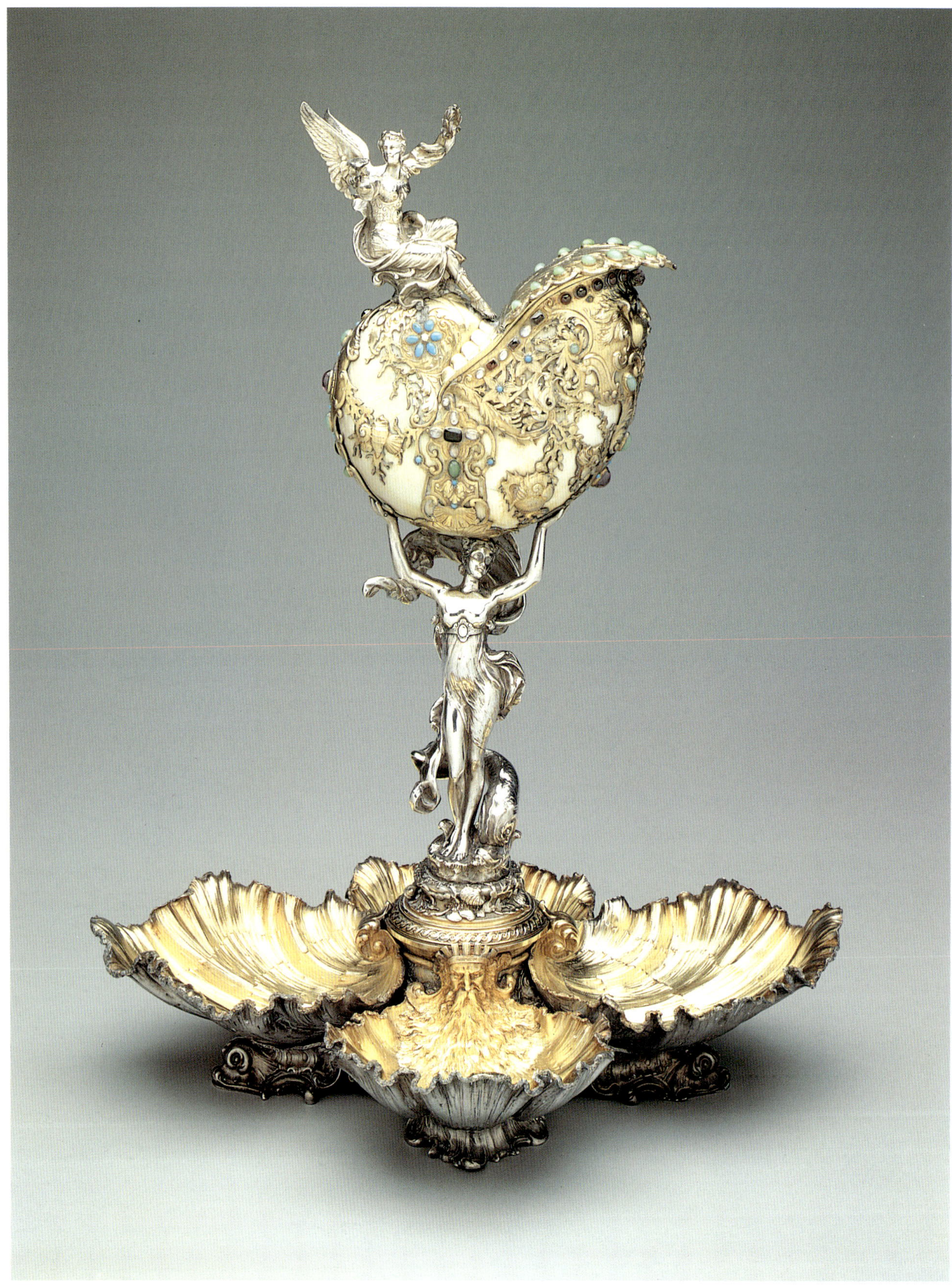

Fig. 12. *Nautilus Centerpiece,* William C. Codman, designer; Gorham Manufacturing Company, maker; Providence, Rhode Island; 1893. Sterling silver, silvergilt, shell, pearls, semiprecious stones, 50.8 × 39.4 × 31.8 cm. Dallas Museum of Art, gift of the 1990 Silver Supper, 1990.176.

(Olympia Museum, Greece), which was dedicated at Olympia in the late fifth century B.C. but not unearthed until after Canova's death. However, Canova had readily available prototypes, since a personification of Victory in this pose appears in numerous examples in Greco-Roman art. Canova's work is symptomatic of an age in which classical memorabilia adorned furniture, architectural details, and other ornamental elements in the neoclassical decorative arts industry. Artists often merged ancient concepts and artistic styles with current fashions and events.

The use of classical motifs in the decorative arts became even more extensive in the nineteenth century. The survival of ancient pottery, silverware, jewelry, and weapons supplied numerous models for decorative motifs, as did the carved ornamental details on stone reliefs and the wealth of painted ornaments unearthed at Pompeii and Herculaneum in the eighteenth century. The Greco-Roman taste for transforming everyday utensils into works of art decorated with human, animal, and floral forms was readily adapted by later European craftsmen. Two exquisite examples of the later nineteenth century from either side of the Atlantic are the silver candelabrum (fig. 11) and *Nautilus Centerpiece* (fig. 12). These finely crafted ornaments have their antecedents in classical antiquity, filtered through several centuries of design after the Renaissance.

The English candelabrum is supported by three classical goddesses holding symbolic attributes. The candleholders are decorated with stylized rosettes and palmettes copied from classical ornament. The nautilus centerpiece depicts the myth of Aphrodite's birth from the sea. The theme, so popular in Greek and Roman art and literature, was revitalized in the Renaissance and continued to provide artistic stimulation for several centuries. In this representation, the ornate nautilus shell recalls Dutch and German Baroque table centerpieces, which often feature a Roman type of Venus in billowing drapery. The whole concept displays a late Victorian taste for lavish ornamentation. Dazzling in its profuse display of mythological symbolism, the design is punctuated with dolphins, seashells, and Triton heads. It culminates in the luxuriant figure of the love goddess holding up the jewel-encrusted nautilus shell, which brings the wavelike composition to a breathtaking conclusion.

While Greek and Roman myths maintained a solid foothold in neoclassicism, another movement embraced a different approach. Romanticism replaced archaeological authenticity with allegorical fantasy. The Romantics mingled mythological tales with historical accounts to create pictorial allegories, sometimes for political purposes. Although an atmosphere of melancholy reverence pervades the Romantics' use of themes and motifs from classical antiquity, purity of form or narrative is often sacrificed to achieve it. Concerned with provoking emotional responses to their art, the Romantics radically altered aspects of classical myths or adapted mythological iconography to suit their needs. The eloquent personification of America by Hiram Powers is an example. Powers, an American who spent most of his successful professional life in Italy without ever learning Italian, adapted ancient sculptures as a sign of "serious" art. His bland idealizations were phenomenally popular. *America* (fig. 13) is interchangeable with works like *Faith* (1866–1867, Museum of Fine Arts, Boston), *Hope* (1866–1891, Brooklyn Museum), and *Diana* (1853, Corcoran Gallery of Art, Washington, D.C.). Each chaste marble bust is based on a composite of Roman imperial portrait heads and classical sculptures like the Venus of Capua in Naples. They vary only in their symbolic headdresses; *America* has a starry crown.

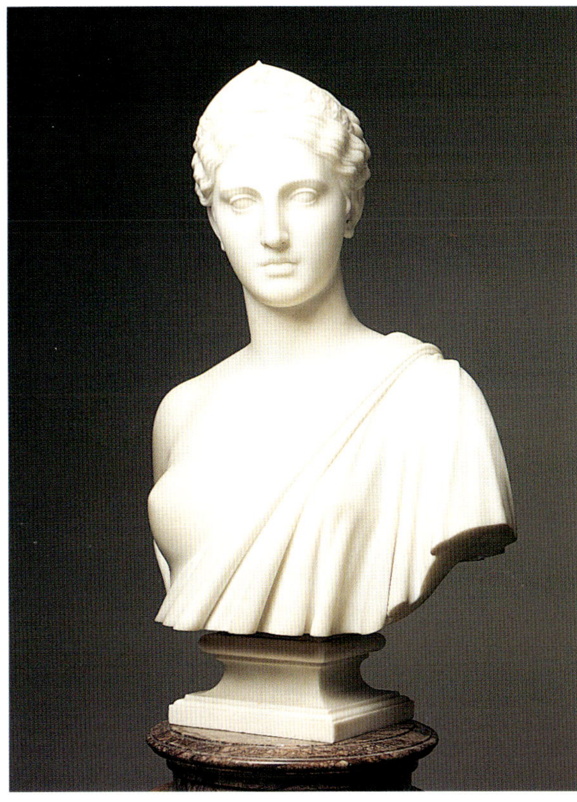

Fig. 13. Hiram Powers, *America*, 1860. White and polychrome marble, 71.1 cm. Dallas Museum of Art, gift of Eleanor and C. Thomas May, Jr., 1983.147.

The ingrained tradition of basing artworks on classical prototypes —a process built into academic art training, which involved copying

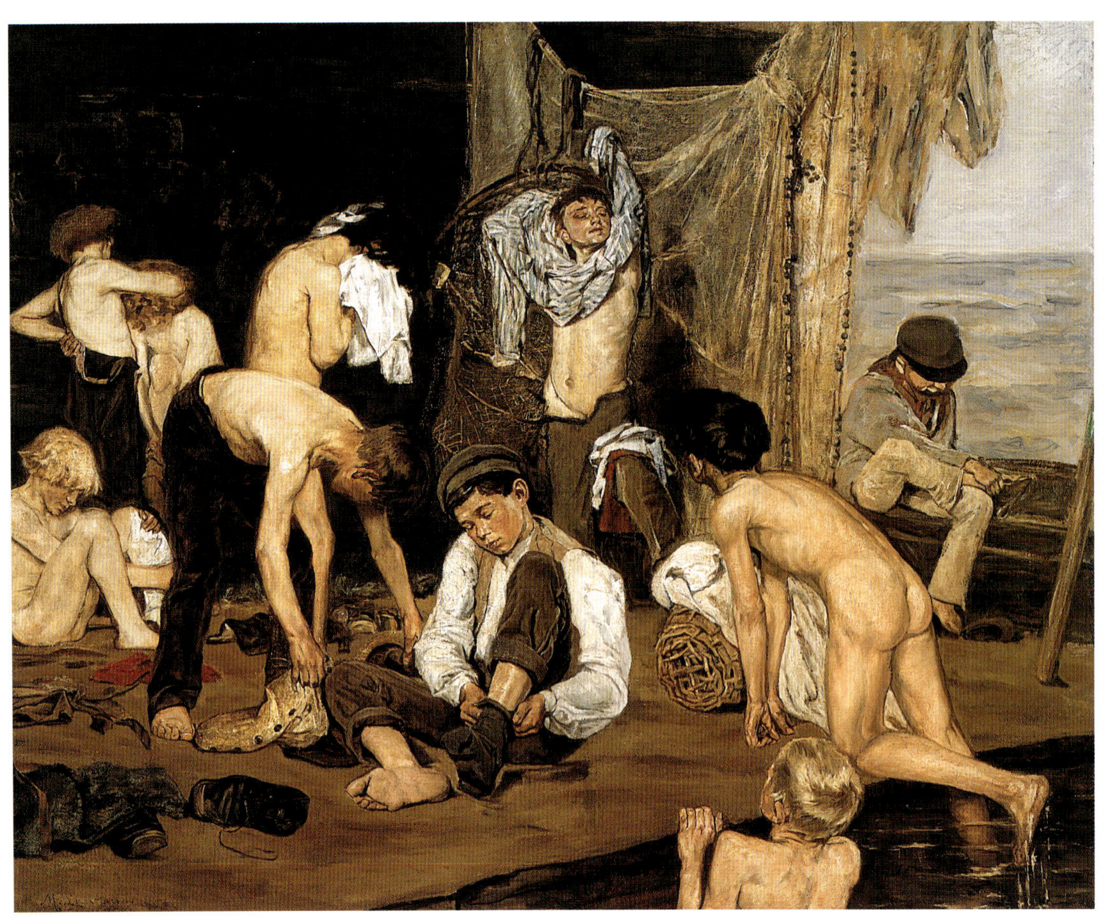

Fig. 14. Max Liebermann, *Im Schwimmbad,* 1875–1878. Oil on canvas, 181 × 225.1 cm. Dallas Museum of Art, Foundation for the Arts Collection, Mrs. John B. O'Hara Fund, 1988.16.FA.

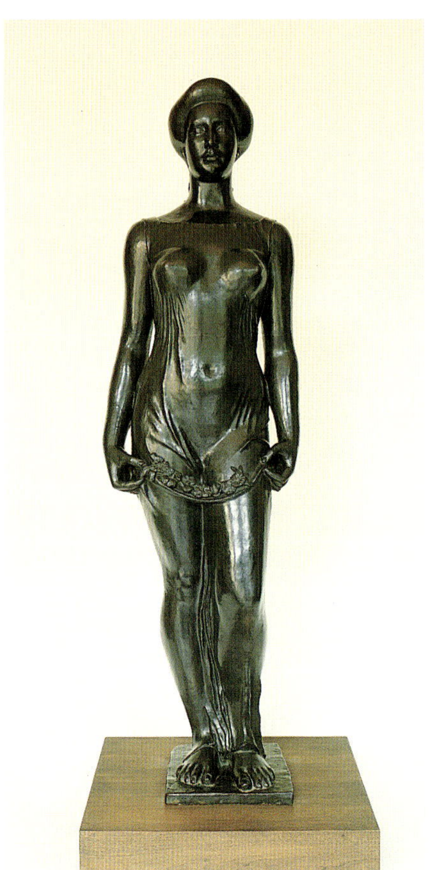

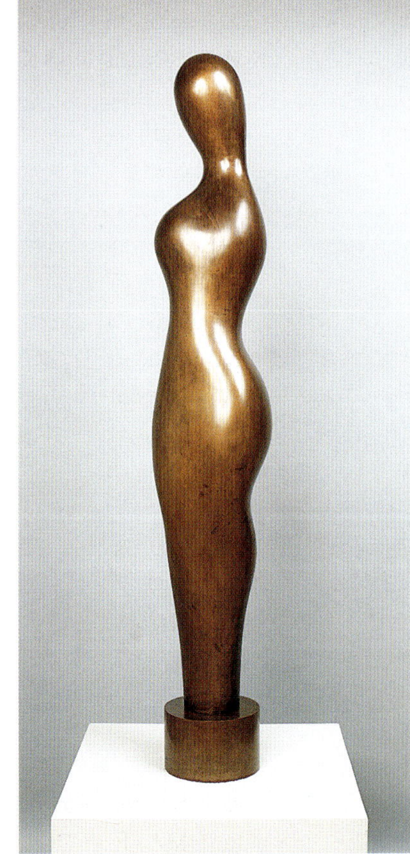

Fig. 15. Aristide Maillol, *Flora,* 1911. Bronze, 165.1 × 48.3 × 34.3 cm. Dallas Museum of Art, gift of Mr. and Mrs. Eugene McDermott, 1960.70.

Fig. 16. Jean Arp, *Sculpture Classique,* 1960. Bronze, 127 × 22.2 × 20.3 cm. Dallas Museum of Art, Foundation for the Arts Collection, given in memory of Mary Seeger O'Boyle by her family and friends, 1966.13.FA.

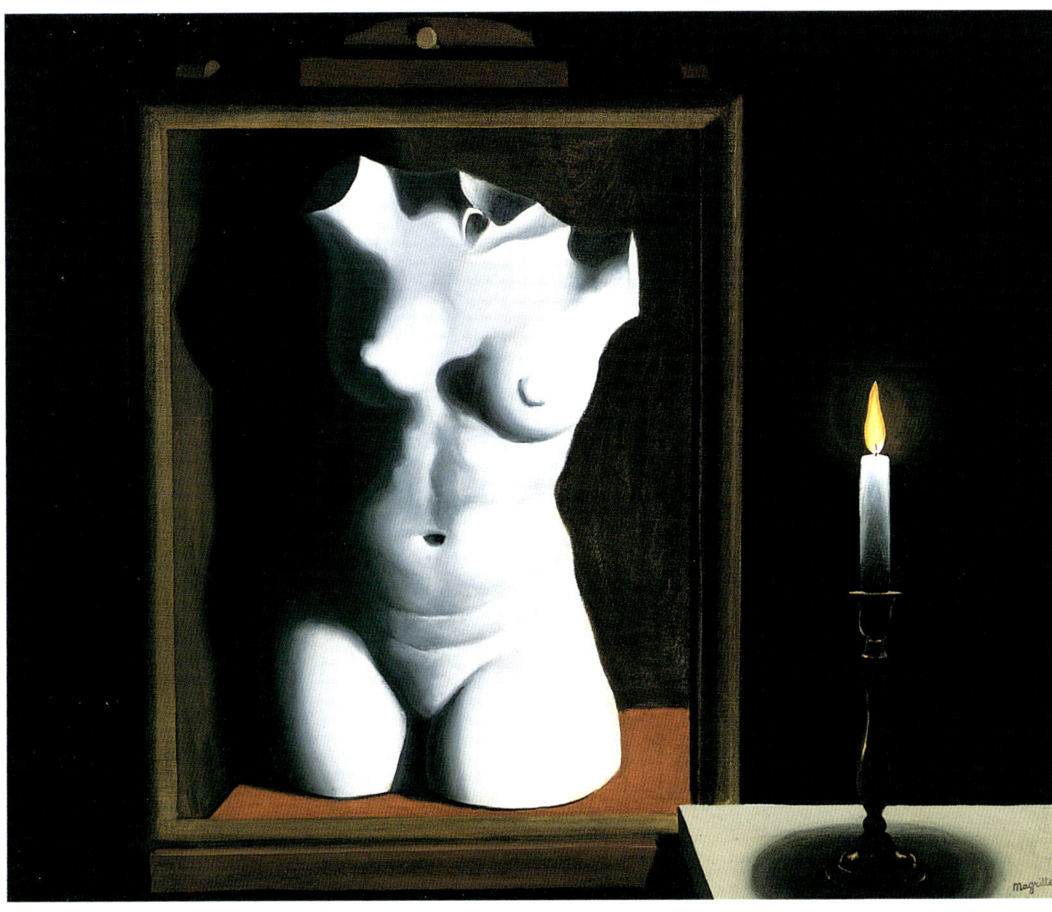

Fig. 17. René Magritte, *The Light of Coincidences*, 1933. Oil on canvas, 60 × 73 cm. Dallas Museum of Art, gift of Mr. and Mrs. Jake L. Hamon, 1981.9.

antique sculptures—appears in surprising places. The realist painting of German artist Max Liebermann, as seen here in *Im Schwimmbad* (The Swimming Hole; fig. 14), presents a scene of young boys bathing. Several of the boys hark back to Michelangelo's nude figures and even further back to ancient art. The youth sitting cross-legged is modeled after ancient versions of the Spinario (third century B.C., Museo Capitolino, Rome), which depicts a boy pulling a thorn from his foot.

Twentieth-century artists engaged in more radically abstract ways of reimagining ancient art. The earthy grace of Aristide Maillol's *Flora* (fig. 15) returns to the nature cults of antiquity. This personification of Spring is depicted with all the elements of freshness and fertility that characterize the maiden daughter of Demeter, Persephone. Evoking the vitality of youth through the vision of the classical past, the eternally young girl, poised erect and facing front with arms at her sides, is the modern version of ancient kore (maiden) statues, which once epitomized the feminine beauty of Archaic Greece. Maillol was inspired by Auguste Rodin's sculpture and by Archaic Greek statues to produce a smoothly abstract, columnar female form. The piece is a statuesque descendant of the DMA's stylized marble fertility figurines (cat. nos. 15 and 16).

In Jean Arp's work *Sculpture Classique* (fig. 16) the classical double S curve of the DMA's fourth-century-B.C. Attic grave figure

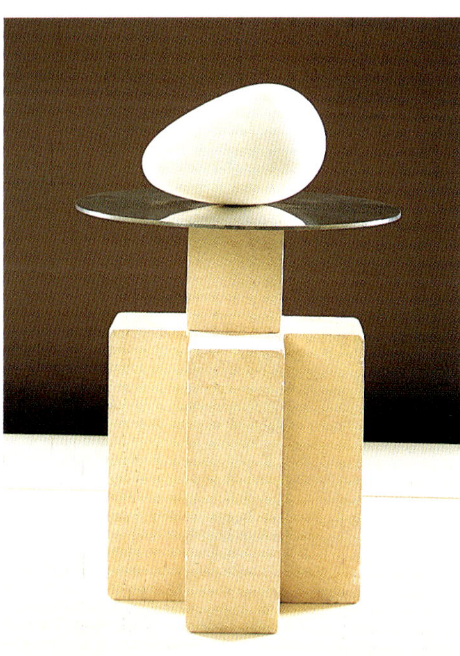

Fig. 18. Constantin Brancusi, *Beginning of the World*, c. 1920. Marble, metal, and stone, 76.2 × 50.8 × 50.8 cm. Dallas Museum of Art, Foundation for the Arts Collection, gift of Mr. and Mrs. James H. Clark, 1977.51.FA.

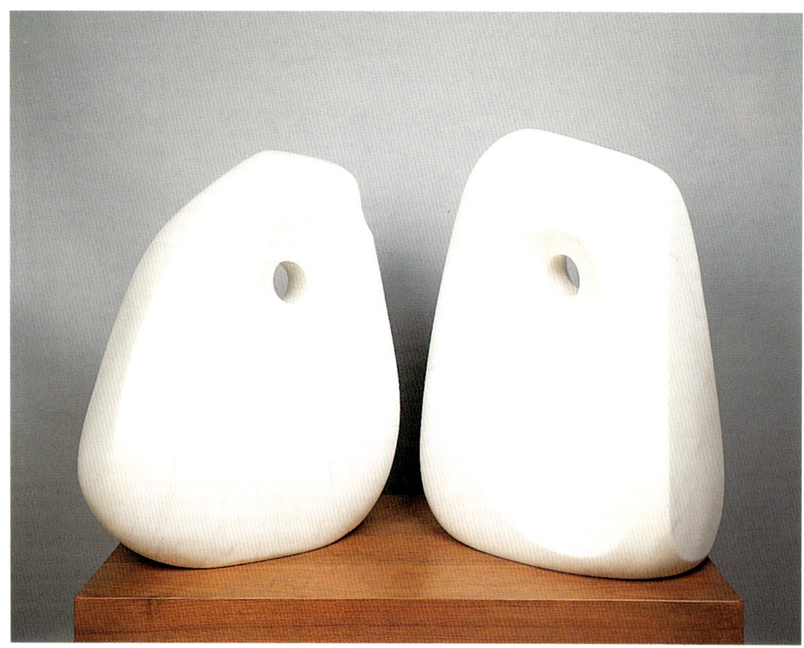

Fig. 19. Barbara Hepworth, *Contrapuntal Forms (Mycenae)*, 1965. Carrara marble and teakwood, 95.3 × 130.8 × 64.8 cm. Dallas Museum of Art, gift of Mr. and Mrs. James H. Clark, 1971.94.

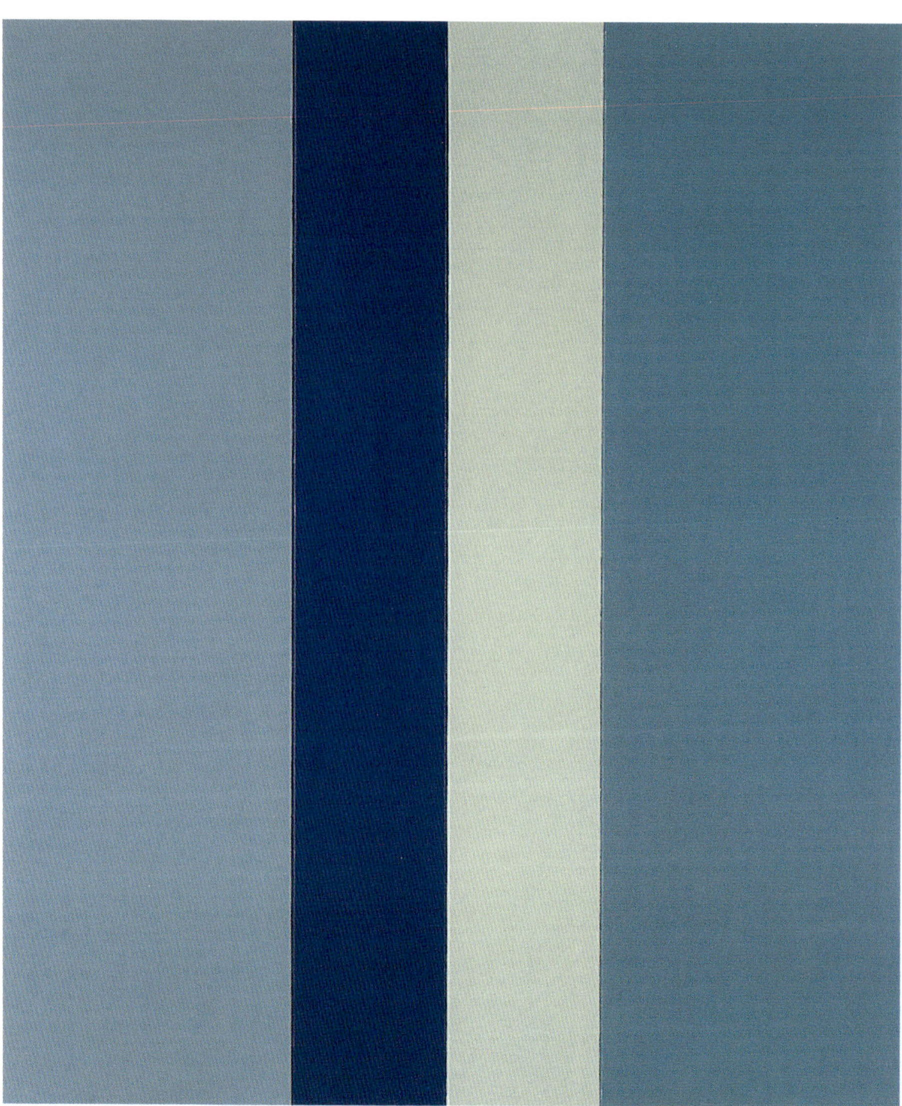

Fig. 20. Brice Marden, *To Corfu*, 1976. Oil and wax on canvas, 213.4 × 184.2 cm. Dallas Museum of Art, Foundation for the Arts Collection, anonymous gift, 1976.23.FA.

(cat. no. 30), which exhibits such a noble *contrapposto* of forms, is reduced to a purely abstract shape. Unlike the Maillol figure, the human body is barely indicated. The classical reference is pure form alone.

Other twentieth-century artists were equally abstruse in their invocations of the classical past. René Magritte's *The Light of Coincidences* (fig. 17) displays the classical nude torso of a woman in a way that cannot be understood logically. While the figure refers to fragmented statues of Aphrodite, the harshly illuminated image placed within a box removes the ancient image from accepted contexts and places it in an illusionistic world similar to surrealism. What is art and what is the real world become interchangeable. Although Magritte himself denied his connections with surrealism per se, saying "the mind loves the unknown" and "it is the power of enchantment which matters" (Ashton 1985, 47–48), he devoted his life to creating fantastic conjunctions that transform the everyday into a dream world. Ancient sculpture becomes one more detached object in this hallucinatory scene.

Abstraction freed artists from the literalism of copying the antique. If the Liebermann painting (fig. 14) very distantly recalls a classical statue, Constantin Brancusi's *Beginning of the World* (fig. 18) is Platonic in the truest sense. The Greek philosopher Plato considered circle and sphere to be the most perfect geometric forms and mathematics to be a paradigm of ultimate reality. Brancusi's splendidly austere marble egg, metal disk, and cross-shaped stone pedestal are a twentieth-century visual equivalent of Plato's divine geometry.

The sense of nature and place in ancient art, which was a fundamental part of Greco-Roman religion, also inspired contemporary artists. The purity and power of Mediterranean landscapes still appeals to the imagination. Barbara Hepworth's sculpture *Contrapuntal Forms (Mycenae)* (fig. 19) and Brice Marden's encaustic painting *To Corfu* (fig. 20), both in the DMA collections, reflect a profound immersion in the natural world of Greece, with its brilliant light and clarity of form.

Classical myth speaks to us today, as Plato does, because it deals with universal human experiences. The great cultural images of the ancient world were not about received truths or consoling faiths. They were about painful conflicts, unanswerable questions, ambiguous gods, and suffering human beings. Out of this somber view of human life, ancient artists created sublimely beautiful forms, testaments to the power of human will and imagination. It is that tension between form and content that still inspires people today. As William Butler Yeats said, "a terrible beauty is born"; it is an epitaph for the twentieth century.

References

Adcock 1967: Adcock, F. E. *The Greek and Macedonian Art of War* (Berkeley 1967).

Amandry 1953: Amandry, P. *Collection Hélène Stathatos: Les bijoux antiques* (Strasbourg 1953).

Amyx 1965: Amyx, D. A. "Some Etrusco-Corinthian Vase-Painters." In G. Becatti, et al., eds. *Studi in onore di Luisa Banti* (Rome 1965).

Amyx 1988: Amyx, D. A. *Corinthian Vase-Painting of the Archaic Period*. Vol. 2 (Berkeley 1988).

Anderson 1961: Anderson, J. K. *Ancient Greek Horsemanship* (Berkeley 1961).

Andrén 1940: Andrén, A. *Architectural Terracottas from Etrusco-Italic Temples* (Lund, Sweden 1940).

Ashton 1985: Ashton, D. *Twentieth-Century Artists on Art* (New York 1985).

Athanassakis 1976: Athanassakis, A. N., trans. *The Homeric Hymns* (Baltimore 1976).

Axmann 1986: Axmann, U. *Hellenistische Schmuckmedaillons* (Berlin 1986).

Basta 1982: Basta, M. *Saqqara*. Simpkins Splendor of Egypt, bk. 2 (Salt Lake City 1982).

Beazley 1951: Beazley, J. D. *The Development of Attic Black-Figure* (Berkeley and Los Angeles 1951).

Beazley 1956: Beazley, J. D. *Attic Black-Figure Vase-Painters* (Oxford 1956).

Beazley 1963: Beazley, J. D. *Attic Red-Figure Vase-Painters*. 2d ed. Vol. 2 (Oxford 1963).

Beazley 1971: Beazley, J. D. *Paralipomena: Additions to Attic Black-Figure Vase-Painters and to Attic Red-Figure Vase-Painters*. 2d ed. (Oxford 1971).

Bianchi Bandinelli 1971: Bianchi Bandinelli, R. *Rome: The Late Empire, Roman Art* A.D. *200–400* Trans. by P. Green (New York 1971).

Bieber 1962: Bieber, M. "The Copies of the Herculaneum Women." *Proceedings of the American Philosophical Society* 106, no. 2 (1962): 111–34.

Boardman 1974: Boardman, J. *Athenian Black Figure Vases* (New York 1974).

Boetzkes 1921: Boetzkes, R. "Kerykeion." In A. F. von Pauly and G. Wissowa, *Real- Encyclopädie der klassischen Altertumswissenschaft*. Vol. 11 (Stuttgart 1921).

Bothmer 1965: Bothmer, D. von. Letter to M. C. Rueppel. 21 September. DMA object file no. 1965.29.M.

Bothmer 1990: Bothmer, D. von, ed. *Glories of the Past: Ancient Art from the Shelby White and Leon Levy Collection* (New York 1990).

Bottini 1988: Bottini, A. "Apulisch-korinthische Helme." In *Antike-Helme: Sammlung Lipperheide und andere Bestände des Antikenmuseums Berlin*. Romisch-Germanisches Zentralmuseum, Forschungsinstitut für Vor- und Fruhgeschichte, Monographien, Band (Volume) 14 (Mainz 1988).

Bourriau 1988: Bourriau, J. *Pharaohs and Mortals: Egyptian Art in the Middle Kingdom* (Cambridge 1988).

Brendel 1978: Brendel, O. J. *Etruscan Art* (New York 1978).

Bromberg 1979: Bromberg, A. *A Guide to the Collections: Dallas Museum of Fine Arts* (Dallas 1979).

Bromberg 1983: Bromberg, A. R. *Dallas Museum of Art: Selected Works* (Dallas 1983).

Bromberg 1990: Bromberg, A. R. *Gold of Greece: Jewelry and Ornaments from the Benaki Museum*. Rev. text (Dallas 1990).

Brommer 1973: Brommer, F. *Vasenlisten zur griechischen Heldensage*. 3d ed. (Marburg 1973).

The Brooklyn Museum 1966: The Brooklyn Museum. *The Pomerance Collection of Ancient Art* (Brooklyn 1966).

Brovarski 1989: Brovarski, E. "The Tomb of Ny-Ankh-Nesut." Abstract presented at the annual meeting of the American Research Center in Egypt, Philadelphia, Penn., 21–23 April 1989.

Brown 1960: Brown, W. L. *The Etruscan Lion* (Oxford 1960).

Brown 1972: Brown, A. C. "Recent Museum Acquisitions." *Burlington Magazine* 114, no. 831 (1972): 399–404.

Brown 1973: Brown, B. R. *Anticlassicism in Greek Sculpture of the Fourth Century* B.C. (New York 1973).

Cameron and Kuhrt 1983: Cameron, A., and A. Kuhrt, eds. *Images of Women in Antiquity* (Detroit 1983).

Carducci 1963: Carducci, C. *Gold and Silver Treasures of Ancient Italy* (Greenwich, Conn. 1963).

Carnegie Institute 1964: Carnegie Institute, Museum of Art. *Ancient Bronzes: A Selection from the Heckett Collection* (Pittsburgh 1964).

Carpenter 1986: Carpenter, T. H. *Dionysian Imagery in Archaic Greek Art: Its Development in Black-Figure Painting* (Oxford 1986).

Carravetta 1991: Carravetta, P. *Prefaces to the Diaphora: Rhetorics, Allegory, and the Interpretation of Postmodernity* (West Lafayette, Ind. 1991).

Chesterman 1974: Chesterman, J. *Classical Terracotta Figures* (London 1974).

Clairmont 1966: Clairmont, C. *Die Bildnisse des Antinous: Ein Beitrag zur Porträtplastik unter Kaiser Hadrian*. Bibliotheca Helvetica Romana, vol. 6 (Rome 1966).

Clairmont 1993: Clairmont, C. *Classical Attic Tombstones*. Vol. 2 (Kilchberg, Switzerland 1993).

Coldstream 1977: Coldstream, J. N. *Geometric Greece* (New York 1977).

Comstock and Vermeule 1971: Comstock, M. and C. Vermeule. *Greek, Etruscan, and Roman Bronzes in the Museum of Fine Arts Boston* (Greenwich, Conn. 1971).

Cristofani and Martelli 1983: Cristofani, M. and M. Martelli, eds. *L'Oro degli Etruschi* (Novara, Italy 1983).

Crome 1938–39: Crome, J. F. "Kerykeia." *Mitteilungen des Deutschen Archäologischen Instituts, Athenische Abteilung* 63–64 (1938–39): 117–26.

Curtis 1988: Curtis, J., et al. *Bronzeworking Centres of Western Asia, c. 1000–539 B.C.* (London 1988).

Cygielman 1990: Cygielman, M. *Ori e argenti nelle collezioni del Museo Archeologico di Firenze* (Florence 1990).

D'Auria, Lacovara, and Roehrig 1988: D'Auria, S., P. Lacovara, and C. Roehrig. *Mummies and Magic: The Funerary Arts of Ancient Egypt* (Boston 1988).

Deppert-Lippitz 1985: Deppert-Lippitz, B. *Griechischer Goldschmuck* (Mainz 1985).

Diepolder 1931: Diepolder, H. *Die attischen Grabreliefs des 5. und 4. Jahrhunderts v. Chr.* (Berlin 1931).

Dils 1991: Dils, P. "Twee sarcofagen van Iahtesnacht." In E. Guleb, ed., *Van Nijl tot Schelde* (Brussels 1991).

DMA 1992: Dallas Museum of Art. "What's New." *Dallas Museum of Art Agenda* 1, no. 4 (March/April 1992): 2–8.

DMFA 1966: Dallas Museum of Fine Arts. "New Accessions." *Dallas Museum of Fine Arts Newsletter* (February 1966).

DMFA 1968: Dallas Museum of Fine Arts. "New Accession." *Dallas Museum of Fine Arts Newsletter* (November 1968).

DMFA 1970: Dallas Museum of Fine Arts. "New Accession." *Dallas Museum of Fine Arts Newsletter* (April 1970).

DMFA 1973: Dallas Museum of Fine Arts. "New Accession." *Dallas Museum of Fine Arts Newsletter* (March 1973).

Doeringer 1970: Doeringer, S., et al., eds. *Art and Technology: A Symposium on Classical Bronzes* (Cambridge, Mass. 1970).

Dörig 1975: Dörig, J. *Art Antique: Collections privées de Suisse romande* (Geneva and Mainz 1975).

Doumas 1983: Doumas, C. *Cycladic Art: Ancient Sculpture and Pottery from the N. P. Goulandris Collection* (London 1983).

Dover 1978: Dover, K. J. *Greek Homosexuality* (London 1978).

Egyptian Museum Berlin 1990: *Egyptian Museum Berlin*. 4th ed. (Berlin 1990).

Fantham 1994: Fantham, E., et al. *Women in the Classical World: Image and Text* (New York 1994).

Fazzini 1989: Fazzini, R., et al. *Ancient Egyptian Art in the Brooklyn Museum* (New York 1989).

Finkenstaedt 1988: Finkenstaedt, E. "Egyptian Pottery." *The Bulletin of the Cleveland Museum of Art* 75, no. 3 (1988): 74–94.

Fitts 1956: Fitts, D. *Poems from the Greek Anthology*. 3d ed. (New York 1956).

Fittschen and Zanker 1985: Fittschen, K., and P. Zanker. *Katalog der römischen Porträts in den Capitolinischen Museen und den anderen kommunalen Sammlungen der Stadt Rom*. Vol. 1, Tafeln (Plates) (Mainz 1985).

Forbes 1966: Forbes, J. R. *Studies in Ancient Technology*. Vol. 5 (Leiden 1966).

Freed 1987: Freed, R. *Ramses II: The Great Pharaoh and His Time* (Denver 1987).

Friis Johansen 1951: Friis Johansen, K. *The Attic Grave-Reliefs of the Classical Period: An Essay in Interpretation* (Copenhagen 1951).

Furtwängler 1890: Furtwängler, A. *Die Bronzen und die übrigen kleinenen Funde von Olympia*. Vol. 4, Tafelband (Plates) (Berlin 1890).

Gardiner 1933–1958: Gardiner, A. H., ed. *The Temple of King Sethos I at Abydos*. 4 vols. (London and Chicago 1933–1958).

Gazette des beaux-arts 1973: *Gazette des beaux-arts supplément*. "La Chronique des arts: Editorial." 81, no. 1249 (1973): 1–279.

Gazette des beaux-arts 1985: *Gazette des beaux-arts supplément*. "La Chronique des arts: Principales acquisitions des musées en 1984." 105, no. 1394 (1985): 1–84.

Ghirshman 1964: Ghirshman, R. *The Arts of Ancient Iran: From Its Origins to the Time of Alexander the Great*. Trans. by S. Green and J. Emmons (New York 1964).

Godard 1965: Godard, A. *The Art of Iran* (New York and Washington, D.C. 1965).

Grace 1939: Grace, F. R. *Archaic Sculpture in Boeotia* (Cambridge, Mass. 1939).

Greenhalgh 1973: Greenhalgh, P. A. L. *Early Greek Warfare: The Horsemen and Chariots in the Homeric and Archaic Ages* (Cambridge, England 1973).

Greifenhagen 1929: Greifenhagen, A. *Eine attische schwarzfigurige Vasengattung und die Darstellung des Komos im VI Jahrhundert* (Königsberg 1929).

Greifenhagen 1970: Greifenhagen, A. *Fundgruppen*. Vol. 1 of *Schmuckarbeiten in Edelmetall* (Berlin 1970).

Grimm 1974: Grimm, G. *Die römischen Mumienmasken aus Ägypten* (Wiesbaden, Germany 1974).

Grummond 1981: Grummond, N. Thomson de. "Reflections on the Etruscan Mirror." *Archaeology* 34, no. 5 (1981): 54–58.

Grummond 1982: Grummond, N. Thomson de. *A Guide to Etruscan Mirrors* (Tallahassee, Fla. 1982).

Hall 1987: Hall, E. S., ed. *Antiquities from the Collection of Christos G. Bastis* (Mainz 1987).

Harden 1956: Harden, D. B. "Glass and Glazes." In *The Mediterranean Civilization and the Middle Ages c. 700 B.C. to c. A.D. 1500*, vol. 2 of *The History of Technology* (Oxford 1956).

Harden 1969: Harden, D. B. "Ancient Glass, II: Roman." *Archaeological Journal* 126 (1969): 44–77.

Harris 1964: Harris, H. A. *Greek Athletes and Athletics* (London 1964).

Harrison 1953: Harrison, E. *Portrait Sculpture*. The Athenian Agora, vol. 1 (Princeton 1953).

Hase 1969: Hase, F. W. von. *Die Trensen der Früheisenzeit in Italien*. Prähistorische Bronzefunde, Abteilung (Section) 16, vol. 1 (Munich 1969).

Hase 1982: Hase, F. W. von. "Ein unbekannter apulisch-korinthinischer Helm im Reiss-Museum." *Mannheimer Hefte* 2 (1982): 99–108.

Hayes 1990a: Hayes, W. C. *The Scepter of Egypt: A Background for the Study of the Egyptian Antiquities in The Metropolitan Museum of Art*. Part 1. Rev. ed. (Cambridge, Mass. 1990).

Hayes 1990b: Hayes, W. C. *The Scepter of Egypt: A Background for the Study of the Egyptian Antiquities in The Metropolitan Museum of Art*. Part 2. Rev. ed. (Cambridge, Mass. 1990).

Haynes 1985: Haynes, S. *Etruscan Bronzes* (London 1985).

Herrmann 1968: Herrmann, H.-V. "Frühgriechischer Pferdeschmuck vom Luristan-typus," *Jahrbuch des Deutschen Archäologischen Instituts* 83 (1968): 1–38.

Higgins 1967: Higgins, R. A. *Greek Terracottas* (London 1967).

Higgins 1980: Higgins, R. A. *Greek and Roman Jewellery*. 2d ed. (London 1980).

Hill 1955: Hill, D. K. "Six Early Greek Animals." *American Journal of Archaeology* 59, no. 1 (1955): 39–44.

Hoffmann 1964: Hoffmann, H., ed. *Norbert Schimmel Collection: Fogg Art Museum of Harvard University* (Mainz 1964).

Hoffmann 1970: Hoffmann, H. *Ten Centuries That Shaped the West: Greek and Roman Art in Texas Collections* (Houston 1970).

Hoffmann and Davidson 1965: Hoffmann, H., and P. Davidson. *Greek Gold: Jewelry from the Age of Alexander* (Mainz 1965).

Hornbostel 1979: Hornbostel, W. "Syrakosion Damosion: Zu einem bronzenen Heroldstab." *Jahrbuch der Hamburger Kunstsammlungen* 24 (1979): 33–62.

Hornung 1991: Hornung, E. *The Tomb of Pharaoh Seti I* (Zurich 1991).

Hôtel Drouot 1972: Hôtel Drouot (Paris). "Bronzes antiques des steppes et de l'Iran: Collection D. David-Weill." Sale catalogue (28–29 June 1972).

Inan and Rosenbaum 1966: Inan, J., and E. Rosenbaum. *Roman and Early Byzantine Portrait Sculpture in Asia Minor* (London 1966).

Israel 1966: Israel, G. *The Art of Amlash: From the Collection of Galerie Israel* (New York 1966).

Jucker 1991: Jucker, I. *Italy of the Etruscans* (Jerusalem and Mainz 1991).

Juliis 1984: Juliis, M. de, et al. *Gli ori di Taranto in età ellenistica* (Milan 1984).

Kilinski 1978: Kilinski, K., II. "The Boeotian Dancers Group," *American Journal of Archaeology* 82, no. 2 (1978): 173–91.

Kilinski 1981a: Kilinski, K., II. "Boeotian Black-Figure Tripod-Kothon." In H. A. Shapiro, *Art, Myth, and Culture: Greek Vases from Southern Collections* (New Orleans 1981).

Kilinski 1981b: Kilinski, K., II. "Attic Black-Figure Eye-Cup." In H. A. Shapiro, *Art, Myth, and Culture: Greek Vases from Southern Collections* (New Orleans 1981).

Kilinski 1981c: Kilinski, K., II. "Attic Black-Figure Column Krater." In H. A. Shapiro, *Art, Myth, and Culture: Greek Vases from Southern Collections* (New Orleans 1981).

Kilinski 1983: Kilinski, K., II. "An Archaic Etruscan Head of Terra Cotta," *Dallas Museum of Fine Arts Bulletin* (Spring 1983): cover, 1–2.

Kilinski 1990: Kilinski, K., II. *Boeotian Black Figure Vase Painting of the Archaic Period* (Mainz 1990).

Kleiner 1992: Kleiner, D. E. E. *Roman Sculpture* (New Haven and London 1992).

Klengel 1972: Klengel, H. *The Art of Ancient Syria* (South Brunswick, N.J. and New York 1972).

Kozloff and Mitten 1988: Kozloff, A. P., and D. G. Mitten. *The Gods Delight: The Human Figure in Classical Bronze* (Cleveland 1988).

Kraiker 1930: Kraiker, W. "Pheidippos," *Mitteilungen des Deutschen Archäologischen Instituts, Athenische Abteilung* 55 (1930): 167–80.

Kraus 1967: Kraus, T., ed. *Das Römische Weltreich*. Propyläen Kunstgeschichte, vol. 2 (Berlin 1967).

Kurtz 1983: Kurtz, D. C. Review of *Art, Myth, and Culture: Greek Vases from Southern Collections*, by H. A. Shapiro. *The Journal of Hellenic Studies* 103 (1983): 220.

Kurtz and Boardman 1971: Kurtz, D. C., and J. Boardman, *Greek Burial Customs*. Aspects of Greek and Roman Life (Ithaca, N.Y. 1971).

Lacey 1968: Lacey, W. K. *The Family in Classical Greece*. (Ithaca, N.Y. 1968).

Lawler 1964: Lawler, L. B. *The Dance in Ancient Greece* (Middletown, Conn. 1964).

Leipen 1994: Leipen, N. "Atlas, the Titan Who Supported the Sky." In *Tranquillitas: Mélanges en l'honneur de Tran tam Tinh*. Collection Hier pour aujourd'hui (Quebec 1994).

Leoni 1726: Leoni, G., trans. *De re aedificatoria* by Leon Battista Alberti (London 1726).

Lichtheim 1973: Lichtheim, M. *Ancient Egyptian Literature: A Book of Readings*. Vol. 1, *The Old and Middle Kingdoms* (Berkeley and Los Angeles 1973).

LIMC 1981: *Lexicon Iconographicum Mythologiae Classicae*. Vol. 1, part 1 (Zurich and Munich 1981).

LIMC 1988: *Lexicon Iconographicum Mythologiae Classicae*. Vol. 4, parts 1 and 2 (Zurich and Munich 1988).

LIMC 1990: *Lexicon Iconographicum Mythologiae Classicae*. Vol. 5, part 1 (Zurich and Munich 1990).

Littauer and Crouwel 1979: Littauer, M. A., and J. H. Crouwel. *Wheeled Vehicles and Ridden Animals in the Ancient Near East*. Handbuch der Orientalistik (Leiden and Köln 1979).

Marshall 1911: Marshall, F. H. *Catalogue of the Jewellery, Greek, Etruscan, and Roman, in the Departments of Antiquities, British Museum* (London 1911).

The Metropolitan Museum of Art 1968: "Anatolia." *The Metropolitan Museum of Art Bulletin* 26, no. 5 (January 1968).

The Metropolitan Museum of Art 1992: "Ancient Art: Gifts from The Norbert Schimmel Collection." *The Metropolitan Museum of Art Bulletin* 69, no. 4 (1992): 1–64.

Michalowski 1969: Michalowski, K. *Art of Ancient Egypt* (New York 1969).

Mitten and Doeringer 1967: Mitten, D. G., and S. F. Doeringer. *Master Bronzes from the Classical World* (Cambridge, Mass. and Mainz 1967).

Moorey 1971: Moorey, P. R. S. *Catalogue of the Ancient Persian Bronzes in the Ashmolean Museum* (Oxford 1971).

Moorey 1981: Moorey, P. R. S., et al. *Ancient Bronzes, Ceramics and Seals* (Los Angeles 1981).

Muscarella 1974: Muscarella, O. W., ed. *Ancient Art: The Norbert Schimmel Collection* (Mainz 1974).

Muscarella 1981: Muscarella, O. W., et al. *Ladders to Heaven* (Toronto 1981).

Muscarella 1988: Muscarella, O. W. *Bronze and Iron: Ancient Near Eastern Artifacts in The Metropolitan Museum of Art* (New York 1988).

Nash 1984: Nash, S. A. "Egyptian Bust of Seti I Acquired in Honor of Betty Marcus." *Dallas Museum of Art Bulletin* (Fall 1984): 1.

Neugebauer 1931: Neugebauer, K. A. *Die Minoischen und Archaisch Griechischen Bronzen*. Vol. 1 of *Katalog der Statuarischen Bronzen im Antiquarium: Staatliche Museen zu Berlin* (Berlin 1931).

Oakley 1993: Oakley, J. H. *The Wedding in Ancient Athens* (Madison, Wis. 1993).

Oliver 1966: Oliver, A. "Greek, Roman, and Etruscan Jewelry." *The Metropolitan Museum of Art Bulletin* 24, no. 9 (May 1966): 269–84.

On View 1974: *On View: A Guide to Museums and Gallery Acquisitions in Great Britain and America* 8 (London 1974): 79.

Pallottino 1975: Pallottino, M. *The Etruscans*. Rev. ed. (Bloomington, Ind. 1975).

Parlasca 1966: Parlasca, K. *Mumienporträts und verwandte Denkmäler* (Wiesbaden 1966).

Petrie 1891: Petrie, W. M. F. *Illahun, Kahun and Gurob 1889–90* (London 1891).

Piggott 1983: Piggott, S. *The Earliest Wheeled Transport: From the Atlantic Coast to the Caspian Sea* (Ithaca, N.Y. 1983).

Pomeroy 1975: Pomeroy, S. B. *Goddesses, Whores, Wives, and Slaves: Women in Classical Antiquity* (New York 1975).

Porada 1965: Porada, E. *The Art of Ancient Iran* (1962; reprint, New York 1965).

Price 1976: Price, J. "Glass." In D. Strong and D. Brown, eds., *Roman Crafts* (New York 1976).

Rawlinson 1910: Rawlinson, G., trans. *The History of Herodotus* (London and New York 1910).

Reeder 1995: Reeder, E. *Pandora: Women in Classical Greece* (Baltimore 1995).

Renfrew 1991: Renfrew, C. *The Cycladic Spirit: Masterpieces from the Nicholas P. Goulandris Collection* (New York 1991).

Richardson 1964: Richardson, E. *The Etruscans: Their Art and Civilization*. (Chicago 1964).

Richter 1940: Richter, G. M. A. *Handbook of the Etruscan Collection: The Metropolitan Museum of Art* (New York 1940).

Richter 1951: Richter, G. M. A. "Who Made the Roman Portrait Statues—Greeks or Romans?" *Proceedings of the American Philosophical Society* 95 (1951): 184–208.

Rieu 1945: Rieu, E. V., trans. *The Odyssey*, by Homer (Harmondsworth, England and New York 1945).

Roberts 1978: Roberts, S. R. *The Attic Pyxis* (Chicago 1978).

Roberts 1982: Roberts, H. S. "Later Etruscan Mirrors: Evidence for Dating from Recent Excavations." *Analecta Romana Instituti Danici* 11 (1982): 31–54.

Robertson 1975: Robertson, M. *A History of Greek Art*. Vol. 1 (London and New York 1975).

Saleh and Sourouzian 1987: Saleh, M., and H. Sourouzian. *The Egyptian Museum Cairo* (Mainz 1987).

Scott 1986: Scott, G. D., III. *Ancient Egyptian Art at Yale* (New Haven 1986).

Seeberg 1971: Seeberg, A. *Corinthian Komos Vases* (London 1971).

Shapiro 1981: Shapiro, H. A. "Greek Vases in Southern Collections." *Arts Quarterly of the New Orleans Museum of Art* 3, no. 4 (1981): 1, 3–5.

Smith 1976: Smith, H. R. W. *Funerary Symbolism in Apulian Vase-Painting* (Berkeley 1976).

Smith 1978: Smith, W. S. *A History of Egyptian Painting and Sculpture in the Old Kingdom* (1946; reprint, New York 1978).

Snodgrass 1967: Snodgrass, A. M. *Arms and Armour of the Greeks*. Aspects of Greek and Roman Life (Ithaca, N.Y. 1967).

Sotheby Parke Bernet 1978: Sotheby Parke Bernet & Company (London). "Egyptian, Middle Eastern, Greek, Etruscan and Roman Antiquities." Sale catalogue (10 April 1978).

Spanel 1988. Spanel, D. *Through Ancient Eyes: Egyptian Portraiture* (Birmingham, Ala. 1988).

Stary 1986: Stary, P. "Italische Helme des I Jahrtausends vor Christus." In J. Swaddling, ed., *Italian Iron Age Artifacts in the British Museum* (London 1986).

Stewart 1990: Stewart, A. *Greek Sculpture: An Exploration*. Vol. 1 (New Haven, Conn. 1990).

Stupperich 1994: Stupperich, R. "Fragmentanpassungen bei attischen Grabreliefs." *Thetis: Mannheimer Beiträge zur Klassischen Archäologie und Geschichte Griechenlands und Zyperns*. Band (Volume) 1 (1994): 53–62.

Sweet 1987: Sweet, W. E. *Sport and Recreation in Ancient Greece* (New York 1987).

Szilágyi 1967: Szilágyi, J. G. "Etrusko-korinthische polychrome Vasen." *Die Griechische Vase: Wissenschaftliche Zeitschrift der Universität Rostock* 16, Heft 7/8 (1967): 543–53.

Szilágyi 1975: Szilágyi, J. G. *Etruszko-Korinthosi Vázafestészet* (Budapest 1975).

Szilágyi 1976: Szilágyi, J. G. "Entwurf der Geschichte der etrusko-korinthischen figürlichen Vasenmalerei." In A. Alföldi, ed., *Römische Frühgeschichte: Kritik und Forschung seit 1964* (Heidelberg 1976).

Taylor 1991: Taylor, J. H. Letter to Nicholas Reeves. December 1991. DMA object file no. 1994.184.

Ternbach 1969: Ternbach, J. "Technical Notes on the Restoration of a Greek Marble Statue." *Collection Latomus* 103 (1969): 651–54.

Terrace 1962: Terrace, E. *The Art of the Ancient Near East in Boston* (Boston 1962).

Terrace 1964: Terrace, E. L. B. "Recent Acquisitions in the Department of Egyptian Art." Museum of Fine Arts, Boston *Bulletin* 62, no. 328 (1964): 48–64.

Thimme 1977: Thimme, J., ed. *Art and Culture of the Cyclades: In the Third Millennium* B.C. (Chicago 1977).

Tiverios 1976: Tiverios, M. A. *Ho Ludos kai to Ergo Tou* (Athens 1976).

Tiverios 1981: Tiverios, M. A. *Provlēmata tēs melanomorphēs Attikēs keramikēs* (Thessalonika 1981).

Trendall 1985: Trendall, A. D. "An Apulian Loutrophoros Representing the Tantalidae." In *Greek Vases in The J. Paul Getty Museum*. Vol. 2. Occasional Papers on Antiquities, 3 (Malibu, Calif. 1985).

Trendall and Cambitoglou 1982: Trendall, A. D., and A. Cambitoglou. *The Red-Figured Vases of Apulia*. Vol. 2, *Late Apulian*. Oxford Monographs on Classical Archaeology (Oxford 1982).

Ure 1934: Ure, P. N. *Aryballoi and Figurines from Rhitsona in Boeotia* (Cambridge, England 1934).

Vellacott 1954: Vellacott, P., trans. *The Bacchae and Other Plays*, by Euripides (Baltimore 1954).

Vermeule 1965: Vermeule, C. "A Greek Theme and Its Survivals: The Ruler's Shield (Tondo Image) in Tomb and Temple." *Proceedings of the American Philosophical Society* 109, no. 6 (1965): 361–97.

Vermeule 1968: Vermeule, C. *Roman Imperial Art in Greece and Asia Minor*. (Cambridge, Mass. 1968).

Vermeule 1969: Vermeule, C. "A Greek Hero of Alexander the Great's Age." *Collection Latomus* 103 (1969): 648–50.

Vermeule 1981: Vermeule, C. *Greek and Roman Sculpture in America: Masterpieces in Public Collections in the United States and Canada* (Malibu and Berkeley 1981).

Vermeule and Ternbach 1972: Vermeule, C., and J. Ternbach. "A Greek Heroic Statue in Dallas," *Archaeology* 25, no. 3 (1972): 216–221.

Verner 1982: Verner, M. *Altägyptische Särge in den Museen und Sammlungen der Tschechoslowakei*. Corpus Antiquitatum Ägyptiacarum (Prague 1982).

Walker 1985: Walker, S. *Memorials to the Roman Dead* (London 1985).

Webster 1972: Webster, T. B. L. *Potter and Patron in Classical Athens* (London 1972).

Wegner 1939: Wegner, M. *Die Herrscherbildnisse in antoninischer Zeit* (Berlin 1939).

Weiss 1985: Weiss, H., ed. *Ebla tō Damascus, Art and Archaeology of Ancient Syria* (Washington, D.C. 1985).

Williams and Ogden 1994: Williams, D., and J. Ogden. *Greek Gold: Jewellery of the Classical World* (London 1994).

Woldering 1967: Woldering, I. *Gods, Men and Pharaohs: The Glory of Egyptian Art* (New York 1967).

Index

Main headings in italic type are catalogue entries. Numerals in italic type are page numbers of illustrations; numerals in bold type are page numbers of catalogue entries, each accompanied by one or more illustrations.